Practising Social Work Law

Second Edition

Suzy Braye

and

Michael Preston-Shoot

MACMILLAN

First published 1992
Reprinted 1994
Second edition published 1997

Published by
MACMILLAN PRESS LTD
Houndmills, Basingstoke, Hampshire RG21 6XS
and London
Companies and representatives
throughout the world

ISBN 0–333–69383–3

A catalogue record for this book is available
from the British Library.

10   9   8   7   6   5   4   3   2
06   05   04   03   02   01   00   99   98

Copy-edited and typeset by Povey–Edmondson
Tavistock and Rochdale, England

Printed in Malaysia

Contents

List of Abbreviations

AA	Adoption Act 1976
ASW	Approved Social Worker
CA	Children Act 1989
CAYP	Children and Young Persons Act 1933; 1969
CCETSW	Central Council for Education and Training in Social Work
CI	Chief Inspectors Letter
CJA	Criminal Justice Act 1982; 1991; 1993
CJPOA	Criminal Justice and Public Order Act 1994
C(RS)A	Carers (Recognition and Services) Act 1995
CSDPA	Chronically Sick and Disabled Persons Act 1970
DipSW	Diploma in Social Work
DoH	Department of Health
DPA	Disabled Persons (Services, Consultation and Representation) Act 1986
DPMCA	Domestic Proceedings and Magistrates' Court Act 1978
DPP	Director of Public Prosecutions
DVMPA	Domestic Violence and Matrimonial Proceedings Act 1976
ECT	electro-convulsive therapy
EPO	Emergency Protection Order
FLA	Family Law Act 1996
HA	Housing Act 1996
HASSASSA	Health and Social Services and Social Security Adjudications Act 1983
HO	Home Office
HSG	Health Service Guidelines
HSPHA	Health Services and Public Health Act 1968
LAC	Local Authority Circular
LASSA	Local Authority Social Services Act 1970
LASSL	Local Authority Social Services Letter
LEA	Local Education Authority
MAHA	Matrimonial Homes Act 1983
MHA	Mental Health Act 1983

MH(PIC)A	Mental Health (Patients in the Community) Act 1995
MHRT	Mental Health Review Tribunal
NAA	National Assistance Act 1948
NHS	National Health Service
NHSA	National Health Service Act 1977
NHSCCA	NHS and Community Care Act 1990
NR	nearest relative
PACE	Police and Criminal Evidence Act 1984
PCCA	Powers of Criminal Courts Act 1973
RRA	Race Relations Act 1976
SOAD	second opinion appointed doctor
SSD	Social Services Department

Table of Cases

AC   Appeal Cases
All ER   All England Law Reports
CO   Crown Office
Cr App R (S) Criminal Appeal Reports (Sentencing)
Crim Law   Criminal Law Review
ELR   Education Law Reports
FCR   Family Court Reporter
FLR   Family Law Report
HL   House of Lords
HLR   Housing Law Reports
QB   Queens Bench
WLR   Weekly Law Reports

Circulars

Preface to the Second Edition

Since publication of the first edition much has changed in social work law. The NHS and Community Care Act 1990 has been fully implemented, followed by a burgeoning number of research and evaluation studies and a hotly contested debate about the effectiveness of community care. Nowhere has this debate been sharper than in mental health, where highly publicised assaults by mentally disordered people have prompted arguments about registers and supervised discharge orders and led to new legislation (Mental Health (Patients in the Community) Act 1995) and guidance. Meanwhile, concerns about resources have come to permeate the entire community care field.

Similar fierce debates have characterised criminal justice, for instance around secure training orders and the right to silence (Criminal Justice and Public Order Act 1994), and the process of securing antidiscriminatory legislation for disabled people (Disability Discrimination Act 1995). The jury is still out on whether either Act will prove effective.

The needs of carers have been recognised but without the provision of additional resources for already hard-pressed local authorities (Carers (Recognition and Services) Act 1995). The balance between the interests of children and parents continues to evoke strong emotions in the area of family support. The Children Act 1989 has generated a substantial volume of case law, not all of which interprets the Act in ways that social work and legal practitioners would believe to be consistent with the spirit and purpose of the legislation. Nonetheless the Act continues to enjoy a positive consensus. This cannot be said for reforms to the law on divorce, domestic violence, asylum and housing homeless people. Increasingly, vulnerable people are being denied the social care assistance they need.

Not that social work and social work education have escaped major change. Social services departments have experienced major upheavals, reflected in local government reorganisations, and divisions into purchaser/provider functions and/or children's and adult services. They are also subject to increasing regulation, as for example in the development of national standards. The requirement for probation officers to hold a social work qualification has been rescinded by the Home Office, despite near unanimous opposition. Social work education has been reviewed, in part because of the rapidly changing legislative framework, but also because of government unease with its anti-oppressive practice agenda.

The period between the two editions has also witnessed the emergence of a new discipline: social work law. A social work law association (Preston-Shoot, 1993) has brought together academics, practitioners, trainers and researchers around two themes: teaching and assessment of competence to practise social work law; and developing a critical awareness of the interface between the law and social work practice. CCETSW, through the social work law research group, has revised and extended its guidance to Diploma in Social Work programmes on teaching and assessing social work law (Ball *et al.*, 1995), coinciding with an increased prominence for the law in the requirements for social work qualification. The emergence of this new discipline has involved defining its scope. CCETSW's guidance defines the discipline narrowly, as the powers and duties given to local authority social services departments, whilst acknowledging the importance of social workers having knowledge of wider social welfare law provisions. This book takes a wider view, including within its definition not only those powers and duties which social workers implement directly but also those mandates in the operation of which they must take an interest when working with service users and their carers. Accordingly, the law relating to homelessness, divorce and special educational needs is included. The focus of the book remains the law in England and Wales.

Each chapter has been thoroughly revised to take account of these changes and developments. The intervening period between the two editions has seen us on an upward learning curve and, perhaps, even more appreciative of the fact that competence to practise, in social work law as elsewhere, should be a lifetime journey. One of us (SB) has moved from academe to management of social services provision; the other (MPS) has engaged in research with users and carers into the effectiveness of social work law practice. Both of us have continued to engage in critical reflection of law and practice, whilst also negotiating our way around the minutiae of law as a discipline. Law reports and transcripts of judgements have become as much a part of our reading as social work practice texts and have made us keenly aware of the inadequacy of much reporting in social work journals and literature of legal judgements.

We have continued to benefit from the encouragement and friendship of colleagues, friends and family. We would like to thank Jo Campling for her continued support and friendship, and Stuart Vernon both for his lawyer's perspective and his enthusiasm for bridging law and social work. We would like to thank Stuart and Sue, Vic and Linda, Margaret and Bill, and Eileen and John for practical and moral support in our work on this new edition. Finally, Hannah and Sebastian deserve a special mention for their patience and love.

SUZY BRAYE
MICHAEL PRESTON-SHOOT

1

Towards Practising Social Work Law

The relationship between law and social work

Increasingly from the early 1980s the relationship between the law and social work was critically scrutinised. Research highlighted deficiencies in social workers' knowledge and use of legislation. It identified practitioners' concerns about the practice relevance of their learning about law, and unease about acting as statutory agents (Ball *et al.*, 1988; Davies and Brandon, 1988; Vernon *et al.*, 1990). Reports into child abuse tragedies criticised the failure of practitioners to identify and observe their legal duties, and to use positively their available legal powers (DHSS, 1982; Beckford Report, 1985; Carlile Report, 1987). They suggested that social workers disliked an authoritarian role and the use of legal intervention in social work practice.

By contrast, other reports criticised social workers for being over-zealous and ill-advised in their use of the law, and found that using statutory controls can be counter-productive to risk management and decision-making in child care (DHSS, 1985; Butler-Sloss, 1988). The paradox was stark: social workers appear damned if they act and damned if they do not act. They were portrayed as doing both too little too late and too much too soon (Freeman, 1990). This paradox continues, reflected for example in government-endorsed research (DoH, 1995a) which criticises social workers for focusing more on child abuse and child protection than on the support needs of children and families, without examining the context in which this situation has been reached, and which advocates an increased emphasis on preventive services without indicating how an apparent preoccupation with abuse is to be modified. In simply calling for a more balanced service, reflected in sensitive professional–family relationships, appropriate use of power, a broad perspective and services designed to enhance quality of life, the Department of Health research has failed to address the roots of the paradox in the legal mandate and its relationship with social work.

The prescribed remedies for this 'malaise' differ fundamentally. The Beckford Report (1985) argued that social work can only be defined in terms of the functions required of its practitioners by their employing agencies operating within a statutory framework. The law is social work's mandate, the pivot around which social work practice should be based. What is required, since social workers only have a function because of the law (Howe, 1980), is a higher degree of proven competency in relation to statutory duties, an ability to interpret and exercise legal responsibilities within a conception of social work which emphasises social control and inspection (Beckford Report, 1985; Blom-Cooper, 1988). This legalistic model is reflected in *Working Together* (DoH, 1991e) and *The Law Report* (Ball *et al.*, 1988) which allocate knowledge of the law to the central position in social work. It is clearly expressed in an increasing concentration by local authorities on statutory duties, cutting back on other activities with the result that services appear less user-oriented (Flynn, 1993).

An alternative pivot was offered by Stevenson (1988): an ethical duty of care. Here the law is one framework, alongside key social work values and skills, including user self-determination, professional judgement, assessment and working for both individual and social change, within which good practice can develop (Stevenson, 1986; Freeman, 1990). This position, that the law alone is insufficient, also has government endorsement: the care of children requires professional skill and judgement in addition to legal regulations and guidance (DoH, 1989a). Rather than an ideology of legalism, which stresses the preeminence of the law in defining social work, the counter-view is of social workers as problem-solvers rather than law enforcement officers (Parton, 1986). A close fit between the law and appropriate courses of action is not assumed. The law is seen only as one resource, ambiguous, open to interpretation, and not always effective.

The legalistic model has been challenged, also, for undermining preventive work with families at risk who do not fulfil legal criteria for intervention (Freeman, 1990); for prioritising work away from older and disabled people since legislation is largely discretionary in their cases (Braye and Preston-Shoot, 1994); and for creating an impression that social workers have greater powers than they have (Lyon, 1989; Braye and Preston-Shoot, 1990). The criticism extends to challenging the dogmatism, which the law often represents, about what the dominant sectors of society want (Stevenson, 1986), a challenge which may take social workers into the realms of deviance (Pearson, 1975) as they work to empower disadvantaged people and to change the structures which oppress many users of social services.

These positions on the relationship between the law and social work may now be seen in several on-going debates. Some commentators (for example, Adcock *et al.*, 1991) have argued that the law, reflected through court orders, can assist social work's purposes. Others (for example, Walrond-Skinner and Watson, 1987; King and Trowell, 1992; Jones, 1993) have argued that reliance on the law fails to address the problems people face and may, indeed, exacerbate them. This is because, by naming as individual and/or family problems issues which originate in social problems, social work risks colluding with oppression. From this viewpoint welfare interventions are a deception and diversion from moral and political questions, masking deprivation, disadvantage and the damage done by inequitable social structures and discriminatory social policies.

When this critical line of argument focuses on the effect on individuals, commentators point for example to the failure of anti-discriminatory legislation to reduce discrimination and inherited disadvantage (Banton, 1994). Community care law does not secure even the limited objectives of government on need and choice, such that policy and practice have been challenged for a meanness of spirit and poverty of provision (Utting, in Ellis 1993). In child care the legal system, instead of promoting the welfare of children, can lose it amidst rules of evidence, courtroom procedures, adversarial tactics and binary decision-making (King and Trowell, 1992). Thus, despite the wording of guidance, the use of corporal punishment by child-minders has been sanctioned in a judgement (*Sutton LBC* v. *Davis* [1994]) which fails to protect children from legally condoned violence and abuse (Rickford, 1993). Furthermore, the United Nations has alleged that the best interests of children are not reflected in health, education, criminal justice or social security law, and that government has repeatedly violated the *Convention on the Rights of the Child* to which it is a signatory (Cloke and Davies, 1995).

Other commentators point to the detrimental effect on social work of its close proximity to local and central government. The overarching theme here is central government's mistrust of, and antipathy towards, the public sector and professional groups (Flynn, 1993). One outcome of this has seen training and practice increasingly removed from professional control. A review of qualifying training was imposed by government earlier than CCETSW and Diploma in Social Work programmes thought necessary, whilst the Home Office has removed probation training from the Diploma in Social Work framework despite universal condemnation and research evidence on the effectiveness of training programmes. The relative autonomy of the probation service has been eroded by the imposition of national standards which have elevated coercion, diminished the importance of the relationship between probation officer and offender, and heavily circumscribed the sensitivity and flexibility necessary for informed practice (McWilliams, 1992; Ward, 1996). Similarly, social work has been characterised as ineffective and burdensome, unaccountable and out of control (Howe, 1994; Parton, 1994). Its discretionary power has been curbed by regulations, national standards, inspection and dependence on judicial decision-making (Parton, 1991; Valentine, 1994), not all of which facilitates sensitive, flexible and informed practice. Indeed, this emphasis on legalism is often characterised by government refusal to accept practice wisdom or engage with contrary research evidence, as in the imposition of registers of severely mentally ill people (HSG(94)5), who represent a significant risk of suicide, of serious violence to others, or of severe self-neglect, without the definition of terms, objectives and criteria for success. It constrains social work's legitimacy to comment on whole areas which it has seen as its legitimate concern (Preston-Shoot, 1996a).

Another outcome has been a reduction in the state's role from primary to residual provider of preventive, supportive and protective services. One effect here is that social workers may have increased reliance on statutory powers in child-care services (DoH, 1995a) and under the Mental Health Act 1983 in order to obtain resources for people. Another is that reliance on a mixed economy of welfare is resulting in many people's long-term care needs not being met, either because of non-provision or inappropriate provision. The report into the murder of Jonathan Zito by Christopher Clunis (Ritchie *et al.*, 1994) warned that thresholds for receiving mental health services were becoming higher with the result that people were not securing access to much needed services. The Commission on Social Justice (1994) concluded that community care policy is a nightmare and a failing system.

This connects with a third outcome, the imposition on local authorities of tight financial controls. Resources have become a dominant theme in health and welfare provision. In some health authority districts the NHS can no longer claim to provide a comprehensive service. Within local authorities the picture is marked first by calls for more resources. The Commission on Social Justice (1994) argued that, without extra resources, community care policies would fail and the needs of children would not be met. It pointed to the economic folly of children living in financial, emotional and educational impoverishment. Researchers in community care have pointed to principles of quality, choice and needs-led assessments and provision becoming secondary to concerns about resource constraints (Knapp *et al.*, 1992; Hoyes *et al.*, 1994; Braye and Preston-Shoot, 1995), whilst reports on assaults committed by mental health service users discharged from hospital (see, for example, Ritchie *et al.*, 1994) consistently emphasise the paucity of provision and the impact of resource shortage on the appropriateness of the initial discharge, of the subsequent placement, and of follow-up support services. In services for children and families evidence indicates that:

1. some decisions about the need for family proceedings are influenced by resource issues (SSI, 1992a);
2. children with special needs are not being assessed within timescales laid down by government;
3. children are being inappropriately placed in residential care, with local authorities failing to take account of the suitability of a placement and/or of its current staff and residents to the needs of the young person to be placed, as required by guidance (DoH, 1991i);
4. more resources should be invested in residential child-care services to ensure appropriate quality care for looked-after children (SSI, 1993a);
5. available provision is failing disabled children and their families (SSI, 1994a);

6. the quality of services for children in need is adversely affected by resource constraints (Colton *et al.*, 1995), with attention consequently focused on children at risk of abuse and neglect at the expense of other areas which might reduce the need for statutory intervention;
7. inexperienced practitioners are dealing with difficult situations alone, the consequences of which include the neglect of important issues in assessment and intervention, and a failure to engage significant people (DoH, 1995a);
8. the effectiveness of child protection services is adversely affected by resource constraints (Fox Report, 1990).

This picture indicates the necessity of rethinking funding arrangements. The system of Standard Spending Assessments, the primary means of funding local authorities, may be criticised on the grounds that it is confusing, complicated and produces inadequate outcomes. Perhaps of most concern, however, is the apparent validation of reduced provision. Despite evidence that existing resources cannot accommodate the new duties of assessment, there will be no extra resources to implement the Carers (Recognition and Services) Act 1995. The House of Lords has ruled that the duty on housing authorities to provide accommodation for homeless people is met if accommodation is suitable. It does not have to be permanent, despite the impact this can have on the welfare of children whose needs, elsewhere in legislation, are paramount (*R* v. *L B Brent, ex parte Awua* [1995]). Similarly, judicial review decisions in community care have allowed local authorities to consider their resource position when setting and reviewing eligibility criteria, and when deciding how to meet with services those needs which they are prepared to accept fall within their statutory duties (*R* v. *Gloucestershire County Council, ex parte Mahfood and others* [1995]; *R* v. *Lancashire County Council, ex parte RADAR and Another* [1996]; see Preston-Shoot, 1996b). This undermines the emphasis in guidance on needs-led services and choice. Yet the Chief Inspector, in his annual report (SSI, 1995a), makes no mention of resource difficulties in community care and surprisingly feels able to assert that assessments are still needs-led. He does, however, note a tendency for slippage into service-led provision.

These polarities serve to reinforce two stereotypes about the relationship between social work and the law. Either law is knowledge to be crammed in, if not embraced uncritically, as it offers certainty and direction in an uncertain and confusing world, as if it is somehow obvious when and how practitioners must act. Or law may be an obstacle to practice and an understanding of it may be unnecessary. Both views are simplistic. Neither provides guidance on how social workers should respond to responsibilities which involve questions of liberty and custody, rights and risks. Nor do they address the context of practice: stress, low morale, organisational resource constraints and an ambiguous mandate from a society which, overall, has little confidence or trust in social work. Nor do they suggest how social workers should respond when financial considerations rather than people's needs dominate decision-making, and when social policies appear to neglect people's basic needs and social rights. Consequently neither view is likely to resolve questions of social work or public confidence, or to overcome the defensive practice which is such a feature of child protection work (Harris, 1987; Preston-Shoot and Agass, 1990).

Nonetheless this dichotomy was reflected in the requirements for social work training (CCETSW, 1989). A key requirement was that social workers should be competent to 'protect the vulnerable and exercise authority under statute'. This required an ability to invoke legal powers where appropriate and competence in applying knowledge of statutory powers and duties in social work practice. However the requirements failed to recognise that the legal powers and remedies available to social workers do not always empower them to protect vulnerable people, and they perpetuated the illusion that it will be clear, and can be learned, when it is appropriate to invoke legal powers. Nor in its discussion of ethical issues and practice dilemmas did this CCETSW report appear to recognise any disjunction between the responsibility to protect vulnerable people by exercising statutory authority and the apparent absence of consensus regarding when social workers should so act. Nor did it address the conflict between 'working in accordance with statutory requirements' and the parallel requirements to demonstrate:

1. commitment to natural justice and human rights;
2. competence in maximising people's rights to protection from abuse, exploitation and violence;
3. competence in facilitating individuals and groups; and

4. commitment to and skills in addressing the multidimensional nature of social need and challenging forms of structural oppression.

The statutory requirements, in accordance with which social workers must work, at times create or maintain the very structures and inequalities which disempower people, and which social workers are required to influence or challenge.

These concerns have not been answered by CCETSW's revised requirements for DipSW training (1995). Competence in social work law is strongly emphasised. All students must be provided with opportunities to apply and deepen in practice the broad understanding of legislation acquired through the academic curriculum. Moreover, with knowledge and understanding of statutory responsibilities given central importance, students must demonstrate through formal written assessment their understanding and application of the law relating to social work in the country in which they train. Law is the *only* subject so emphasised.

The emphasis is further strengthened by the practice requirement, attached to the core competence 'assess and plan', that students must be able to work in accordance with statutory and legal requirements, and to carry out orders of the court. The evidence indicators for this specify the ability to identify, discuss with service users, and adhere to legal and policy requirements and procedures.

If these requirements emphasise conformity to officially sanctioned rules, procedures, structures and relationships, elsewhere the stress is on practising anti-oppressively, counteracting discrimination, and contributing to an enabling environment for individuals and families. This must recognise, but in CCETSW's requirements does not, that the law, which gives students a mandate to practise, may be oppressive, both in intent and application, and that social and legal institutions are frequently discriminatory in their operation (Ball *et al.*, 1995). It also involves challenging the poverty, poor housing, unemployment and racism which even government (DoH, 1989a) acknowledges affect people's behaviour. It involves exploring the political context explicitly, and identifying how power is used to define people's interests and needs. This activity falls outside the legal mandate, which does not extend to sanctioning intervention in social, political and economic systems (Kingston, 1982). Rather, it requires practitioners to intervene on the basis of how people behave and are, not why; to treat the act, not the person in situation; the offence, not the offender (Howe, 1990, 1994). Not surprisingly, then, there is little reference in the requirements for qualifying social workers to community development, community action, and work aiming for social and organisational change.

The revised requirements continue to juxtapose the interests of service users, agencies, courts and society as if there is no conflict. They juxtapose a traditional value base, which emphasises paternalism and protection, professional domination of decision-making, needs and participation, alongside a more radical value base with its emphasis on rights, equality, partnership, and service-user power to influence decisions, without any apparent recognition that social work goals, and the relationship between law and social work, will differ depending on which value base is drawn upon (see Braye and Preston-Shoot, 1995).

This discussion highlights the need for a conceptual frame which moves beyond a legalistic approach to teaching, assessing and practising social work law, towards addressing the dilemmas of practice by means of a decision-making framework. This will draw on values, a knowledge base informed by research and theory, and skills in conceptualising and negotiating the connections between social work tasks and social work law. It will be accompanied by a critical appraisal of local authority powers and duties, and by skills in gaining information, reflecting on events, identifying and taking action, and developing clarity about the reasons for the action which is proposed (Braye, 1993).

Where does this leave social workers? Clearly, an exclusively legalistic model, where the law is elevated to the centre of practice and becomes the main form of admissible knowledge, is inadequate for the complexities which social workers face. First, the law is neither simple nor unproblematic to apply. It cannot be assumed that if the legal mandate is known and followed practitioners will provide appropriate types and levels of intervention. Social workers operate with legal clauses which are open to interpretation, and where what is included and excluded is a matter of judgement on which professionals do not necessarily agree (Norman, 1980). The child protection mandate is now being challenged by calls for a lighter touch, for a renewed emphasis on prevention (DoH, 1995a), without the guidance and resources to assist practitioners with the difficult question of what to do and when. The differential meanings which may be attributed to partnership, choice, empowerment and quality are further examples of ambiguity. Indeed, both inquiries (Ritchie *et al.*, 1994) and judges (*R* v. *Gloucestershire County Council, ex parte RADAR* [1995]) have criticised Department of Health guidance for being difficult to understand and couched in unhelpful jargon. Practice is suffused with dilemmas and choice points, a complexity which requires judgement, analysis, assessment and problem-solving, and which means that equally possible and appropriate but different definitions of a situation will take workers in different directions. When and how to intervene is not always obvious, yet there continues an unreal belief that tragedies can be prevented and that they are due to bad practice (Reder *et al.*, 1993).

If the law is an ambiguous mandate, it can also be an ineffective remedy. Social workers' legal options to protect older, abused people are very limited. Victims of domestic violence do not find the law particularly effective if their abusers fail to be bound by legal injunctions. Nor is the law the only difficulty in knowing when to intervene. There are few cases where outcomes are predictable and clear-cut (Stevenson, 1974); the prediction of risk is hazardous; there is no empirical support for it (Parton, 1986); there is no definition of what constitutes high or unacceptable risk, nor a single factor or cluster of variables which always indicate action. Risk cannot, therefore, be eliminated, however elaborate and extensive the procedures (Parton, 1991; SSI, 1992a). Professional skills, a knowledge base and judgement are all necessary in order to determine what the problem is, where and when to intervene, and when to implement available powers and duties. An emphasis on legalism, which equates the law to the appropriate course of action, perpetuates two myths: of the law providing right answers; and of omnipotence, that social work can tidy away social problems (Preston-Shoot and Agass, 1990; Valentine, 1994).

Second, a breadth of knowledge is required. Human growth and development, multidisciplinary teamwork and the effects of social and economic policies and structures on individuals and families are but three examples. The dynamics and emotions which can be aroused by the work require access to knowledge, skills and support to enable practitioners to identify, negotiate and hold to the task. The law alone is insufficient protection or guide. Legislating to promote inter-agency cooperation will not of its own accord make it happen. The courts have had to intervene to mediate between agencies, for instance in relation to housing children in need and their families (*R* v. *Northavon District Council, ex parte Smith* [1994]), and government has had to emphasise the importance of maintaining and improving cooperation between agencies responsible for health and social care services (DoH, 1993a). The barriers to collaboration include resource levels and arrangements, differing status and levels of knowledge, lack of role clarity, overlap of functions, stereotyping and competitiveness, attitudinal and value differences. These have to be addressed by managers in the respective services. Collaboration will not be realised without discussion of values, power, objectives, expertise, knowledge and structures.

Third, a simple legalistic model does not take account of the range of roles that social workers perform and the skills required by them: negotiating tensions between helping individuals and acting for society; between enforcing clients' rights, affording them protection and securing social control; between being an agent of the client and of social services (Stevenson, 1988; Braye and Preston-Shoot, 1990). Which role when is a complex matter of values and judgement.

Fourth, the emphasis on legalism places inappropriate trust in the law. The continuing adversarial nature of the court system, together with its rules of evidence and procedures, is inappropriate to deal with the complexities of child abuse cases (King and Trowell, 1992). Equally, judicial review decisions in community care (see for instance *R* v. *Gloucestershire County Council, ex parte Mahfood and Others* [1995]; *R* v. *Wandsworth LBC, ex parte Beckwith* [1996]) appear limited in the scope they offer for challenging a government policy which purports to endorse needs-led services but actually undermines people's rights to satisfaction of their needs through the emphasis on resources and an imposition on local government of political objectives and ideology.

Fifth, any emphasis on working in accordance with statutory and agency requirements assumes that powers and duties expressed through statute and local authority circulars are mirrored in agency procedures and performance. Practitioners may rightly doubt that agency procedures accurately reflect or interpret the powers and duties imposed by social work law. Research evidence (Rickford, 1992), ombudsman decisions (Age Concern, 1995) and judicial review cases (for example, *R* v. *Avon County Council, ex parte Hazell* [1993]; *R* v. *Gloucestershire County Council, ex parte Mahfood and others* [1995]; *R* v. *Bexley LBC., ex parte B* [1995]; *R* v.

Islington LBC., ex parte Rixon [1996]) demonstrate that some agencies are failing to assess need in a structured way, to interpret law and guidance accurately, to provide sufficient assistance and to provide help within a reasonable time period, to conduct regular reviews or to provide written plans, to report deficits in service provision, to consult with users and carers and to take their views fully into account, and to manage complaints procedures fairly. The dangers of practice becoming defined by agency policies and priorities are obvious.

Finally, major themes in contemporary social work – partnership, empowerment and antidiscriminatory practice – highlight both developments and inadequacies in the legislative framework. Some major enactments, for example, the Disabled Persons (Services, Consultation and Representation) Act 1986 and the Children Act 1989, incorporate themes of empowerment and partnership, and may be enabling in the sense that individuals may participate in assessment and service design. Others highlight either the inability of the law to remove discrimination and provide redress for victims of discriminatory practices, for example the Sex Discrimination Act 1975, or the use of the law to promote dominant societal values and to discriminate against groups of people – immigration rules, legislation relating to sexuality, and the racism and sexism in social security provisions (Alcock and Harris, 1982; Dominelli, 1988). In this latter respect the law effectively denies the importance or existence of groups of people, and embodies value judgements about their behaviour and choices, their needs and goals, which practitioners might wish to challenge. Even the law's enabling potential is constrained by government policies which discourage formal intervention in people's lives and which, by reducing public expenditure, have narrowed the range and quality of services which agencies can provide. Combined with narrow legal definitions of need and the influence, if not primacy, of resource considerations in policy development, practice becomes service-led and residual rather than orientated around considerations of quality of life.

How then should social workers practise within and interact with the law and a legal system which discriminates against or fails to protect people on the basis of ethnicity, gender, sexuality, age, poverty and disability? How should social workers intervene in the context of an unequal society where the law is made by and frequently benefits those with social, economic and political power?

Once again social workers are faced with both implementing and challenging the law.

A legalistic model, founded on a premise of right answers to specific questions, is inapplicable to social work. The law draws a fine line between what is permissible or 'right' and what is not. However, as we shall demonstrate, that line is obscure owing to an absence of clarity and consensus. Even where it can be identified, and a situation falls on the 'right' side of it, permitted or mandated action may not be the 'right thing to do'.

Training for and practising social work law

Why another book on the law and social work? Previous publications reflect the polarities discussed above. Some provide detailed descriptions of the legislation (see Brayne and Martin, 1995; Vernon, 1993) but omit a critical framework within which to locate the law and do not integrate case studies with the legal commentary. This is unlikely to make legal knowledge stick or appear relevant (Braye and Preston-Shoot, 1990). Moreover it promotes the assumption that application of the law in social work practice is unproblematic when, in fact, practice often highlights the difficulty of knowing with any certainty when to intervene. It divorces the law from the real context of practice, as if assuming that the law can be assimilated and practised out of its context (Kent, 1989).

Other texts (see Alcock and Harris, 1982; Brophy and Smart, 1985; King and Trowell, 1992; Kaganas *et al.*, 1995) provide a critical analysis of the context, the values and ideologies underpinning legislation. This analysis pinpoints the inadequacies of the law as it affects and defines the needs of users of welfare services. It elaborates ideologies, for instance about the role of women, within different areas of the law. However these texts are less informative on where and how social workers should intervene: on the skills necessary for antidiscriminatory practice, for making empowerment work in a statutory context, and for challenging the social and economic consequences of attitudes, policies and structures. Moreover the law tends to be presented in discrete areas when the reverse is the more usual practice reality: a breadth of knowledge, legal and otherwise, is required by social workers for effective practice.

Practitioners appear uncertain about working in the legal arena. Even highly experienced practitioners, and those whose role carries positional authority, such as guardians *ad litem*, report considerable stress from their contact with the law (Jones *et al.*, 1991). They perceive that social work practice, experience, training and evidence have limited credibility compared with that of other professional groups, a view that finds echoes in some case law (DoH, 1994a; Foster and Preston-Shoot, 1995). This may be the result of limited opportunities through which practitioners can develop and update their knowledge and skills for interacting in the legal arena. However, it also suggests that attention should be given by all involved in the legal arena to the culture and attitude of the law and courts towards social work. What is written and taught about social work must leave practitioners certain in relation to 'knowing what' and 'knowing how'. It must also enable them to question the roles prescribed for them in law and to debate how legislation defines problems and solutions.

Thus a broader model is required. It must address contemporary social work issues, practice dilemmas and anxiety. It must promote confidence and competence in both knowledge of the law and skills in identifying its relevance to practice. It must therefore connect theory and practice by providing critical frameworks in which to experience, make sense of and resolve dilemmas of applying law in practice, and by describing skills and principles for positive, effective intervention. It must encourage practitioners to move beyond narrowly defined agency functions of interpreting and implementing legislation based on dominant social values towards debating issues of crucial importance. These include all forms of discrimination and structural oppression, pervasive social constructions of older age, class, disability, sexuality, race and gender, and the principles and skills of antidiscriminatory practice and social action which follow.

This broader model must answer six questions clearly:

1. What do social workers need to know?
2. What helps social workers acquire and retain knowledge of social work law, and turn knowledge into understanding?
3. What values should they carry into their interaction with and application of the law?
4. In what skills do they need to be competent?

5. What agency structures influence social workers' understanding of, and competence for, the practice of social work law?
6. How might antidiscriminatory and anti-oppressive perspectives be integrated into social work law practice?

One model for social work law proposes that social workers should possess legal knowledge pertinent to client groups and legal knowledge which transcends these groups. They should understand legal processes and procedures, social work legal roles and the values which underpin them, and have relevant skills for 'legal competence' (Vernon, 1993). This model is too narrow, since it promotes the law as determinative in understanding the relationship between it and social work practice. Following the arguments developed in this chapter a broader model of social work law comprises eight components.

First, the law relating to specific user groups is essential knowledge for effective social work practice. It provides a degree of confidence by clarifying the rights, duties and powers of those involved and the circumstances in which these may be invoked. However practice-relevant knowledge extends further than the ability to quote Acts of Parliament. Factual legal knowledge, whilst important, is only part of the story. Surrounding its application, the dynamics of the encounter between practitioner and user are such that legal knowledge alone will not guarantee that practitioners feel confident or intervene appropriately. A second requirement, therefore, is knowledge of and skills in managing the processes which occur. Social workers encounter frightening and horrifying behaviour, and frequently work where violence is explicitly or implicitly threatened. They inherit an ambiguous mandate which requires certainty before action but the minimum of risk and time delay. Continuing emphasis on the importance of the family can promote over-optimism about the care available therein, which contrasts with the pessimism which follows from recognition of the frequent abuse of power in familial relationships. The dynamics of the helping encounter and the anxiety created by the work can lead social workers away from the legal authority vested in them or to over-emphasise it via directive authoritarianism as a hoped-for means to control the dynamics and minimise stress. The dynamics and anxiety can create defensive practice (Harris, 1987), inappropriate investigative measures or removal into care, or delayed rehabilitation – measures to minimise risk-taking, when risk may be justified but carries the possibility of an adverse outcome. Individuals and organisations may adopt procedures to distance themselves from clients, or become entangled because they fail to recognise and use transference, counter-transference and mirroring processes (Preston-Shoot and Agass, 1990). If these 'forces' are not understood, and that understanding is not integrated into procedures such as practice guidelines, agency policy statements on risk-taking and supervision, work is more likely to become purposeless, stuck and ineffective.

This extension beyond legal knowledge also applies to the third requirement: knowledge which transcends specific groups. Clearly social workers must possess knowledge of the law which affects their work with users, such as knowledge of rights, of risks and when rights may be overruled, and of procedures for obtaining evidence. However, as the law provides insufficient knowledge regarding when and how to intervene, a practice as well as a legal rationale is consequently required for intervention. Knowledge from social sciences and from social work theory and practice is required too. This knowledge may relate to specific user groups or transcend them. Knowledge of internalised oppression, the accommodation syndrome (Summit, 1983), triangular relationships and conflicts (Preston-Shoot and Agass, 1990) and defence mechanisms will help to explain the position and needs of victims in abusive relationships. Indicators and contra-indicators for rehabilitation of abused children and for significant harm have been developed (Bentovim *et al.*, 1987; Adcock *et al.*, 1991). These inform practice and give meaning to such legal concepts as 'welfare of the child' and 'significant harm'. So too does knowledge of human growth and development and of indicators of risk of abuse or family breakdown.

Such knowledge is a useful corrective or addition to legal knowledge. The law assumes, indeed appeals to, the reasonable person. Psychodynamic theories alert us, however, to the irrational and the unreasonable. The law deals mainly with individuals and with presenting problems or symptoms rather than with structures and with the relationships and systems which have an impact on individuals. Systems theories alert us, however, to a circular view of causation which emphasises the interaction between individual difficulties and internal processes, such as historical experiences, and/or social difficulties and issues, such as class, poverty and structural oppression. Whilst legal measures promote an individual focus, more effective or durable change follows from a person-in-situation focus where both the individual and social dimensions of problems are addressed, where the whole context, rather than just one, individual, part of it is confronted, where underlying relationships and systems are tackled in addition to immediate presenting symptoms (Yelloly, 1980; Preston-Shoot and Agass, 1990). The limited effectiveness of race and sex discrimination legislation, and the failure of initiatives to curb child abuse or crime and of measures to reduce poverty, are the result of just such a failure to look beyond the individual to the environment and to the impact of each on the other.

Fourth, social workers must understand legal processes and procedures. This includes familiarity with court structures, rules of evidence and limits to confidentiality. However it also requires a critical appreciation of the dilemmas inherent in legal processes, such as the rights of victims in giving evidence versus the rights of the accused. It requires practitioners to challenge assumptions about the neutrality and impartiality of the law, and to understand and work to improve the current position of social work *vis-à-vis* other professions within the legal system. Medical and psychiatric evidence has higher status (*Re R (A Minor) (Disclosure of Privileged Material)* [1993]; *B* v. *B (Procedure: Alleged Sexual Abuse)* [1994]), yet this evidence is also open to contradictory opinion. Nor is there any evidence to indicate that doctors or lawyers are any more likely to avoid errors of judgement; or to collect evidence more effectively; or to interpret the 'truth' of a situation more accurately. Rather, different professions are judged by different assumptions and standards.

This relates to the fifth component, understanding of the relationship between the law and social work. This understanding operates at two levels. The macro level involves not only identifying the practice relevance of the law but also the ways in which the law contributes to or exacerbates social work's practice dilemmas, role conflict, uncertainty and ambiguity. This requires analysis of the law as a social construct, reflecting dominant (sometimes discriminatory) assumptions about, for instance, the role of women, appropriate needs, ageing, rights and responsibilities of parents, and disability. This understanding, that the law is not immune from social processes and that it is a value-laden entity, must incorporate the concept of conflicting imperatives which are the outcome of compromise and conflicts between value systems and which result in contradictory expectations of welfare services. From understanding of the relationship between law, social work and society practitioners must develop strategies for change at individual and social levels which give life to principles of empowerment, advocacy and antidiscriminatory practice.

The micro level relates to the ethical questions and value and practice dilemmas which the law poses for each practitioner. Each must question where he or she stands on equal opportunities, the law and sexuality, the law and antidiscriminatory values, on rights versus risks, on welfare versus justice, on political action concerning resources and attitudes versus working within agency constraints, and on conflict between valued courses of action (Horne, 1987). This last conflict is endemic in social work: when does a commitment to user self-determination, for example, give way to protection against risk or to the rights of another individual? These issues must be faced if practitioners are to manage the personal experience of work and be effective rather than inconsistent, defensive and/or dangerous.

The sixth component is the development of a decision-making framework. This must integrate legal and other forms of knowledge to formulate what may/must be done (users' and workers' statutory rights, duties or powers; requirements, such as needs and risks, which arise from practice knowledge and interaction between workers and users); why (the legal and practice rationale for action); when and how (skills for the effective practice of social work law). Such a framework is imperative to assess risk and need, to guide action and to minimise error.

A decision-making framework is only as good, however, as the competence of practitioners in relevant skills and social work roles – the seventh and eighth essential components of a model for effective practice in social work law. The relevant skills include legal skills – collecting and giving evidence; applying the law where those to whom it is applied may wish to reject it – and practice skills in removing a child on an emergency protection order, in applying for compulsory admission to psychiatric hospital, or in encouraging but not coercing an older person to accept domiciliary services or residential care. They also include generic social work skills: information gathering, formulating assessments, intervening on the basis of assessment and evaluating that intervention, recording and report-writing, working in partnership, transferring learning from one context to another, and establishing and maintaining relationships with professionals and users. The practice of social work law requires competency in all these skills.

By social work roles is meant not just legal roles, such as carrying out orders of the court and working in accordance with statutory and legal requirements (CCETSW, 1995) which deprive people of their liberty, provide financial benefits or change their status in law. If competence here is one requirement, subsumed under headings of protection, enabling and social control, then a second is to express the commitment to antidiscriminatory practice by means of social action, advocacy and empowerment. These roles, not all of which appear to be validated by CCETSW, focus on individual and community realisation, political awareness and action, and on social change, and may involve challenging agency policies and procedures. Herein lies a major tension. The more practitioners emphasise a legal role, the more they are likely to incur user displeasure; the more they emphasise social action, the more they risk government or agency displeasure. To hold the middle ground, and to avoid a continuing dive in credibility, requires that social workers, individually and collectively, implement strategies which make empowerment and antidiscriminatory practice a reality in the statutory context; develop a political awareness which connects the individual and the social, and raises consciousness about the law, about unmet needs, about inadequate resources and structural inequalities; make sense of and promote that understanding of social work's position and engage in debate about social work's mandate.

In summary, this book aims to develop the subject of social work law and to empower social workers in their practice. Specifically it aims to provide a critical understanding and appraisal of social work law, including the values it upholds, its provisions, the knowledge required and its usefulness. This will provide practitioners with one foundation stone: knowing 'what'. It also aims to provide a practical text which will illuminate the relevance and application of the law to social work situations. This is the second foundation stone: knowing 'why'. Finally it aims to connect the law with social work practice principles and skills in order that a practitioner's approach is informed and rigorous, retains core social work values and practice-relevant knowledge, and implements legal duties. It is inspired by the anxieties and difficulties faced by practitioners and addresses these by providing conceptual frameworks with which to make sense of and work through them. This is the third foundation stone: knowing 'how' and 'when'.

Since, in our view, knowledge is retained and understanding promoted when it has significant emotional impact on the recipient (Braye and Preston-Shoot, 1991) and when couched in a framework directly relevant to everyday practice, case studies and exercises will be used at various points. These are clearly marked off from the text and readers will derive greater benefit from the book and become more directly involved in their own learning if they focus on them before reading on. There are, of course, few right answers in social work. There is no substitute for finely tuned judgements; no remedy for the inevitability of risk. However this book provides a more rounded model as a solid foundation for practice.

2

Values and Functions within the Law

In debates about the relationship between social work and the law, the law is presented as a given fact, a clear set of rules of self-evident and unquestionable integrity, which need only to be negotiated with technical skill for helpful solutions to emerge. This chapter challenges this view of the law as firm ground, and likens it more realistically to shifting sand, the reflection of dominant ideologies, attitudes and values which themselves change and develop over time. Ideology shapes and penetrates the law (Alcock and Harris, 1982). Far from being synonymous with justice (Zander, 1974), the law as a paradigm of social relations is influenced by dominant forces which perpetuate injustice (Carlen, 1976) and emerges as a statement of what is rather than of what should be. That statement is written not on tablets of stone but in 'a malleable plasticine which is kneaded to reflect the political, legal and professional exigencies of the day' (Harris, 1990a). Most welfare law is the product of complex interactions between social, economic and political factors (Busfield, 1986), thrown into sharp relief by key events, such as the death of a child or vulnerable adult, which crystallise public and political opinion. The uneasy coalitions which result between shared interests produce a semblance of consensus which hides the deeper contradictions and conflicts beneath.

Questions about values are valuable questions. Values influence what legislation is prioritised, what judgements are passed. Considerable legislation exists which regulates family relationships and protects children, but very little to protect adults who are vulnerable through age or disability. Values affect what legislation is enacted and how sanctions for non-observance are imposed. Despite being on statute, key sections of the Disabled Persons (Services, Consultation and Representation) Act 1986 relating to advocacy will not be implemented. The Mental Health (Patients in the Community) Act 1995 permits measures to control the activities of people with severe mental disorder but does nothing to secure their access to appropriate levels of service provision. Discrimination under the Sex Discrimination Act 1975 and Race Relations Act 1976 is notoriously difficult to prove, and penalties imposed are often minimal with little benefit to the individual.

Exercise 2.1

Before reading further, reflect upon the following three questions, and notice how you justify your views.

1. Should social workers intervene in decisions made by parents about their children?
2. Should social workers prioritise child protection?
3. Should people have a right to die rather than submit to medical treatment?

At the level of professional practice, such questions confront individual workers with the value base of the available legislation, of their professional culture and of personal belief systems. Decisions made will reflect not only public concerns and priorities but also private attitudes and values. The daily interpretation of the law, the 'law in practice', is far from being a value-free activity and cannot be negotiated by reference merely to technical knowledge. Critical appraisal of the assumptions and potential effects of the law is essential. Only through such an appraisal can understanding become the foundation for applying the law in practice, understanding based on awareness of the law's underlying social functions and of the influence on practice of personal values.

The functions of law in society

The purposes that law fulfils in society are multiple, and at times contradictory. Some major themes may be identified.

Preservation of power structures

The law preserves the status quo within the power structures of society. Its principles reflect prevailing economic and political arrangements, thus preserving the interests of powerful groups in society (Bynoe *et al.*, 1991). Whilst predicated upon the rhetoric of freedom, justice and equality, the law colludes with inequalities between women and men, black people and white people, disabled and non-disabled people, young and old. In promoting a view of women's role it orders relationships between the sexes (Edwards, 1985a) in such matters as financial security, child care, work patterns and male domination by violence. Class, gender and racial biases in the judiciary and in the law-making machinery of Parliament are matched by complementary over-representation of disadvantaged and less powerful groups in the statistics of those selected for compulsory intervention by the state (Parton, 1985). Psychiatric hospital admissions, for example, show compulsory powers used disproportionately in respect of young Afro-Caribbean men (Rogers and Faulkener, 1987; Cope, 1989; Barnes *et al.*, 1990) and lend weight to a view of psychiatry, social work and the law harnessed to racist systems of social control (Francis *et al.*, 1989; Sashidharan, 1989). Black children are more likely to be taken into care (Barn, 1993).

The law remains relatively silent on who has what rights. Rarely does it enshrine rights for individuals, and in the absence of any Bill of Rights it remains open for the assumed rights of powerful groups to influence how the law is applied. There is evidence that the property rights of (male) respondents in proceedings for ouster injunctions frequently dominate over children's rights and needs in situations of domestic violence (Edwards and Halpern, 1988). Whilst protection and ouster orders have been obtainable because of violence or abuse, used or threatened, against an applicant or a child (DVMPA 1976; DPMCA 1978), these orders have only been granted after consideration of the parties' conduct, the children's needs, the parties' needs and the available financial resources (section 1 (3), MAHA 1983). Since these criteria are of equal standing, the needs of children are not paramount. Thus adults' accommodation rights may mean children having to be removed from their home in order to ensure protection. This position was reinforced in *Nottinghamshire County Council* v. *P* [1993] which held that a local authority could not use prohibited steps order or specific issues order applications (section 8, CA 1989) to regulate residence. If a child needed protection, measures under parts IV and V (CA 1989) were to be used, involving potentially removal of a child for her own protection. Similarly, in *Re F (Minor) (Parent Home – Ouster)* [1993] the court refused to make a specific issues order which would have amounted to an ouster order although it could have been of benefit to the children.

The Family Law Act 1996 seeks to amend this position. It repeals two Acts (DVMPA 1976; MAHA 1983) and codifies the general principle (section 1 (d)) that any risk to one of the parties to a marriage, and to children, of violence from the other party should be removed or diminished. However, this is only so far as reasonably practicable. It includes provision for occupation orders (section 33) which will regulate rights to occupy a home, but the child's welfare is not paramount when a court is determining whether or not to make this order (section 33 (6)). Rather, courts must also consider the housing needs of all the parties involved, their financial resources, the conduct of the parties, and the effect an order would have on them. The Act includes provision for non-molestation orders (section 42) prohibiting a person from molesting another, including a child. These orders may be made on the court's own motion in family proceedings (section 42 (b)). A child of sufficient age and understanding may also apply (section 43), and such orders may be made *ex parte* in situations of risk of significant harm to the applicant or a child. However, courts must have regard to all the circumstances of the case, including the need to secure the health, safety and well-being of the applicant and/or a child. Schedule 6 of the Act amends the Children Act 1989 by providing courts with the power to include an exclusion requirement when making an interim care order or an emergency protection order. A power of arrest may be attached to this requirement which would prohibit residence, entering a house, or entering the surrounding area. This potentially preserves the child's right to occupation of the family home.

Social engineering

The law undertakes a social control function, establishing norms of behaviour, proscribing and prescribing certain lifestyles. The law may be used to promote traditional virtues (Parton, 1981) or to lure individuals back into a conventional way of life (Wootton, 1959). Legal sanctions are used to coerce non-conformists. Legality is thus drawn as a boundary around what is normal and permissible, and becomes a threshold for societal intolerance (Parton, 1985). The law dictates who may marry, requiring marriage partners to be hetero-sexual and to have been born male and female (*Cossey* v. *The United Kingdom*, European Court of Human Rights [1990] – people who have changed sexual identity through gender reassessment surgery may not legally marry someone of the opposite sex). It regulates who may have children, by allowing for sterilisation without consent (*F* v. *West Berkshire Health Authority* [1989]) and by promoting a norm of heterosexual parenthood. Lesbianism is the single identifi-able factor which reverses the common bias in favour of women gaining custody of their children in divorce, despite, in some cases, proven violence from the father (Garlick, 1990). The Human Fertilisation and Embryology Act 1990 requires fertility clinics to consider the need for a father when taking a future child's welfare into account before deciding to offer a woman treatment (Dyer, 1991a). These norms are fuelled by strong anti-gay and anti-lesbian sentiments (Whitefield, 1991) and mirrored by overt control of sexuality in section 28 of the Local Government Act 1988 which attempts to curtail and suppress homosexual lifestyles (Romans, 1991) referring to 'pretended family relationships'. There is some evidence of a gradual shift however. Lesbian women and gay men may foster children (DoH, 1991a) following protest about draft guidance which expressly excluded 'equal rights and gay rights from any place in fostering services'. Although the norm of heterosexual parenthood remains a moral standard, an ideal which the law will consider in assessing where a child's welfare lies (*Re C (A Minor)* [1990]), lesbian couples have been successful in gaining joint resi-dence orders (CA 1989) (*Re C (A Minor) (Residence Order: Lesbian Co-Parents)* [1994]), giving both partners parental responsibility (Dyer, 1994).

The function of the law in prescribing conformity to established dominant norms was well-illustrated in debates surrounding divorce law reform and legislation on domestic violence. Opposition to proposals for reform was expressed on the grounds that they gave too many rights of property occupation to unmarried partners who were seeking protection from domestic violence, thus devaluing marriage. The Family Law Act 1996 reflects this by requiring that courts (section 41 (2)), in determining occupation orders that could exclude perpetrators of domestic violence from their own property, should take into account that unmarried couples have not made the same commitment to the relationship. Similarly, measures to remove the concept of fault in divorce, to promote mediation and ensure that reflection rather than recrimination informs discussion on the position of children and finances, have been criticised on the one hand as making divorce too easy and elicited counter-proposals to ban divorce for couples with children and to extend minimum waiting times. On the other hand there has been criticism that mediation favours the more powerful partner in a marriage, often the man, and that focus on reaching agreement, any agreement, is not necessarily in children's best interests (Mason, 1995).

Solutions to 'social problems'

The law provides for society's response to 'social problems'. These solutions are based on the assumption that the problems are caused by individuals deviating from the pre-given 'norm' of behaviour or failing to be bound by the constraints of the social engineering function. The moral panic aroused by deviance is calmed by the existence of measures to cure individual pathology or contain 'the incurables'.

The law provides the 'machinery for the suppression of unusual, eccentric or inconvenient behaviour' (Hoggett, 1990). The Mental Health Act 1983 enables madness to be contained behind locked doors; the National Assistance Act 1948 provides for the removal of sick people in the interests of public health. Professionals have an important function here, in locating and treating social problems in the individual (Wilding, 1982), in tidying away the disturbed and disturbing images (Preston-Shoot and Agass, 1990). The legal mandate to professionals is not, however, a consistent one. If professionals assume too much autonomy in interpreting it, they may come to be seen as part of the problem rather than the solution. Harris (1990a) demonstrates the variation between proposals to use legislation on the one hand to gain 'more control' over the problem of child abuse by creating wider powers of investigation and on the other hand to free families by controlling excesses of professional intervention.

Thus the regulation of professional activity is an allied function of the law in the field of social problem-solving. Legislation confirms and legitimises professional power in providing the mandate or permission to act. However professional power and status in itself affects both the perception of the social problem and the nature of the mandate (Sheppard, 1990). The historical development of certain areas of welfare legislation shows persistent tension and conflict between the relative power of professional ideologies, for example, legalism versus medicalism in mental health legislation (Bean, 1980) and their interaction with social and political forces (Busfield, 1986).

Legislation is often at the mercy of public and political opinion about what is defined as a social problem. Thus, child maltreatment is recognised as a socially constructed phenomenon which reflects current values and opinions (DoH, 1995a). Following the 1991 Criminal Justice Act's removal of custody as a sentencing option for young people under 15, it took only three years and a few high-profile young criminals, together with government anxiety about votes, to produce children's prisons – secure training centres (Criminal Justice and Public Order Act 1994). The level of feeling about the 'social problem' of youth crime has been described as reaching the scale of a moral panic, with young offenders as the 'folk devils' (Pitts, 1995). There has been a concerted political campaign to demonise young people and put them at the centre of draconian measures of punishment (Grewcock, 1995). In such a context of fear, increasing powers of coercion and control seek to reassure that 'something is being done'. Similarly, a small number of murders committed by people with severe mental illness were instrumental in defining them as a social problem to be addressed by increased measures of control.

Shaping attitudes and behaviours

The law can take a proactive role in shaping attitudes and behaviours. Notable here are the prohibitions on direct and indirect discrimination in the Race Relations Act 1976 and Sex Discrimination Act 1975 (amended 1986), and the provisions of the Equal Pay Act 1970 (amended 1983). More recently the Disability Discrimination Act 1995 has prohibited discrimination against disabled people in certain circumstances. These attempts can be criticised on a number of grounds, particularly for their emphasis upon restraining and remedial action rather than upon reform (Carlen, 1976) and for their provision of only individual remedies rather than class actions to benefit greater numbers of people. Individualised remedies are often ineffective and have had little impact on, for example, the position of women in the labour market (Equal Opportunities Commission, 1995). There is evidence of continuing barriers to equality in access to high status professional roles (Fothergill, 1994), of increased racial discrimination against staff in social services departments (Francis, 1995), and of a failure by the majority of local authorities to recruit a workforce that reflects the ethnicity of the local population (Commission for Racial Equality, 1995). A survey of social services departments' compliance with section 71 of the Race Relations Act (which requires that local authorities secure that their various functions are carried out with due regard to the need to eliminate unlawful racial discrimination and to promote equality of opportunity and good relations between people of different racial groups) found that 66 per cent did not even have an articulated policy (CRE, 1989) and service delivery continues to reflect low prioritisation of appropriate and diverse services (Hughes and Bhaduri, 1987). Problems in accessing racially appropriate services are even more acute in areas of relatively low black population (Rickford, 1995). Women who bring discrimination cases against employers have found that the cost of successful action is continued victimisation (Coles, 1991).

Current legislation does little to challenge the structures that maintain inequality. The Equal Opportunities Commission has called for prohibition within the legislation to be replaced by prescriptions, declarations of rights to equal treatment (EOC, 1988). The Disability Discrimination Act 1995 has been the subject of extensive criticism, a package of 'ifs, buts and maybes' (Robinson, 1994) which does little to promote a social model of disability or a civil rights perspective (Brindle, 1994). Powers of enforcement are woefully inadequate. The opportunity to address structural disadvantage has been missed by the focus on individual remedies (Thornton and Lunt, 1995). Calls for a more robust legislative structure have been met with government reluctance, emphasising (in defiance of the evidence) voluntarism and persuasion as more potent forces for change (George, 1991). The fierce debates on disability discrimination legislation that preceded the 1995 Act testified to the level of resistance, and it is unlikely that the tentative, individualised measures in that Act will be any more successful than the Race Relations Act 1976 or the Sex Discrimination Act 1975 have been in tackling the many barriers to fundamental change in attitude and behaviour.

Avoidance

The law assists in avoiding the confrontation of discrimination and disadvantage by, in effect, 'sins of omission'. The legislation that does not exist, or is not implemented, is as significant as that which is available. There is, for example, no legislation which prohibits discrimination on grounds of sexuality, age or (other than in Northern Ireland) religion. Although the Disabled Persons Act 1986 applies to 70 per cent of Social Services users (Kelly and Johnson, 1989) the government will not implement the key sections 1–3 relating to participation and advocacy. Observance of the implemented sections of the Act is very patchy, characterised by a lack of policy statements, reluctance to make the key operational changes required and low levels of funding (Warburton, 1990). The Disabled Persons (Employment) Acts of 1944 and 1958 required a 3 per cent quota of employees with disabilities, yet less than a third of eligible employers achieved this, such were the loopholes and absence of sanctions (*Employment Gazette*, 1991). The Disability Discrimination Act 1995 has abolished this quota. It prohibits less favourable treatment in employment of a person by reason of their disability if the employer cannot demonstrate that such treatment is justified (section 5), or if an employer fails to make a reasonable adjustment to the working environment and cannot justify that omission (section 6). However, this only applies to organisations employing more than twenty people. The Act has been criticised as insufficient protection for disabled people and as compounding disability by vagueness in drafting and the weakness of its employ-ment and services provisions (Gooding, 1996).

The emphasis in remedies for domestic violence has primarily been upon welfare services to women and civil action by them, rather than arrest and prosecution of the abusers (Hanmer *et al.*, 1989). In legislation relating to adults vulnerable through age, sickness or disability, there is a major omission of powers to protect from abuse or harm, currently under process of review (Law Commission, 1993a, 1993b).

Ideology

The law functions as a tool for furthering ideology. It is one means whereby beliefs about how society should be run may be turned into action. Thus social welfare legislation now embodies concepts such as 'the primacy of markets, the need to work and make self provision' (Freeman, 1990). The NHS and Community Care Act 1990 brought about fundamental changes to the health and welfare economy, rerouting its funding through purchaser and provider organisations, promoting a contract culture in which the local government service monopoly of the welfare state makes way for the questionable benefits of choice, flexibility, innovation and competition (Bamford, 1989). Community care legislation is an interesting example of law as a vehicle for ideology, in that the policy of community care represents a broad and unusual consensus between differing ideologies, between politicians, professions and people who use services that it is 'a good thing'. It is framed both as enabling people to achieve maximum autonomy and independence, and as ensuring cost-effectiveness and value for money in spending from the public purse (Braye and Preston-Shoot, 1995). That such benefits are subsequently seen to be illusory is evidence of the rhetoric rather than substance on which the policy is based, and of the primacy of monetarist ideology in the setting of objectives for welfare policy.

The common thread which unifies the functions of law in society is its emphasis upon individual solutions for individual problems. The law in effect colludes with an avoidance of the deeper underlying problems inherent in society's structures and institutions. Thus, whilst the Children Act 1989 provides for the support and protection of individual children, it does not tackle the underlying structural causes of impaired health and development. The position of women and children in relation to male violence remains unaddressed by the individual reactive remedies available in law (Freeman, 1984b). The legal framework for social work intervention focuses on individuals and families, not social and economic systems (Kingston, 1982), and on people-processing, not social change.

Value assumptions in the law

The functions that welfare law fulfils are underpinned by values and assumptions about people, relationships and their place in society. These assumptions are pervasive and influential in both the letter of the law and in its interpretation at an individual level.

Images of competency

The law assumes that people are rational and able to take responsibility for running their own lives and making their own decisions. The common law test of capacity requires only that people understand what they are doing, and the likely effects of their actions. The quality of the decision is irrelevant to the question of their capacity to make it (Law Commission, 1991). Many users of social services, however, are deemed not to have the right to exercise such choice; social workers and others are empowered to make decisions on their behalf and about them if certain conditions exist.

A diagnosis of mental disorder is a major disqualifier. There exists, under the Mental Health Act 1983, a complex statutory regime for the deprivation of liberty and treatment without consent, provided the proposed treatment is in respect of the mental disorder. Users of psychiatric services discover that few professionals question the basic assumption that people with a mental illness are incapable of defining their own best interests (Chamberlin, 1988). Powers to detain people compulsorily in hospital, even to treat, are unique in that predictive professional opinion of harm provides sufficient grounds. And yet there is no definition in law of mental illness – 'the law pays too little attention to the precise mental qualities which add up to disqualification from the right to make a choice about treatment' (Hoggett, 1990). The arena of decision-making is heavily dominated by medical paternalism – that a proposal to admit to hospital and treat is in someone's best interests – despite a marked lack of evidence to instil confidence that professional power is governed by adequate safeguards (Fennell, 1990). The Mental Health (Patients in the Community) Act 1995 extends even further the realm of professional influence, allowing for after-care under supervision in respect of patients where there is a substantial risk of serious harm to their, or other people's, health and safety. The purpose is to ensure that they accept services, including a requirement to reside in a particular place and to attend for treatment. There are by comparison very few powers to overrule the will of a physically ill person, although those that exist in section 47 of the National Assistance Act 1948 are sweeping. The British Association of Social Workers expects its members to avoid the use of such compulsion because of concerns about the section's effects and ethics.

Mental incompetence through psychiatric disorder also carries with it the negative stereotype of dangerous behaviour. Whilst this is rooted in fear rather than in fact, it is a powerful contributory factor to the extensive powers of control available. The early 1990s saw a stream of inquiries into circumstances in which people discharged from psychiatric hospital had killed others in the community. The common themes of these inquiries were the risk assessment and decision-making of professionals, the availability of suitable resources in the community and the coordination between services. The legislative response was to focus on the control of individual patients through supervision registers (HSG (94)5) and supervised after-care under the Mental Health (Patients in the Community) Act 1995, rather than upon the level and nature of service provision.

People with learning difficulties are commonly assumed to have limited 'competence' for decision-making, again with far-reaching consequences. They too may be compulsorily admitted to psychiatric hospital for assessment, and for treatment too if their behaviour is 'abnormally aggressive' or 'seriously irresponsible'. Until the early 1990s, people with learning difficulties could be detained in hospital without hope of release or trial on the grounds that they had committed an offence, often of a minor nature, but were deemed unfit to plead in court proceedings (Barry, 1990). This injustice may have become less likely through the Criminal Procedure (Insanity and Unfitness to Plead) Act 1991, which allows a trial of the facts to establish whether or not someone unfit to plead because of mental illness committed the offence, and gives courts sentencing disposals ranging from an absolute discharge, through supervision, treatment and guardianship orders, to a hospital order.

There is no specific legislation to cover treatment which is not for mental disorder, and for people who are not compulsorily detained under the Mental Health Act 1983 but who are incapable of consenting. The regime which has developed piecemeal under common law, and which is currently under review (Law Commission, 1993a, 1993b), is similarly dominated by medical paternalism (Fennell, 1990). Judgement in the case of *F* [1989], a woman with learning difficulties in respect of whom application was made for leave to perform sterilisation, clarified the legality if not the ethical issues. In the absence of any positive power for the courts to consent or give mandatory approval on behalf of people not capable of consenting, medical interventions must be carried out in the best interests and for the welfare of the person concerned (Shaw, 1990). Certain categories of treatment, including sterilisation but not abortion (*Re G* [1991]), should be referred to the courts for confirmation that the proposed operation is in the patient's best interests and therefore lawful (Official Solicitor, 1989). The confirmation will be sought by way of further medical opinion, continuing the pattern established in such cases of courts considering principally the views of clinicians (Carson, 1989), despite the finding that those views may be informed more by the ability to treat than by individuals' needs (Carson, 1990a). Thus professional dominance is reinforced in an arena where users' rights or, to be more precise, women's rights, do not have a powerful voice. Analyses of the judgement in the case of *F* [1989] (Carson, 1989; Morgan, 1990; Shaw, 1990) reveal bland assumptions about the woman's wishes, about where the responsibility for contraception lay, and failure to consider alternative courses of action. Legal backing for decision-making in this arena is given on the basis of best interests as determined by an expert, rather than substitute judgement as articulated by an advocate. It can be as far-reaching as to determine whether someone should live or die, as in the withdrawal of treatment to sustain life (*Airedale NHS Trust* v. *Bland* [1993]), or forcible tube feeding of women with anorexia.

A further major influencing factor in relation to competency is the concept of childhood. This itself can be seen as a social construct, rooted in cultural norms and values rather than biological capacities (Freeman, 1983a). Childhood carries implications of maturational incompleteness justifying the presence of a higher authority, be it parental or in other ways adult, and contributing to a view of children as unreliable in the legal arena (*Childright*, 1990a). The concept of absolute adult authority has become something of a battleground between competing perspectives on the decision-making capacity of children. The progressive erosion of the concept was accelerated by judgement in *Gillick* v. *West Norfolk and Wisbech Area Health Authority* [1986], which stated: 'parental right yields to the child's right to make his [*sic*] own decisions when he reaches sufficient understanding and intelligence to be capable of making up his mind on the matter requiring decision'.

A parallel shift of thinking about parental status was hastened by the same judgement: 'parental rights to control a child do not exist for the benefit of the parent. They exist for the benefit of the child and are justified only insofar as they enable the parent to perform his [*sic*] duties towards the child'. The emphasis on the child's views and the concept of parental responsibility find legislative expression in the Children Act 1989, and the Gillick judgement has had far-reaching consequences for a review of children's 'competency' in matters of medical treatment (Hoggett, 1987) and court processes. Children are no longer automatically presumed to be incompetent witnesses (CJA 1991).

The checklist of circumstances to which a court must have regard in determining a child's welfare under the Children Act 1989 is headed by the ascertainable wishes and feelings of the child. The Act allows a young person, of sufficient age and understanding to make an informed decision, to refuse examinations and assessment (sections 38 (6), 43 (8) and 44 (7)), and to refuse psychiatric and medical treatment (Schedule 3). Moreover the Act allows children, with the court's permission, to seek an order about the future and, in the event of disagreements with the guardian *ad litem*, to directly instruct a solicitor to represent them (DoH, 1989b). However the child's preferences are not determinative (Bainham, 1990). Judgement in the case of *B* aged 12 [1991] in line with whose wishes the court sanctioned abortion, against the express wishes of the parent, has reinforced the right of children's voices to be heard, but the abortion was ordered because it was in her best interests, not merely because she wanted it. Subsequent judgements have appeared to recapture some of the adult authority ground eroded by Gillick. In *Re R* [1991], the Court of Appeal overruled a 15-year-old's lucid withdrawal of consent to anti-psychotic drug treatment, indicating that refusal by a 'Gillick competent' child could be overruled by someone with parental responsibility. In this case, where the child was a Ward, the court also emphasised its power to override the decisions of 'Gillick competent' children as well as those of parents. In *Re W* [1992] the Court of Appeal ruled that legislation distinguishes between a minor's right to consent and their right to refuse, thus establishing that a competent minor's refusal could be over-ruled by someone with parental responsibility. In addition a court may overrule either consent or refusal on the part of a minor. This judgement has precipitated an 'extraordinary muddle' about the rights of young people to control their treatment (Hodgkin, 1994).

Recent legal decision-making on children's competence in the field of medical consent is in stark contrast to that in youth justice where the age of criminal responsibility has remained low in inter-national comparison, despite provision in the Children and Young Persons Act 1969 (repealed by section 72, CJA 1991) to raise it from 10 to 14. A child between the ages of 10 and 13 can still be convicted of an offence provided that they knew their actions to be seriously wrong (*C (A Minor)* v. *DPP* [1995]). Reliance may be placed on what a young person does or says, to indicate their state of mind and their appreciation of the seriousness of their behaviour. Responses to direct questions may be relied on as insight into this (*L* v. *DPP* [1996]; *T* v. *DPP* [1996]; *W, GH, and CH* v. *DPP* [1996]).

Images of moral worth

Much welfare legislation contains expressions, if not definitions, of the concept of 'need'. Section 21 of the National Assistance Act 1948 provides for accommodation for people 'in need of care and atten-tion'. Section 1 of the Chronically Sick and Disabled Persons Act 1970 requires local authorities to identify the needs of certain groups of people. The Education Act 1993 talks of special educational need, the NHS and Community Care Act 1990 imposes a duty to assess need for community care services, and section 17 of the Children Act 1989 refers to 'children in need'. In a society which promotes a self-help, enterprise culture, valuing responsibility and the ability to provide for oneself from the fruits of one's labours, to be publicly identified as 'needy' has an inevitably stigmatising effect. The stigma of public provision has a long history from Poor Law eligibility rules and Victorian beliefs about the links between poverty and indolence and immorality (James, 1987) through to modern-day criteria for state benefits and welfare provision. The inclusion of children with disabilities by definition in the Children Act as 'in need' has provoked anxiety (Martin, 1990) – to be chosen for state interven-tion lowers one's station as a citizen, confirming the neediness as some form of personal pathology. Whether the state's response to the pathology is punitive or benevolent depends both upon the legislative framework and upon personal and professional ideologies. Moral assessments, whether positive (more deserving) or negative (less deserving) have been shown to be potent in decision-making by courts (Parker *et al.*, 1989), by the police (Hanmer *et al.*, 1989; Smith, 1989) and by social workers in child protection (Dingwall *et al.*, 1983) and after-care provision (McCluskey, 1994).

Images of race

One of the functions of the law is to maintain the privileges and power of dominant groups in society. Within a racialised social hierarchy, public power and authority are used to legitimise and maintain the subordination of black people to white (Dominelli, 1988). The law, as one such mechanism, is both founded upon and in turn reinforces the individual, institutional and cultural manifestations of racism which interact to continue oppression.

At one level, the law appears benign: the Race Relations Act 1976 makes direct and indirect discrimination on grounds of race illegal in a range of situations – employment, education, the provision of goods, services and facilities. However this must be matched against the existence of other legislation controlling immigration, nationality, access to income support and welfare benefits, all of which have the effect of imposing constraints upon the freedom of movement, citizenship status, opportunities and eligibility of black people, and in particular of black women, owing to the interaction of racism and concepts of roles and relationships within families (WING, 1985). Race and class have been found to be powerful mediators of police responses to domestic violence, where the first official response has been to check women's immigration status (Hanmer and Statham, 1988). Women have been trapped in situations of violence by the one-year rule in immigration, whereby to have residential status confirmed women have to prove that they remain married and that they have no recourse to public funds (Mama, 1989; Redding, 1991a). Families are permanently separated by rules limiting women's rights to be joined by children and older dependent relatives (WING, 1985). Black families are placed under considerable financial pressure by the requirement to sponsor and support dependent relatives (Dominelli, 1988).

What appears as an inconsistency of intention between liberal and humanitarian race relations legislation and harsh and oppressive immigration law (Alcock and Harris, 1982) in fact can be seen as two interrelated developments – liberalism balanced by assurance that numbers will be restricted. Indeed the very existence of the race relations legislation is only possible politically in a context of strict immigration controls (Layton-Henry, 1984). The discrimination in immigration law conflicts with both the European Charter of Human Rights and the United Nations Convention on the Rights of Children (*Childright*, 1990b).

Within the field of welfare law there are inconsistencies in the profile held by issues of race. The Children Act 1989 takes a proactive stance to bring consideration of race, language, religion and culture to the fore in decision-making about children. The NHS and Community Care Act 1990, by contrast, is silent on the issue.

It is also necessary to consider how effectively the legislation operates in practice. The Race Relations Act has not changed the employment profile of black people, and services are still dominated by white norms. Major problems exist around enforcement, which is left to individual complainants who have to prove discrimination, with all the attendant problems of evidence, rather than employers demonstrating an absence of discrimination. Not surprisingly, complaints have a low success rate (Banton, 1990) and, as more overt forms of racism are identified and proscribed, more subtle forms appear (Alcock and Harris, 1982). Images of race also influence the ways in which general legislation which permits the control of 'problematic' behaviour such as madness, child abuse or criminal offending is consistently used with disproportionate frequency in respect of black people. The social system which excludes black people from power and resources then pathologises and blames them for 'failure' (Dominelli, 1988). Thus at the levels of both ideology and practice stereotypical images and assumptions about race are woven into the law, which not only fails to challenge white racism but accepts and condones it (Alcock and Harris, 1982).

Images of gender

'The legal system is constantly re-creating a particular ideological view of relationships between the sexes, best expressed as an ideology of patriarchalism' (Freeman, 1984b). It is hard to avoid in law the stereotypical image of women as the property of men, economically and emotionally dependent, with primary responsibility for child rearing. This is despite the reality of the experience of women, the majority of whom return to the labour market after having children, making vital contributions to the domestic economy and often not maintained by men at all (Smart, 1990). Arrangements under the Child Support Act 1991 require women claiming state benefits to reveal the identity of the child's father or potentially to be financially disadvantaged, preserving dependency links despite the real risks of subsequent harassment or violence. The absence of any broad duty to provide pre-school facilities is arguably predicated upon the expectation that family care is available and that women construct their working lives around the availability of child care, not the reverse.

The legal framework for responses to domestic violence provides a major example of institutionalised collusion with women's subordination and rich evidence of how women are viewed within the law. No statute has ever repealed the common-law privilege of men to inflict 'domestic chastisement' upon their wives (Freeman, 1984b) and it was only under the Criminal Justice and Public Order Act 1994 (section 142 (2)) that statute withdrew the right of a man to rape his wife following a House of Lords judgement (*Regina* v. *R* [1991]). Domestic violence has commonly not been classed as a crime, and therefore has not qualified as 'legitimate' police work (Smith, 1989). Yet the remedies available to women under civil law (DVMPA 1976; DPMCA 1978; HA 1985; FLA 1996) have failed to provide adequate solutions. By focusing on the victim, they do nothing to tackle the underlying structural issues of power which maintain the inequality. Awareness of this has led to mounting pressure for more effective action to be taken under criminal law. Police reluctance to arrest male perpetrators of violence has been widely criticised (Smith, 1989) and increasing emphasis has been placed upon reviewing the Force Orders which regulate the pattern of operational policing at local level (Bourlet, 1990). In some areas schemes promoting a more interventionist police approach have been instituted (Bourlet, 1990; Campbell, 1990) and Home Office guidelines now prescribe an approach which emphasises the criminal aspects of domestic assaults (Knewstub, 1991). Responses, however, are still often imbued with assumptions about the seriousness of the crime, which are reinforced by deferred cautioning or 'cooling off in the cells' approaches. Claims of 'success' for these schemes often simplify the interactive processes which follow such interventions, and in which the power relationship remains unchanged. Similar criticism has been levelled at the provision under the Police and Criminal Evidence Act 1984 to compel women to give evidence in criminal proceedings against their partners. This was heralded as an advance to help persuade the police to more interventionist approaches, but does little to remove the underlying disincentives for women to give evidence (Brownlee, 1990), and when they do women remain disappointed and let down by the leniency shown in the criminal courts (NCH, 1994). There is also concern that the 'reforms' do not necessarily benefit all women, but merely make it easier for white middle-class heterosexual women to complain of only the more obvious and excessive forms of male violence (Hanmer *et al.*, 1989).

The domestic violence arena provides ample evidence of the influence of value assumptions on the 'law in practice'. 'Where the legal system fails is in the application, operation and interpretation of legislative provisions' (Smith, 1989). Even where effective legal remedies exist, police responses have been shown to be powerfully influenced by individual officers' personal experiences, attitudes and stereotypical assumptions about the patterns of relationships and respective rights of women and men (Hanmer *et al.*, 1989). They may be summarised as the belief that domestic violence is of a trivial nature, that it is a family matter in which the law should not interfere, that the victims are usually 'undeserving' women, and that they are unreliable and uncooperative as witnesses (Smith, 1989). The police response has been described as a lottery (Appio and Rudgard, 1995). Legislative and policy changes have yet to make a demonstrable impact at the level of individual attitudes. Such negative stereotyping of women permeates the judicial statements which gain occasional press notoriety – images of women as devious, manipulative, fickle, and ultimately responsible for male excesses. Of equally serious concern is the failure to take account of the power dynamics of gender and age within families, and of how these are shaped by male dominance (O'Hara, 1994). Thus, the links between men's violence to women and their abuse of children have been slow to be recognised. The Children Act 1989 contributes to the difficulty of promoting safe and appropriate responses to male violence by its erroneous assumption that separated parents can behave reasonably and that children's interests are served by retaining contact with men who have abused their mothers (Harne and Radford, 1994). Gendered assumptions influence the implementation of community care legislation also, where the promotion of independent lifestyles within a mixed economy of welfare reflects a reliance on the continued availability of cheap or free women's labour (Grimwood and Popplestone, 1993).

At a more systematic level there is ample evidence of the influence of institutionalised values. Allen (1986) gives an analysis of patterns of court disposals in relation to female and male offenders, where women were twice as likely to receive a psychiatric disposal that could not be accounted for by differences in the respective mental health of the women and men concerned. She concludes that decision-making was constrained by a complex interaction between biases in the legal and medical provision on the one hand and gendered understandings about the nature of human beings on the other. The law in effect operationally differentiates at a deep structural level, despite stated neutrality in relation to the sexes. Harris (1990b) provides similar evidence in relation to juveniles, with adolescent young women propelled into supervision or care more quickly than young men, and receiving tutelary disposals for lesser offences. Edwards and Halpern (1990), in a national survey of financial provision in divorce, found wide geographical variations in the orders made, not attributable to economic or demographic differences. They conclude that the high degree of discretion exercised by court registrars was the most influential factor, and that this discretion was informed by varying views on the place and role of the family, the position of women in the home and at work, and attitudes both to divorced women and to the second wives of the men concerned.

A final example of gendered images in law is provided by the differential experiences of women and men accused of murder. Women driven to kill as an ultimate self-defence against domestic violence but who, because of differences in strength, take action as the man sleeps, have found grounds of self-defence not open to them. The law was constructed to take account of male capacity for action, not female (Miller, 1991). A defence of provocation has, until the mid-1990s, relied on the violent response to the provocation being immediate, involving a sudden and temporary loss of self-control or an act of self-defence in the face of imminent danger. A series of appeals has more recently established that provocation can be cumulative, that the reaction in self-defence need not be immediate, and thus opened the door to women previously convicted of the murder of their violent partners.

Images of disability

Available legislation provides for services to address problems experienced as a result of disability rather than to promote change through addressing the interaction between society and disabled people, and the social and economic factors which create and exacerbate disability. The definition of disability used in legislation reinforces this perspective and may be criticised for its narrow focus (AMA, 1994). The underlying principle of normalisation contributes to the emphasis on convention and conformity in the experience of disabled people to the standards of a non-disabled world, rather than an acknowledgement of society's need to change (Ryan and Thomas, 1993). The Chronically Sick and Disabled Persons Act 1970 and the Disabled Persons Act 1986 are concerned with numbers, assessment of individual need and, therefore, with care, adjustment and rehabilitation. The emphasis is upon what people with disabilities can or cannot do through their impairment rather than upon inequality of opportunity, what they are prevented from doing through a hostile environment. Local authorities have considerable discretion, being required to provide services *where satisfied that it is necessary to do so* in order to meet the needs of a disabled person. However, an applicant who wishes to appeal a decision must not only identify a present unmet need but prove that refusal of a local authority to meet that need is irrational and perverse (*R* v. *Kent County Council and Others, ex parte Bruce* [1986]). Key aspects of the 1986 Act concerned with advocacy, involvement in assessment and representation will not be implemented, yet these would move legislation away from an individual dependency and medical model towards a focus upon empowerment and partnership in decision-making.

Even more recent legislation, the Disability Discrimination Act 1995, does little, if anything, to promote a social model of disability, to further understanding of disability not as an individual problem but as one 'concerned with the effects of hostile physical and social environments upon impaired individuals, or even a societal one concerned with the way society treats this particular minority group' (Oliver, 1983). Indeed there appears to be an absence of commitment to look beyond arrangements based on dominant images of 'normality'. The Disability Discrimination Act 1995 reflects the government's ongoing reluctance to give legislative backing to disability rights, and it reinforces the preoccupation with individual disadvantage. Without such a focus on the structural position of disabled people, protective legislation requires that an individual has to identify and associate him/herself with a stigmatised state in order to gain protection.

During the passage of the NHS and Community Care Act 1990, an amendment proposing a duty on housing authorities to develop policies to meet the housing needs of those covered by the community care legislation was overturned in the Commons. Even legislation (Community Care (Direct Payments) Act 1996) to allow local authorities to make cash payments to disabled people, instead of arranging services, in order to promote choice, independence and autonomy, fails to establish such a mechanism as a right for disabled people, and may by Statutory Instrument exclude large groups from its remit (Waters, 1995).

Whilst the above themes have been separated for exploration, they interact and impact together to create overlapping layers of discrimination. Thus women's oppression within the law is powerfully mediated by images of race; the images underlying law in the field of disability will operate differentially for women and men. In a social system where the validated and respected norms are white, able-bodied, male, competent and responsible, negative images of deviations from these norms are powerful influences, both within the law itself and in the decision-making of those who implement it.

Conflicting imperatives

The complexity of the law's functions in society results in a number of forceful demands which contradict each other. These conflicting imperatives are contained within the law and emanate from it in such a way that obeying one set of principles forces the abandonment of another.

Needs v. rights/citizenship

In 1991 the government ratified the United Nations Convention on the Rights of the Child. The convention (1989) sets out standards for children's welfare and civil rights in four broad areas – survival, development, protection and participation. Its underlying principles emphasise the paramountcy of the child's welfare, and the child's right to:

1. express views and be permitted freedom of expression, thought and association;
2. be free from discrimination, inhumane treatment, unlawful restrictions of liberty and all forms of sexual, physical and mental violence;
3. information, education and health care;
4. have these rights widely known (Lindsay, 1992).

The convention has, in itself, no legal authority. It must be incorporated into member states' national law in order to progress from its position as a moral imperative. Progress, however, is monitored by the United Nations Committee on the Rights of the Child, and the United Kingdom has been severely criticised for its record on ensuring that policy and legislation complies with the convention. Furthermore, some developments may be criticised as being directly contradictory to its principles – in particular provisions of secure training centres for young offenders (CJPOA 1994), the law's tolerance of reasonable chastisement by parents and childminders, lack of consultation with young people in the education system, immigration and asylum-seekers provisions which can separate children from their parents, the number of children living in poverty due to benefit cuts, the impact of legislation (CJPOA 1994) on travellers' children, and the tightening of provisions for homeless people (*Childright*, 1995a). These findings have fuelled calls for a Children's Rights Commissioner or Ombudsperson (Levy, 1995; George, 1995).

The United Nations has been influential in promoting the development of a European Convention on the Exercise of Children's Rights, available for member states to ratify from 1996. The convention contains procedural measures to ensure that children's rights are respected, and establishes a standing committee (*Child-*

right, 1995b). United Kingdom ratification is undecided. A route that is available to UK citizens is to the European Court of Human Rights. This may hear submissions that the European Convention on Human Rights and Fundamental Freedoms has been breached. Whilst not a route of appeal from UK courts for individuals, the court's findings are influential, and national legislation must be amended to take account of them. In more than two-thirds of UK cases heard by the court up to 1990, there was held to be a violation of human rights. The UK has had the highest number of findings against it (Pritchard, 1992).

This broad emphasis on the rights of all children should be contrasted with the emphasis in UK law on a more selective response to some children – those defined as children in need (CA 1989). Establishing need is a prerequisite to a child falling within the local authority's range of duties (as opposed to powers). Even then there is no individual enforceable right to services. A court cannot, for instance, make a specific issues order (section 8, CA 1989) to compel a local authority to provide services to a child or family (*Re J (A Minor: Specific Issue Order)* [1995]). Challenging such local authority decisions has to be through judicial review and courts are reluctant to overturn the exercise of discretion by local authorities in pursuit of their duties unless such exercise has clearly been unreasonable (see Preston-Shoot, 1996b).

In the field of community care there are similarly no rights enshrined in law. Legislation which attempts to recognise rights of citizenship, such as the Disabled Persons Act 1986, is in tension with the requirement to prove individual need in order to gain resources, for example the NHS and Community Care Act 1990. Services are provided under the latter not because people have an active right, but because a passive need has been established. Individual detriment has to be proved rather than membership of a group with rights. The further one moves from the dominant image of competency and self-provision, the fewer rights one has. To be old, disabled or poor is to be less of a citizen.

The concept of need in itself gives rise to further conflicts. Need is not self-evident (Smith and Harris, 1972); methods of identifying and defining it have differing implications for intervention and provision. There is tension, for instance, between need as an expression of individual incompleteness and need as an expression of structural inequality. The dominant medical model of welfare, where need is seen to arise from individual pathology, informs much of the legal framework which allows for individual but not group provision and leaves hierarchical power structures intact. The rule of economy is a major influence on definitions of need, whereby needs-led assessments are required but then compromised by what resources can be provided. Government statements on community care (DoH, 1989c) exemplify the conflict. Key concepts such as 'the careful assessment of need' are juxtaposed with the 'aim to ensure that all available resources are put to best use'. 'Assessment should not focus only on the user's suitability for an existing resource' but 'decisions on service provision will have to take account of what is available and affordable'. Subsequent guidance (DoH, 1990) goes one stage further: assessors (of need) should have available to them information about the cost of services 'to assist them in arriving at cost-effective proposals'. There lies, therefore, a fundamental contradiction within community care law and policy – the open-ended obligation on social services departments to meet growing needs from increasingly smaller budgets (Clements, 1995). It is a contradiction on which courts are increasingly being asked to rule (see Chapter 5).

Children's services are similarly beset. The Audit Commission (1994) encourages a needs-led approach but advocates decision-making on what needs can and should be met. In special education services similar compromises occur, with pressure upon professionals to 'amend' assessments to bring them in line with what is already available within the authority (K. Jones, 1991). In relation to eligibility for medical treatment the Court of Appeal ruled that it was not for the court to overrule a health authority's decision over the non-allocation of funding to treatment for a particular child (*R* v. *Cambridge District Health Authority, ex parte B* [1995]). Thus, need confers no rights, and may be subject to a resource-led response.

Welfare v. justice

The law would prefer intervention to be both fair and beneficial. The conflict between the two imperatives has been widely recognised in the field of youth justice where the Children and Young Persons Act 1969, in attempting to reconcile the demands, succeeded in merely blurring the distinctions and provided justice masquerading as welfare (Harris, 1982). Subequent policy developments have increasingly separated the two strands, fuelled by public concern about youth crime and culminating in the Criminal Justice and Public Order Act 1994 which places young offenders squarely in the justice arena. This makes welfare arguments for provision to address their needs as children even more difficult to sustain. 'Children who offend are offenders first and children second. Punishment takes precedence over welfare' (Crisp, 1994).

The conflict crystallises again in the field of child protection, where the requirement to promote the child's welfare conflicts with the parent's right to the justice of a fair trial, and in debates about the treatment or punishment of abusers. The emphasis on civil remedies in situations of domestic violence gives rise to similar dilemmas: a woman who flees her home with her children because she cannot get legal backing for protection while she remains in the house may be acting for their welfare but can hardly be described as receiving fair treatment. The Mental Health Act 1983 was the result of strong lobbying to enhance the civil liberties of people with mental disorder, but allows welfare to override them, compulsory detention and treatment being possible in the interests of health or safety or the protection of others. Conversely, large numbers of people with mental disorder enter the criminal justice system where their health and welfare needs are ill-served owing to the absence of diversionary schemes offering psychiatric involvement at early stages in the justice process (*The Guardian*, 1991).

The rights of an individual to autonomy v. the rights of the state to intervene

The private/public debate is one which is central to family law. The family has a long tradition of 'privacy' which influences the choice of legal remedies to perceived problems and generates controversy about 'the right solution'. This has been apparent in analyses of police intervention in domestic violence where policies of automatic prosecution to deter and protect are hampered by the belief that what happens between men and women in their own home is private and outside the law (Hanmer *et al.*, 1989; Smith, 1989). Throughout the late 1980s the same debate was integral to the review of children's and family law which resulted in the Children Act 1989.

At its extremes, the debate polarised between those who advocate parental autonomy in child-rearing and those who advocate intervention by the state to protect children from their parents (Freeman, 1983b). Children's rights could be used to justify either position – either that they have a right to family integrity, or that they have a right to protection. A further loop of the argument questions the legitimacy of intervention where there are no uniform standards to trigger it, and where inconsistency of standards is so great as to legislate for child protection in a society which condones corporal punishment (Freeman 1984a; *Childright*, 1989a) and where parents may delegate to others the right to hit their children (*Sutton LBC* v. *Davis* [1994]). The purpose of intervention is also questioned: is it to support or to punish (Parton, 1985)? The law reflects the pendulum of opinion as it swings between views of children's welfare as individuals or as family members (Fox Harding, 1991).

The 1989 Children Act neatly encapsulates the conflict between autonomy and intervention. It is the product of strong criticism of social services departments' failures to protect children (Beckford Report, 1985; Carlile Report, 1987) counterbalanced by outcry at over-zealous attempts to exercise the child protection role (Butler-Sloss, 1988) and of the debate between respect for family life and the duty to protect children from abuse (Lyon, 1989). It attempts both to clarify and to widen the grounds for protection, by providing for situations where harm is anticipated but has not occurred, whilst emphasising the role of parents through the concept of responsibility and enhancing the protection of their rights through early decisions on contact and challenges to emergency protection orders. At a deeper level it reflects and widens the ideological split between child *abuse* as symptomatic of malfunctioning families and child *care* as what happens in good families, regardless of their resources and income (Frost and Stein, 1990).

The divergence between these two concepts has become increasingly apparent. The Act's implementation in 1991 was followed by a dramatic drop in the number of compulsory actions and court cases for children's protection, leading to early claims that the new legislative emphasis on partnership with families to provide family support services was achieving its purpose. Such optimism proved premature. Court figures have risen again. The Audit Commission (1994) published a report critical of local authorities' perceived continued emphasis on intervention to protect children from abuse at the expense of broader family support measures. Social services departments are urged to be less selective, and to support a broad range of options for the support of vulnerable families (Gibbons, 1992).

The outcomes from a range of evaluative studies (DoH, 1995a) have fuelled the debate about whether child protection and family support are conflicting imperatives or merely part of the same spectrum of measures available to the relationship between families and the state. The argument is advanced that social work has become too focused on child protection and that more effective family support strategies are protective in themselves, the general family context being more important than any abusive event within it. Held responsible are prioritisation criteria which place child abuse investigations higher than other services to families, thus limiting the latter when resources are scarce. This is attributed to a misinterpretation of the Children Act itself, an assumption that child protection under Part V is statutory and therefore to be prioritised over non-statutory family support under Part III. In fact both parts of the Act carry equal statutory force and should be integrated and seen as a continuum. Such a view is consistent with the argument that, at the ideological level, welfare has been hijacked by non-interventionism (Adcock *et al.*, 1991). Against this it is argued (Parton, 1995) that the two are, in fact, informed by quite different assumptions, are not compatible, and could be more usefully located in separate agencies. Parton (1995) contends that to argue merely for a shift of balance towards meeting children's needs obscures the more fundamental question of the balance of responsibility between the state and parents, particularly when the concept of need is presented without discussion of poverty and deprivation. To construe need as individualised allows parents to be held responsible, and for family support to be presented as an achievable task, letting wider social and economic policies off the hook.

The trend towards non-intervention in the child-care field contrasts sharply with the position in the mental health arena, where the right of individuals to make autonomous decisions about fundamental issues, such as where they live and how they spend their time, is massively eroded by coercive measures under the Mental Health (Patients in the Community) Act 1995.

Conclusion

This exploration of the functions and the value base of the law has shown that, far from providing solutions to the dilemmas of social work, the law is in fact integral to those dilemmas and carries within itself the conflicting imperatives which influence the day-to-day decision-making of individual practitioners.

3

The Law and Social Work's Practice Dilemmas

The opening chapters analysed the contrasting expectations of social workers in their exercise of statutory powers and duties, and the conflicting imperatives embedded in the law. Here the concern is with how these tensions find expression in social work's practice dilemmas. How should practitioners manage work with disturbing and disturbed people in the context of contradictory public attitudes about intrusive and heavy-handed or dilatory and unconcerned workers? How should they manage the tension between an individual's right to self-determination and right to protection when vulnerable or powerless in the context of such constraints on public expenditure that there must be doubt about whether social welfare organisations can fully implement statutory duties?

This chapter analyses myths about the law and social work and the resulting practice dilemmas which daily confront practitioners and their managers. These must be comprehended and reconciled. Otherwise the inheritance from the social and economic politics of welfare will mean defensive practice which provides but illusory protection from the possibility of failure, and which represents a substantial departure from professional standards.

Myths

Myths are belief systems which govern the behaviour of families, organisations and professional networks. They tend to be impervious to contradictory evidence and to remain unchallenged (Ferreira, 1963; Byng-Hall, 1988). Scripts, a closely related concept, are belief systems which prescribe the action to be taken (Stratton *et al.*, 1990). Work patterns dominated by myths and scripts tend to work to formulas, to generate pressure for conformity and to eschew questioning of what happens. Several such myths about the law and social work follow. They are elaborated because social work must 'name the game', that is, point out such assumptions as part of promoting awareness of what it can and cannot do.

The myth of clarity

The legal framework does not provide clarity for social workers about who is vulnerable and should be protected, or about when and how to exercise authority appropriately. It does not inform social workers as to what they ought to do, only as to what they can do (Howe, 1980). Consequently questions remain about what constitutes sufficient grounds to act (Braye and Preston-Shoot, 1990). The absence of clarity arises partly from the ambiguity of language and legislative drafting.

Exercise 3.1

How would you interpret the italicised phrases?
1. . . . suffering from *grave chronic disease* or, being *aged, infirm or physically incapacitated*, are *living in insanitary conditions* and are unable to devote to themselves, and are not receiving from other persons, *proper care and attention* (section 47, NAA 1948).
2. . . . general duty of every local authority . . . *to safeguard and promote the welfare of children . . . who are in need . . .* (section 17(1), CA 1989).
3. . . . *a reasonable standard of health or development . . .* (section 17(10), CA 1989).
4. . . . *reasonable steps* . . . to prevent children . . . suffering *ill-treatment or neglect* (Schedule 2, Part 1, 4(1), CA 1989).
5. . . . the child is suffering, or is likely to suffer, *significant harm*; and that the harm, or likelihood of harm, is attributable to the care given to the child, or likely to be given to him [*sic*] if the order were not made, not being *what it would be reasonable to expect a parent to give . . .* (section 31(2), CA 1989).

---

6. . . . *mental disorder of a nature or degree which warrants the detention of the patient in a hospital* . . . in the interests of his [*sic*] *own health or safety* or with a view to the *protection of other persons* (section 2(2), MHA 1983).
7. . . . an individual ('the carer') provides or intends to provide *a substantial amount of care on a regular basis* . . . (section 1(1)(b), Carers (Recognition and Services) Act 1995).

The Mental Health Act 1983 does not define mental illness and yet sociological and psychological definitions differ fundamentally about causes and interventions. Norman (1980) has demonstrated the different interpretations which may be placed on section 47, National Assistance Act 1948. Ormiston (1990) similarly criticised the lack of clarity in the NHS and Community Care Act 1990, section 46, regarding the structure, content and processes involved in formulating community care plans, questioning too whether they will ultimately be relevant to users and effective in terms of service delivery. Subsequent experience has demonstrated the appropriateness of this concern. Guidance (LAC(93)4) has been necessary to ensure the involvement of voluntary agencies and the independent sector in consultation processes during the preparation and review of community care plans. The experience of multidisciplinary collaboration has been variable and plans have been criticised for their failure to address performance evaluation and review (Wistow *et al.*, 1993). Knowledge of the needs of particular service user groups varies, consultation has not always been effective, and services have not always been grounded by a well-informed sense of direction (DoH, 1993b; Bewley and Glendinning, 1994). Hoath (1990) has analysed the difficulties in defining intentional homelessness (HA 1996), pointing out inconsistencies in interpretation by courts, and a trend towards outcomes not intended by the legislation. It remains unclear whether services provided under section 2 (CSDPA 1970) are community care services since they are not specifically mentioned in section 46(3) (NHSCCA 1990), which defines such services, but are rooted in section 29 (NAA 1948) which is listed there.

Lack of clarity raises considerable problems in the field of child protection. How are social workers to determine the likelihood of significant harm: balance of probabilities, chance, magnitude? The

Children Act 1989 is silent here. Bainham (1990) suggested that courts would relate the chance of harm occurring to its gravity if it occurred. What may be highly unlikely is nonetheless always possible. What likely risks are unacceptable? Two cases (*Newham LBC* v. *AG* [1993]; *Re H and R (Child Sexual Abuse: Standard of Proof)* [1996]) have clarified that 'likely' should be interpreted as a real possibility which cannot sensibly be ignored, a real or substantial risk, rather than as a balance of probabilities. However, such decisions will remain contentious and fraught with uncertainty. Indeed, concern exists that this definition, when accompanied with the requirement that likelihood requires more than suspicion but facts capable of proof (*Re H and R* [1996]), will fail to protect some children from abuse.

Courts have had to determine that section 31(2)(a)(b) is a two-stage test (*Re H and R* [1996]) and that the words 'is suffering' (section 31(2)(a)), for which the standard of proof is the balance of probabilities, relate to the period immediately before the process of protecting a child is first put into motion by, for instance, an emergency protection order (*Northamptonshire CC* v. *S* [1993]; *Re M (A Minor) (Care Order: Threshold Conditions)* [1994]). Concerns, however, have been expressed here that this weakens the family's power to withstand state intervention (Masson, 1994).

Similar ambiguities arise in section 31(10). What is a similar child with whom a child, who may have suffered significant harm to his or her health and development, may be compared? The guidance given (DoH, 1989b) fails to add clarity, referring to a similar child as one with similar attributes and needs. How are these to be determined? Similarly, when is harm significant (Gibbons and Bell, 1994)? Variations between authorities in the number of children whose names are placed on the child protection register, and in how categories for registration are used, add to questions about their usefulness and point to different interpretations of what is abuse and, if all harm is significant, of when state intervention is required. Such inexplicitness concerning child protection creates stress and uncertainty about whether, how and when to act, and allows subjective values, for example about appropriate parental or gender behaviour, to influence judgements.

Lack of clarity arises also from the task facing social workers. The law presents people as homogeneous groups, promoting assumptions that social workers act as rule enforcers. In fact they are rule interpreters, confronting the task of individualising, of appraising whether legal terminology applies to specific cases. In this gate-keeping and decision-making task the absence of predictive vari-ables and checklists creates additional ambiguity and stress. There are no standards for intervention, thresholds which trigger action (Freeman, 1990). For instance, there is no agreed definition of what is good enough child care, or of child abuse and harm (DoH, 1995a), or when child abuse or neglect is such to warrant removal of the child. Indeed debates about transracial adoption, and the rights of parents and children in child-care or child protection cases, demon-strate the absence of consensus over definitions of the 'child's welfare'. Prediction is characterised by uncertainty. Whilst specific factors, about which practitioners should be knowledgeable, suggest dangerousness and risk, they can never be conclusive. Checklists alone are insufficient evidence for action. Nor is there any legal basis for acting on best guesses, or for statutory intervention 'just in case'.

A particular cause for confusion is the term 'need'. The Children Act 1989 defines children in need (section 17) inadequately, with resulting widespread variation in interpretation by local authorities (Colton *et al.*, 1995). Need is not defined at all in community care law, despite being the springboard for a duty on local authorities to provide services. The problem is compounded by the absence of a detailed theory of human need (Doyal and Gough, 1991) on which assessments can be based. Moreover, even if the basic parameters of need can be agreed, the problem then arises as to what level of satisfaction should be provided.

Nor does available guidance solve this conundrum. It refers to personal autonomy, health, finance, employment/education/leisure, accommodation, transport, personal care and social support needs (DoH, 1990); and to community presence, community participation, fulfilment, independence and dignity (SSI, 1993c). The aim is to provide an acceptable level of social independence or quality of life (DoH, 1991j). However, what is an acceptable level, and to whom? The guidance also lacks clarity because it does not prioritise objectives. In community care guidance, for instance, using available resources in the most effective way to meet individual needs is juxtaposed without comment with individual choice and restoring independence (DoH, 1990); proper assessment of need with deciding provision levels according to what is affordable; tailoring services to meet needs in ways and at times convenient to users with developing priorities and targets defined by fundholders (Audit Commission, 1992).

One danger with ambiguity around key concepts is the risk of muddled, variable or uncertain action. One variant of this is buck-passing. The Commission on Social Justice (1994) complained that too many people are passed between agencies at the expense of provision of appropriate forms of care. Housing authorities and social services departments may dispute who should house young people in need. The House of Lords has ruled (*R* v. *Northavon DC, ex parte Smith* [1994]) that a social services department cannot decline to exercise its protective powers (section 17, CA 1989) for financial or other reasons and seek to transfer responsibility without any offer of contribution. A second variant is duplication. Young carers, for instance, may qualify for assessment and services under three separate provisions (section 17, CA 1989; section 8, DPA 1986; Carers (Recognition and Services) Act 1995) but may find, partly as a result of administrative divisions in departments, that services are not coordinated and that the different obligations arising from different statutes are not appreciated or met (*R* v. *Bexley LBC, ex parte B* [1995]).

Another danger is that the law, far from not being known, does not lend itself to being used. Debate about the failure of the law to prevent the death of Beverley Lewis, a young woman with multiple disabilities, produced the view that the law in itself was not inadequate but that the available powers were not used (Fennell, 1989). Ambiguity and obscurity, as much as ignorance or inapplicability, may have played a role in her death. A third danger is that moral values and financial criteria will fill the vacuum left by lack of clarity and will influence whether and how the law is implemented (Dingwall *et al.*, 1983). For example, in operating Part III, Housing Act 1985 (now HA 1996) local authorities have shown varying approaches to protecting victims of domestic violence or assessing the needs of homosexual couples as compared with heterosexual couples (Arden, 1986; Hoath, 1990). Similarly, children in need policies in some authorities aim to provide a broad range of services; others residual provision. Some local authorities charge for community care services (section 17, HASSASSA 1983); others do not. Social workers are entangled and must practise within such ambiguities. Just how complicated this can be is demonstrated by Fox Harding (1991). Concepts such as 'a child's best interests' are interpreted differently by those who view natural families as the optimum context for a child's growth, and those who place faith in state intervention.

The law, then, can become a vehicle for justifying less, through phrases like 'where appropriate' and 'take into account the results of that assessment in making a decision' (section 1, Carers (Recognition and Services) Act 1995). In the conflict between needs and resources, professional values can become displaced by organisational imperatives (Cornwell, 1992/93; Preston-Shoot, 1996a). The question then arises as to whose interests are being met when assessments are conducted.

The myth of helpfulness

Whom does the law help? About what? To what extent? The law is often presented as a remedy or reform, amending the balance of power between different parties. However the extent to which the law is (or is designed to be) helpful varies; the extent to which it can (and is designed to) challenge inequalities is questionable.

Sometimes vested interests – pressure groups or bureaucracies – succeed in watering down or imposing provisions contrary to the original intentions of the legislators. Local authority insistence on inserting the concept of intentional homelessness into reform of housing law, coupled with confusion about the circumstances councils may take into account, has prevented many people from obtaining help (Arden, 1986). Sometimes the emphasis on value for money and cost-effectiveness closes opportunities for meeting need, marginalises or devalues people, and diverts attention away from the effectiveness of provision towards standardisation. This reinforces arrangements for the majority, with services orientated towards Western European concepts of well-being (Mirza, 1991). Services then are judged as sometimes being culturally insensitive and reinforcing gender differentiation and unequal treatment (Cornwell, 1992/93; *Childright*, 1995c).

Not infrequently duties are couched in such a way as to enable agencies providing services to behave in restrictive rather than enabling ways towards service users. Both the Children Act 1989 and the NHS and Community Care Act 1990, whilst laying various duties on local authorities, allow councils to perform these duties as they consider appropriate. Put another way, the law allows considerable discretion, even with regard to duties, such that the perceptions of bureaucracies rather than service users determine how the law is interpreted and used.

These restrictions find expression in the use of the law to sanction resources when crises are evident, when resources *have* to be spent (Lyon, 1989). It is more hesitant to commit expenditure to prevention, even though this might be more economical and effective in the longer term. The preventive duties in respect of children in need allow local authorities to determine what is reasonable or appropriate. The evidence suggests that these duties, and the quality of such services, are highly vulnerable to resource constraints (Colton *et al.*, 1995). Duties to offer advice, assistance and befriending to young people who have been looked after by local authorities have been strengthened, but doubts continue about how financially hard-pressed social services departments will interpret them. The effect on social work practice is not surprising. Research continues to demonstrate that effort is concentrated around admission to care and investigations of abuse at the expense of prevention, support services and continuing longer-term work (DHSS, 1985; DoH, 1995a).

Similarly section 117, Mental Health Act 1983, which places a duty on district health authorities and social services departments to provide after-care services until satisfied that an individual no longer needs such services, is so non-specific as to be meaningless. The Care Programme Approach (LASSL(90)11) requires collaboration between health and local authorities to plan and provide for the social care needs of people referred to specialist psychiatric services, either as outpatients or inpatients, and empowers local authorities to continue to expand social care services to people being treated in the community 'as resources allow'. However, detailed guidance is lacking, and there is an absence of new resources and confusion about its relationship with section 117 (MHA 1983) and with care management. There remains a hotch-potch of statutory provision here. Four Acts can prompt assessment (MHA 1983; DPA 1986; NHSCCA 1990; C(RS)A 1995); with services additionally also from others (CSDPA 1970; MH(PIC)A 1995). The failure to integrate procedures for care management with the Care Programme Approach and after-care duties, and the failure to consolidate legislative provision, arguably results in poor coordination and confused and fragmented services (Faulkner, 1994). In these respects the law does not provide a continuing or complete framework for welfare.

There can be no doubt that the law will be seen by some as inimical or unhelpful to their welfare (Stevenson, 1988; Freeman, 1990). Survivors of psychiatric treatment would question the good intentions which doctors use to justify professional intervention and deprivation of liberty, seeing in the rhetoric of protection of the individual a harmful paternalism. Few older people, removed from their homes without their consent under section 47, National Assistance Act 1948, live for long (Forster and Tiplady, 1980). People in residential care, young and older, can be exposed to personal and system abuse involving escalating punitiveness and denial of human and legal rights (Moss, 1990; Levy and Kahan, 1991). There is evidence that older people are being evicted from residential and nursing homes because of their inability to meet their care costs (Whiteley, 1995). Some people are refusing community care services because of local authority charging policies (Keep and Clarkson, 1994; Lamb and Layzell, 1995). Research studies continue to show that carers are critical of service provision (Robbins, 1993; Hoyes *et al.*, 1994; Buckley *et al.*, 1995; Warner, 1995): inadequate assistance; poor quality; lack of information; unreliability; lack of consultation or influence; insensitive assessment procedures; delays. Most powers given to guardians under the Mental Health Act 1983 are not enforceable, and the criteria for making a guardianship order may exclude those for whom it might be most useful (Gunn, 1986; BASW, 1990), leaving service users vulnerable to coercion or neglect. It is questionable whether the new supervised discharge powers (MH(PIC)A 1995) will, in the context of over-stretched services, result in fewer inappropriate placements, more appropriately staffed and structured teams, and fuller after-care plans – all concerns highlighted by the enquiry into the death of Jonathan Zito (Ritchie *et al.*, 1994). Legislation available to disabled people does little to challenge the assumptions of able-bodiedness around which housing and transport are organised. Furthermore, the Disability Discrimination Act 1995 fails to provide for a commission with powers to enforce its provisions in connection with employment, access to buildings, and delivery of goods and services (Gooding, 1996), even though reliance on persuasion and education alone proves insufficient in changing attitudes and outcomes.

Similarly child-care legislation (such as the Child Support Act 1991) eschews addressing the social, economic and value assumptions which contribute to family difficulties, preferring to pursue parents for not fulfilling their responsibilities. There remains considerable dissatisfaction with the workings of the Child Support Agency. Children in residential care report critically on their quality of life (SSI, 1993a). In respect of disabled children there is a mismatch between demand and the type and level of services available (SSI, 1994a). Guidance on video interviews of children aims to produce results acceptable in criminal proceedings but has the effect of steering interviewers away from empathy and therapeutic interventions in order not to taint evidence. Concern exists that children suffer as a result (SSI, 1994b). The Audit Commission (1994) has been critical of children's services for being poorly co-ordinated and for failing to help those most in need. It has urged local authorities to identify needs and provide services to meet them rather than to offer services into which people must fit. It has also criticised fragmentation of services and the absence of strategic planning between local authorities and health authorities. Victims of domestic violence find the law is little guarantee of protection. Concern remains that the Crown Prosecution Service fails to take assaults on vulnerable victims seriously. The slim prospects of securing a conviction result in women with learning disabilities or mental health problems being denied justice (Sone, 1995). Finally, probation officers are critical of national standards (Home Office, 1995) for redirecting probation away from rehabilitation towards community-based corrections. As Ward argues (1996), getting tough on crime may not be good for offenders if the context fails to value them as people. Similarly, secure training order provisions for 12- to 14-year-olds (CJPOA 1994) treat them as offenders first and children second, elevate punishment over welfare, ignore disadvantages associated with crime, and demonstrate total disregard for research into the effectiveness of custody. Moreover, there is little evidence to justify such orders (Bell, 1994).

An analysis of what is communicated in legislation reveals how the law influences the core of the social work relationship. The law can confirm or reject an individual's reality or self-view. The Children Act 1989 requires local authorities to give due consideration to a child's racial origin, religion, and cultural and linguistic background (section 22). By contrast, placing children's homes where there are fewer than four residents outside the regulatory system (LAC(93)16), the rejection by government of legislation to implement the Law Commission's proposals on protecting vulnerable adults, and the decision not to implement sections of the Disabled Persons Act 1986 concerned with user involvement and advocacy, all convey the message 'you are not important'. More damaging still is the use of the law to negate an individual's self-concept. The message here is 'you do not exist'. The result can be alienation, loss of self. Examples include legislative attitudes towards transsexual identity, the reduction of the age of consent for gay men only to 18 (CJPOA 1994), and the one-year immigration rule which appears to require abused women to submit to domestic violence or face deportation.

The danger for social work, arising from this analysis, is a narrowing of vision: that social workers only see what they are mandated to see or what they can readily do something about. Put another way, because the law sanctions involvement with some users but not others, and because it focuses on individuals and families rather than social and organisational systems, the danger is that social workers intervene at the level of the 'presented problem' and fail to address underlying relationships between systems which promote or maintain inequality and difficulties. For example, in relation to domestic violence, the failure of the law and of law enforcement agencies to address male abuse of power can result in social workers redefining domestic violence cases as child welfare cases, resulting in little being done to help women victims beyond 'talk about it' interventions, referral on to refuges and, sometimes, an overt emphasis on putting children first and on reconciliation, thereby further disempowering women who are already disempowered by the law and the way it is implemented (Smith, 1989).

Further questions arise about whom the law assists when users, who wish to gain access to services or to rights ostensibly provided by the law, find that the law does not facilitate this. Parents acting as appropriate adults (PACE 1984) may not know what the role involves. Indeed the role is not set out in any clear detail (*Childright*, 1991). The burden of proof, for instance in cases of discrimination or housing need, is on the complainant who may be discouraged by the complicated procedures to follow, difficulty in presenting available evidence, the timescales and the financial costs involved. Organisations are more strongly placed than individuals to use the law. Moreover, successful results, leading to damages, injunctions on people or organisations not to do something, or review of a case do not necessarily mean an end to discrimination or achievement of the original outcome desired by the user.

Concern exists too about the enforcement of rights and redress against the way local authorities interpret their duties. Housing Departments are judge and jury when determining issues of homelessness (Arden, 1986). It is their opinion which counts. The process by which their decisions may be challenged, judicial review, focuses not on the facts or merits of the situation but on whether the local authority has approached its decisions correctly. The focus is on whether there have been errors in law or procedures, and on whether the decision is irrational given current law, procedures and considerations relevant to the case. The process can be costly and lengthy (Hoath, 1990). Similarly the Secretary of State may only intervene, using the default powers in section 7, Local Authority Social Services Act 1970, if satisfied that a local authority has acted irrationally and manifestly failed to discharge its duty. Complainants will have to appeal to the Secretary of State, prior to using judicial review, when these default powers are available. However they must first exhaust the local authority's internal representations and complaints procedures (Cooper, 1990). Indeed, courts have been critical of the use of judicial review (*R* v. *RB of Kingston-upon-Thames, ex parte* T [1994]; *R* v. *LB of Barnet, ex parte* B [1994]; *R* v. *Cambridge District Health Authority, ex parte* B [1995]) and pointed to complaints procedures as more appropriate remedies because of the speed with which they can consider matters afresh, their mandate to exercise an independent judgement on the merits of the facts, and their scope for making recommendations to which the local authority must pay due regard. Judicial review is then reserved for a challenge to the use made by an authority of a complaints panel's findings, or for an authoritative resolution of a legal point. Even if an authority is found to be in default, to have failed to discharge its duties, the complainant may not receive redress without further legal action. Class actions are not permitted. Each individual affected by an authority's inaction or policy will have to initiate his or her own, separate proceedings.

Complaints procedures are not necessarily an adequate safeguard. Both the Children Act 1989 and the NHS and Community Care Act 1990 require local authorities to establish such procedures. However

Bainham (1990) is critical of the procedures in respect of children, concerned that the categories of those entitled to make representations are too restrictive, and that the procedures may not meet the demands of natural justice. Whether the procedure is sufficiently independent of the authority and whether it enables people who are powerless or less powerful to challenge and obtain redress from those who exercise power and on whose services they are dependent is open to doubt. The Ombudsman has been critical of the operation of complaints procedures, for example the failure to gather facts, to use clear criteria for decisions, to convey reasons for decisions, and to consider appropriate membership of a panel (90/A/2675; 92/A/3725; 92/A/2412). Research (SSI, 1993c; Buckley *et al.*, 1995; Simons, 1995) has found poor and insufficient recording, a lack of information held by users, a failure of results to inform planning and service delivery, and user anxiety about the possible consequences of complaining.

The myth of neutrality

An underlying theme has been that the law reflects rather than challenges power relationships. People are not all equal before it. Class, gender, race and economic inequalities make a fiction of the key legal value of equality before the law, the more so given the contraction in the availability of legal aid. Conservative assumptions about the appropriate expressions of power and relationships in society, as reflected in what is classified as lawful and unlawful, underpin the law and judicial judgements (Sachs, 1976).

For example, lesbian women continue to experience difficulties in private law family proceedings (section 8, CA 1989). The right of silence has been removed (sections 34–7, CJPOA 1994) contrary to the recommendations of the Royal Commission on Criminal Justice (1993). Poverty, racism, sexism, class, housing and unemployment all affect parenting and children's development (Hanmer and Statham, 1988; DoH, 1989a) but the responsibility for reasonable standards of care rests individually with parents. Circumstances will not be relevant in judgements about what it is reasonable to expect of *this* parent and whether the threshold of significant harm has been crossed (section 31, CA 1989). The test is what *a* reasonable parent would do. The assumption (DoH, 1991d) is that reasonable parents will (be able to) make use of support services. However circumstances will be relevant when considering then whether an order should be made (Bainham, 1990). Yet the effects of these experiences and circumstances can include alienation, apathy and disillusionment as responses to the disjunction between the goals laid out by society and the means provided to achieve them (Hartman, 1969). Failure is personalised and individual change sought when this must be influenced by structural inequalities, limited resources and prejudiced political judgements. Unless it is diligent, social work can act out these judgements.

The myth of substantial powers

There is noticeable suspicion of social work in the public arena, more than of other professions in the welfare field. This suspicion has less to do with the reality of how social workers operate than with societal ambivalence about the role social work plays in 'tidying away' troubling concerns: mental illness, child abuse, personal vulnerability (Byng-Hall, 1988; Preston-Shoot and Agass, 1990). Concern to regulate and restrict the exercise of professional power was one reforming motive behind the Children Act 1989. The supposed solution to child abuse had become part of the problem.

Whilst it is undeniable that social services departments have powers to intervene in people's lives, there is ample evidence of reluctance to exercise legal authority (DHSS, 1982; Dingwall *et al.*, 1983; Corby, 1987). Only in the mental health field do individual social workers, as Approved Social Workers, have a decision-making mandate within the law. Even here, this power is not confined to professionals but is held also by the nearest relative, giving rise to the anomaly that the final word on compulsory admission to hospital is held equally by either a detached professional or a lay person closely involved with the patient (Hoggett, 1990)!

In terms of guardianship under the Mental Health Act 1983 there is no legal mandate for the guardian to enforce requirements of residence or treatment. The provision of residential, day and domiciliary services under the National Assistance Act 1948 is only enforceable if service users consent, regardless of their circumstances. Under the Children Act 1989 there are numerous checks and balances to the social work role, not least in the form of parental powers and responsibilities, and the court's role in decision-making. Local authorities do not have regulatory or registration powers concerning domiciliary services or children's homes with fewer than four children. Including similar arrangements within contracts negotiated with providers is unlikely to prove sufficient protection against dubious or abusive practice. Finally, local authority powers and duties cannot prevent tragedies. The recognition (DoH, 1995a) that it is therefore inappropriate to pillory agencies and practitioners is long overdue.

The myth of good and right solutions – the law is all that is needed

Knowledge and practice of social work law require more than legal knowledge. The assumption must be challenged that the only problem is social workers' ignorance of the law, and that all would be well if only they would use it appropriately. Questions need to be answered, for instance, about the helpfulness and coherence of available guidance, about the relevance of an adversarial legal system, about appropriate and achievable standards of evidence, and the conditions required for practitioners to protect children. Otherwise practitioners will continue to approach statutory work reluctantly (Trotter, 1991). In other respects, social work practice is in advance of the law. The law's endorsement of antidiscriminatory social work practice (CA 1989; CJA 1991) is recent. The law on adoption does not currently reflect concerns or changing practice based on the benefits gained from openness, the importance of information and contact for identity development, and the changing age of children available for adoption (Redding, 1991b).

If questions should be asked of the law, they exist too regarding the context provided for social workers to exercise authority. Ambiguous and contradictory expectations have allowed systems to develop which compromise practitioners' competence and professional standards (Ruddock, 1988). These expectations have also obscured users' experiences and views beneath individual and agency orientations which emphasise defensive practice, organisational rules and professional definitions of need, economy and control (Whittington, 1977). Despite government rhetoric, the increased responsibilities accompanying legislation are not being adequately resourced. Concerns exist in relation to duties concerning community care and children defined as 'in need' under the Children Act 1989. The differing attitudes and resource positions of each local authority produce a lack of consistency and wide variations in practice even where legislation imposes positive duties.

Finally social work values and skills must be reemphasised: the commitment to antidiscriminatory practice; applying research and theoretical knowledge to practice situations; skills in maintaining relationships, and in releasing the power and authority held by users, in situations where statutory authority is or could be used. At the same time social work must not overreach itself, overplay its skills. There appears sometimes an almost mythical belief in the correct assessment. Neither the law nor social work skills can guarantee outcomes, such is the nature of risk, the inherent unknowability of people and the impossibility of controlling all the variables. Law and social work bring different strengths, weaknesses and qualities to the practice arena. Both are needed in a balanced relationship.

Practice dilemmas

Arising from the conflicting imperatives, myths and debates about the relationship between social work and the law are statutory duties and powers which embody widely differing intentions. Legislation may be prescriptive or proscriptive, preventive or curative, proactive or reactive. The intervention may be to enforce rights or minimise risks, protect individuals or society from them, enforce compliance or establish mechanisms for conciliation and arbitration.

There is no easy exit from these tensions. The resulting practice dilemmas require creative solutions which recognise the tension between the polarities of each dilemma which dominates social work practice, and achieve a balanced consideration of each (Braye and Preston-Shoot, 1990). Rigid adherence to one side of the equation will rarely be appropriate. The weight each polarity carries will vary according to circumstances. The dilemmas represent potential for choice. Sometimes the polarities conflict; sometimes they represent different possibilities; sometimes they are apparent as a hierarchy. Rather than immobilise practitioners in the middle, they point to questions which can inform decision-making and provide coherence to the work.

What is the purpose of using the law?

To promote/preserve rights   *v.*   To control and minimise risk

What rights do those involved
in the situation have?

What risks exist in the
situation and to whom?

At what stage should social workers
intervene? By what criteria? What risks
are acceptable? Are some rights more
important to preserve than others?

Prevention   *v.*   Protection
Care   *v.*   Control

Does this person need
care? Of what nature?
Is this child in need?

Does this person need
controlling? Why? Should
this child be protected?

What values and principles should social workers operate?
What procedures should practitioners follow?
What services should they provide?

Sometimes these dilemmas arise from uncertainty about what services are appropriate and from what an ethical duty of care is and how it should be expressed. For instance, should adolescents who have been sexually abused and who subsequently abuse other children be punished or treated? Debates on child witnesses reflect the tension between fairness to alleged perpetrators and child protection (Spencer and Flin, 1993; SSI,1994b). Similar dilemmas exist in child protection: the need for a thorough assessment, which takes time, conflicting with the need to settle a child quickly, to minimise delay and unnecessary separation of child and family (DoH, 1989a); the requirement to balance considerations of risk of disturbance in removing a child against the risk of abuse if allowed to remain at home (*Re H* [1991]); balancing the potentially beneficial aspects of change against the potential damage of loss of security and disrupted relationships (DoH, 1989a). In residential care, what risks are appropriate and at what point should restraint be used? How may workers determine, often in the absence of departmental guidelines and training, the likelihood of injury to the person or to others and whether that likelihood calls for physical restraint? What methods of restraint are acceptable?

Resolving these dilemmas requires, *inter alia*, knowledge of how vulnerable people respond to different courses of action (Parker *et al.*, 1991), but assessment of risk will also be influenced by pressures experienced from different competing interests and which themselves can be inconsistent and contradictory: public expectations about protection and interference; agency require-ments about financial management, avoidance of scandal and gate-keeping; differences between family members; professional expectations – differences between social workers about desirable outcomes.

Dilemmas arise also because short- and long-term objectives clash. When should the principle of self-determination give way to protective intervention (Horne, 1987)? When is immediate action, which contradicts self-determination, acceptable because it enhances an individual's longer-term opportunities to remain self-directing? This tension between autonomy and paternalism or protection is especially evident in the treatment of mentally disordered people. Paternalism is justified to the point where it frustrates the indivi-dual's exercise of choice. Autonomy is justified to the point where respecting it results in harm to the person (Fennell, 1990). Equally, the dilemmas arise because of pendulum swings. In work with children and families, for instance, there are swings between family rights and state powers, and between child care and child protection (Parton, 1991; Reder *et al.*, 1993). The Department of Health (DoH, 1995a) reflects this ambivalence or uncertainty by retaining child protection guidance (DoH, 1991e), which it implicitly criticises for being a small meshed net which catches a large number of families whose needs are not best met by entrapment in the protection process, whilst requiring practitioners to re-emphasise preventive and supportive services. It fails, when identifying that the challenge is to find the most appropriate balance between a child's views, a parent's views and responsibilities, and a professional's responsibility to make informed and appropriate decisions, to answer the question 'which when?'

Therapy   *v.*   Evidence

Primary objective to facilitate recovery of the abused child

Primary objective to obtain proof of abuse which satisfies the court to convict the abuser

The forensic needs of, and standards demanded by, courts sit uneasily alongside an ethical duty of care towards abused children (Douglas and Willmore, 1987). Social work enjoys an uneasy relationship with the legal emphasis on facts, evidence and definitions (Swain, 1989) and lawyers recognise the difficulty of constructing 'hard' evidence from 'soft' information which itself might have been changed by social work intervention to help a distressed child in the earlier stages of investigation (Lyon, 1988). Social workers have been severely criticised for supposed 'incompetence' in interviewing which gave rise to inaccurate and misleading evidence (*Re E (A Minor) (Child Abuse Evidence)* [1990]; Dyer, 1991b; *Re N (minors) (Sexual Abuse: Evidence)* [1993]; *B* v. *B (Procedure: Alleged Sexual Abuse)* [1994]). The emphasis on legalism, potentially though not necessarily at the cost of the child's welfare, is confirmed by guidance on investigation procedures issued to underpin the Children Act (DoH, 1991e). This states that the primary purpose is to obtain a level of proof of abuse which will satisfy legal scrutiny.

However, the emphasis on legalism has been criticised (King and Trowell, 1992; SSI, 1994b; Preston-Shoot, 1996a). The quest for evidence, the rules for video-recorded interviews, and the adversarial nature of proceedings which will result in defence lawyers seeking to discredit a child's evidence, can disrupt progress for the child in overcoming the effects of abuse.

What informs the decision about using the law?

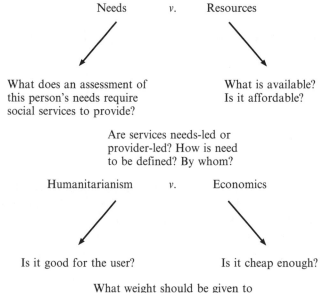

Needs   *v.*   Resources

What does an assessment of
this person's needs require
social services to provide?

What is available?
Is it affordable?

Are services needs-led or
provider-led? How is need
to be defined? By whom?

Humanitarianism   *v.*   Economics

Is it good for the user?   Is it cheap enough?

What weight should be given to
economics as against effectiveness
or efficiency?

Local education authorities have been alleged to tailor statements of children's needs, under the Education Act 1993, to fit what they can provide (K. Jones, 1991). Annual reviews of statements are not being completed, resulting in inappropriate placements. Resources are not available to implement statements (Croall, 1991). Identical resource pressures result in tightly drawn eligibility criteria which exclude people from services, and in agency-informed rather than user-led, needs-based assessments and services in child and adult care (for research evidence of this see, for example, Hoyes *et al.*, 1994; Marchant, 1995). This has led one respected commentator (Utting, in Ellis 1993) to speak of a poverty of provision and a meanness of spirit with which people relying on welfare are regarded. When social workers accept such a gate-keeping, resource-rationing role, they compromise the assessment of need which it is their duty to make, thereby bypassing political questions.

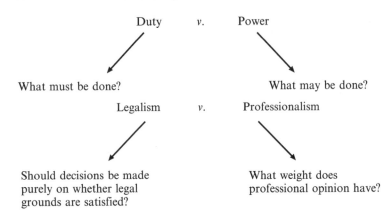

Duty   *v.*   Power

What must be done?   What may be done?

Legalism   *v.*   Professionalism

Should decisions be made   What weight does
purely on whether legal   professional opinion have?
grounds are satisfied?

Permissive powers may not be implemented because of ideologies or financial constraints. Similarly, statutory duties may be implemented restrictively. Ideologies about women, for instance, shape day care for children and psychiatric services, however women recount their experiences and needs (Smith, 1990). When interventions protect ideologies rather than act in the best interests of individuals, arguably practice becomes unethical (Llewelyn, 1987).

Children in need could be defined broadly, with services to match, but Schedule 2, Children Act 1989 endorses a restrictive, individual rather than area-based approach to need. It may help to maintain families, a key child-care principle, but it will not address the poverty, racism, poor housing or unemployment which government acknowledges can undermine parenting capacity (DoH, 1989a). Are services which ignore such structural issues verging on the unethical too? Moreover, since services can be charged for, and a means test applied, need will be equated with a willingness to pay (Gardner, 1990). What price family support?

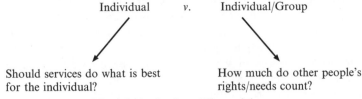

Individual   *v.*   Individual/Group

Should services do what is best   How much do other people's
for the individual?   rights/needs count?

No right is absolute. Whose rights are
paramount or should be considered first?
Are some rights more important to protect than others?

This is a familiar balancing act: between older people and their carers; children and parents; families and the state. It includes the tension between supporting carers (services to preserve and strengthen family units) and placing faith in substitute care (Fox Harding, 1991). It involves the tension between the rule of optimism and the rule of pessimism: allowing intervention only with great care and when necessary (Corby, 1987), against recognition of the need to scrutinise care given to vulnerable people.

Who makes the decisions?

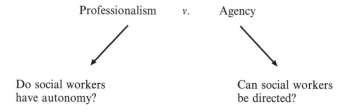

Professionalism   *v.*   Agency

Do social workers have autonomy?

Can social workers be directed?

To whom is the practitioner accountable: user, agency, professional values?

This is the tension between bureaucracy and professionalism. How can social workers, employees of an impersonal agency which retains significant powers of judgement, decision-making and control of service delivery, work within agency guidelines and also become involved with users, involvement which may require challenges to agency policy? It can lead social workers to choose particular legal routes in order to 'work the system' (DHSS, 1985) which in other respects runs counter to professional judgement. Statutory duties attract resources: mental health sections to provide offenders with appropriate placements, or to gain entry to after-care services; guardianship orders to guarantee continuation of services (Dooher, 1989); utilising child protection procedures to secure resources. However, practitioners attempting to promote service users' rights in negotiating with their agencies may find their effectiveness curtailed by their very location in those agencies (Bamford, 1989; Mullender, 1991).

Social workers are being encouraged (for example, see Audit Commission, 1994; Best, 1994) to manage the conflict between meeting need and the careful stewardship of finances. They are not given guidance as to how, with the result that they can become confused about managers' expectations and demoralised or disillusioned as a result of encountering needs which cannot be met (Ellis, 1993).

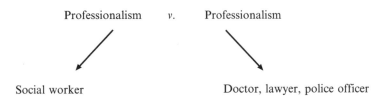

Professionalism   *v.*   Professionalism

Social worker   Doctor, lawyer, police officer

How does status influence the decision-making process? Whose evidence or opinion counts?

Social workers are expected to make judgements about the professional assessments of other professions, to be sufficiently expert in medicine, police work and law to evaluate the accuracy of a doctor's diagnosis of sexual abuse, of a police officer's recommendation for dawn raids, and of a lawyer's uncertainty about whether grounds exist (Lyon, 1989). However, courts are inconsistent in this expectation. There have been cases where experienced non-medical professionals have been adjudged competent to give evidence on a child's mental development (*F* v. *Suffolk County Council* [1981]) and on the question of serious harm to health of a mental or physical nature (*R* v. *Derbyshire County Council, ex parte K* [1994]), because of their experience and knowledge of the people involved. However, there are cases where similar questions have been ruled to require medical or psychological experts (*B* v. *B (Procedure: Alleged Sexual Abuse)* [1994]; *Re R (A Minor) (Disclosure of Privileged Material)* [1993]). This expectation is rendered more difficult because doctors do not agree on diagnoses or interpretation of evidence, or on good practice for intervention (Morgan, 1988). Moreover other professionals' concerns are different. Doctors in compulsory admission to psychiatric hospital are not required to balance their assessment of need for medical treatment against the individual's right to liberty. This is the social work judgement. Medical philosophy is that it is irrational to allow health risks to persist when treatment is possible. Social work upholds an individual's right, to a far greater degree, to disregard their own health or safety (Fisher *et al.*, 1984).

The interface between social workers and other professionals, especially legal practitioners, is rendered more complex by evidence that social workers believe that lawyers and courts hold them, and their evidence, in low esteem. The increase in the use of expert witnesses in care proceedings, by social workers and guardians *ad litem*, is directly linked to this belief (DoH, 1994a; Foster and Preston-Shoot, 1995).

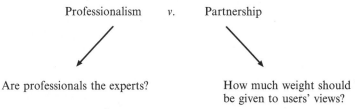

Professionalism   *v.*   Partnership

Are professionals the experts?   How much weight should
                                              be given to users' views?

How does empowerment work within a statutory
framework?
Who defines need?
What level of user involvement is required by law
and by good practice?
When is the imposition on users of opinions about
appropriate action appropriate?

The law provides a variety of decision-making models. The Children Act 1989 emphasises partnership; the Disabled Persons Act 1986, participation; whilst the Housing Act 1996, the Mental Health Act 1983 and the Chronically Sick and Disabled Persons Act 1970 give decision-making powers to professionals. Research indicates the effectiveness of partnership (Corden and Preston-Shoot, 1987). The challenge is to paternalism, and empowering service users when working with statutory and positional authority. However, partnership is not a simple concept (Braye and Preston-Shoot, 1992; 1995). As envisaged in both work with children and families and in community care, partnership leaves the foundation of professional power relatively undisturbed (DoH, 1995b). What is envisaged is participation in processes defined and controlled by others rather than user control or, in any meaningful sense, shared responsibility for constructing the process of intervention, negotiating the agenda or determining how needs are to be addressed.

Triangulation

Thus far the discussion has identified tensions between opposing mandates. The source of these dilemmas and tensions lies partly in the relationships between those who are stakeholders in the practice of social work law – government, professional groups, service users, the public – and in their prominence at any one time in seeking to influence how statutory authority is used. The framework of dilemmas may be taken a stage further by demonstrating how practice is made infinitely more complex by the way in which the tension between two elements can be bypassed by reference to a third mandate. Known as triangulation, any combination of three elements becomes possible, thus keeping all mandates permanently in play (Braye and Preston-Shoot, 1993a, 1994). For instance, the conflict between needs and resources may be detoured through a focus on rights; between needs and rights through resources; between autonomy and protection through empowerment. This can lead to the repetition of old solutions in revised and more elaborate forms as the triangulated nature of the system is not seen as part of the problem, to be a focus itself for intervention. The result is that reforming and practising social work law becomes trapped in more of the same, rather than characterised by informed debate about the balance to be struck between competing imperatives and about the objectives of welfare policy and practice.

Conclusion

The opening chapters have presented a conceptual framework to make sense of social work law. Such a framework is necessary for understanding the role conflict, ambiguity and uncertainty within social work, and for informed decision-making. Without it practice can easily become characterised by a vicious circle.

Subsequent chapters will provide social workers with ways to intervene in this circle, to negotiate the dilemmas which arise in practice, and to formulate professional and legal justifications for decisions taken. This requires a decision-making framework, legal knowledge and practice skills – the focus of subsequent chapters.

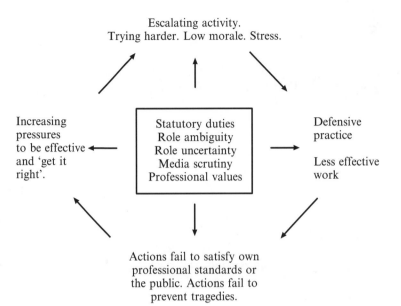

Escalating activity.
Trying harder. Low morale. Stress.

Increasing
pressures
to be effective
and 'get it
right'.

Statutory duties
Role ambiguity
Role uncertainty
Media scrutiny
Professional values

Defensive
practice

Less effective
work

Actions fail to satisfy own
professional standards or
the public. Actions fail to
prevent tragedies.

4

Deciding to Use the Law

The early part of this book explored how the exercise of statutory powers and duties cannot be undertaken in a vacuum, and provided a context for legal knowledge within both the functions of the law in society and the complexity of the social work task. One potential outcome of this is to deny social workers any certainty about what to do and when to do it. Consequently some boundaries must be placed around the uncertainty, a framework provided for the decisions that have to be taken in daily practice.

Why a decision-making framework?

There is considerably more focus by the media upon 'how well' social workers make decisions than upon 'how' – an emphasis on outcome rather than process. Whilst the *outcomes* are clearly of crucial importance to the people who are the subjects of those decisions, it is a study of the key *processes* that will help practitioners find pathways through the dilemmas of practice.

Social workers and their managers have to manage risk, and the concepts of risk assessment, risk-taking and risk management will be explored later in this chapter. Decisions have to be made where the stakes are high: at times, matters of life and death. Acting without a systematic structured approach is a contributory factor to 'professional dangerousness' (DHSS, 1982) in such circumstances. Organisations must develop risk policies and risk procedures that minimise the likelihood of decision error and enable learning from risk decisions to be evaluated and incorporated in future strategies (Carson, 1995). A decision-making framework is both a safety device and a moral imperative. Without such a framework, the nature of the work and the anxiety it evokes are likely to trigger defence mechanisms which result in a stereotypical use of the law, whether this be automatic recourse to it as part of mindless doing or avoidance of it as part of indecisive drift. A further danger is the use of subjective and idiosyncratic criteria in decisions to invoke the law (Wolkind, 1988). Reder *et al.* (1993) identify a range of problems in decision-making: failure to perceive patterns in events and information, selective interpretation of dominant belief systems, and over-reliance on practical and concrete solutions. Research into social work decisions in child care (DHSS, 1985) showed that decisions are made quickly, resulting sometimes in unplanned admissions to care with little observable difference between children admitted and those remaining at home; and the use of compulsory powers not linked to constructive planning. Social workers did not draw on a serious knowledge base in making their decisions, yet bore the responsibility for decisions, and did so under considerable pressure from other people.

Social work intervention is never a matter only of making uniform provision; it is always the result of judgement about unique circumstances (England, 1986). It is a matter of individualising broad criteria, allowing for difference, using judgement. These decisions require a framework not for uniformity but for consistency of practice.

What kind of framework?

A framework for decision-making must take several factors into account. Attention has been drawn earlier to the different emphases of legal and therapeutic purposes. The law aims for the logic and clarity of a positivist approach to decisions, in which ends and means are securely linked, and informed by reified notions of responsibility, reasonableness, equality and justice. Social work has less clarity and agreement about its objectives, knows that human behaviour is at times driven not by reason but by passion, recognises the structured power relations that result in inequality and injustice, and cannot guarantee that certain ends will follow from the chosen means of achieving them. 'The social work role is inevitably one which involves the taking of decisions and the forming of opinions which have legal implications, on the basis of evidence which falls substantially short of legal proof' (Harris,

1982). The dichotomous thinking of the law, where something 'is' or 'is not', is ill-suited to the continuum of uncertainty along which social work decisions are ranged.

A decision-making framework must offer, therefore, opportunities for both these approaches, for legal knowledge and social work practice wisdom, to work together. It must also take into account the 'open texture' of much welfare law, its lack of precision over definitions, and the power it thus leaves to professionals. Wide variations of interpretation by social workers are seen to result, together with the use of additional criteria derived not from the legislation but from other professional concerns to help in the decision-making (Sheppard, 1990).

Finally it must be recognised that decision-making cannot be risk-free: systematic approaches and frameworks can make effective contributions but 'there can be no prescribed formula for balancing the pros and cons of each option . . . this task is, and should remain, a matter for skilled professional judgement' (DoH, 1988).

Factors that influence decision-making

Of the multiplicity of factors that influence decision-making, four have particular relevance to social work decisions and the law. First, there is the influence of prevailing professional cultures and ideologies. Influential during the 1980s, for example, was the 'rule of optimism' (Dingwall *et al.*, 1983) arising from a culture that incorporates assumptions about the natural love of parents for their children, and the belief that standards are relative and therefore difficult to judge. It was offered to explain practitioners' preference for the least stigmatising interpretation of a child's condition and the least coercive form of intervention, and has been held responsible (Beckford Report, 1985) for an observed reluctance to use the law.

Parton (1986) moved the concept out of the realm of individual professional attitudes and saw it more as an institutionalised attempt to resolve a fundamental conflict in societal values between the mandate of family privacy and the mandate for surveillance and intervention. He offered by contrast a rule of pessimism – that social work decisions are influenced by concerns about the poor quality and lack of choice in care provision, a theme subsequently developed in debates about standards (Levy and Kahan, 1991) and outcomes for children in the public care system (Parker *et al.*, 1991; Utting, 1991).

A second major influence upon decision-making lies in the processes of inter-agency collaboration. In the field of child protection, for example, there has been ample evidence of the complex dynamics which operate, of the inter-agency conflicts and professional stereotyping which can distort professional judgement (Hallett and Stevenson, 1980; Dingwall *et al.*, 1983; Dale, 1984). Corby (1987) found that in case conferences agreement over norms was assumed, with little discussion to evaluate the seriousness of abuse or to estimate degrees of risk. Scant attention is sometimes paid to ways of implementing agreed courses of action (Corby and Mills, 1986). Power within the decision-making process was unequally distributed between participants, and was mediated by the regularity of attendance, professional status, seniority and strength of conviction. More recent evidence (Birchall and Hallett, 1995) demonstrates continuing friction within and between professions to do with tasks and priorities, and evident role confusion, exacerbated by factors of power, status and resources. Professional identity was seen to be the most important factor affecting a professional's point of view about a situation, with consensus a rare event.

Similar issues exist in the health-care field where cooperation between social workers and doctors has been characterised by mutual suspicion and criticism (Fisher *et al.*, 1984) and where agreement in decision-making is more likely when, within the law, social workers prioritise medical rather than social risk criteria (Sheppard, 1990).

The third major influence upon decision-making is the style of thinking that the practitioner adopts – the differing qualities of analytical and intuitive patterns (Hamm, 1988). Analytical decision-making breaks decisions down into component parts and applies problem-solving to the parts, which in turn are added together to make the solution. Intuitive decision-making retains the wholeness of the complete picture and applies 'know-how' which does not stem from prior intellectualisation, 'reclaiming the artistic' (England, 1986) in the way knowledge is applied. A similar dichotomy lies in the processes of deductive or inductive problem-solving. In the former, the starting point is a theoretical concept translated into practice and applied to situations. In the latter, observable events are the starting point, related back to the patterns of which they are a part and thence understanding is achieved. A similar distinction is drawn between algorithmic and heuristic problem-solving (Simmonds, 1991). In the former a systematic search of every possibility will be undertaken until the correct solution is found. Impractical in terms of the scale of such a task, it can be argued that the search for *the* correct solution is inappropriate in human systems. The heuristic method involves picking up clues from a situation and matching them to a known pattern. More practically feasible, this runs the risk of searching for evidence based on powerful preconceived notions of what might be found *and* the pressure to make a judgement and act. Both styles of thinking and approaches to problem-solving have advantages and disadvantages. The style adopted will influence the process and possibly even the decision. It is important that logic and intuition, technique and art are integrated (Dowie, 1989b).

Finally, it is vital to recognise the influence on decision-making of the role of the practitioner within a public agency, and the interplay between organisational and personal value systems. Decisions are inevitably role-bound and affected by what it is anticipated may be achieved as well as by the desire to satisfy conflicting pressures (Algie, 1976). Sources of authority are both personal and positional, and it is important for the organisation to be clear about where in the hierarchy different types of decisions should be taken and by whom (Handy, 1985). Other organisational factors affecting decision-making can include access to necessary information, the degree of work overload on individual decision-takers, and evaluative feedback on the success or otherwise of previous decisions (Child, 1984). Judgements about what should be done have to be balanced by knowledge of what can be done. Practice in a public agency must follow policy and procedures, is affected by resource constraints and prioritisation criteria, and must fulfil the organisation's duty of care to those covered by its legislative mandate. As resource constraint has bitten deeper, so eligibility criteria have become more influential. It is not uncommon for local authority community care and children in need policies to set thresholds to assist in prioritising the allocation of scarce resources. The Department of Health has promoted their use, provided they are consistently interpreted and applied (SSI, 1995a) but there have been concerns expressed that their use excludes users with lower-level needs from services, thus enhancing their deterioration and likelihood of requiring services for high-level need at a later date (Clode, 1995). Furthermore, the House of Lords has ruled (*R* v. *Gloucestershire County Council, ex parte Barry* [1997]) that, in relation to the Chronically Sick and Disabled Persons Act 1970, need is a relative expression, and that resources (and by implication the eligibility criteria which reflect them) may be relevant to such a judgement. The logical consequence could be that a local authority without resources could conclude that no disabled person in its area could have any needs. Discretion must, therefore, be used responsibly. In respect of duties owed to individuals (rather than duties owed to groups of people such as children in need), therefore, as in this instance, local authorities will have to exercise care in their use of thresholds and eligibility criteria.

A number of these factors, in particular those of professional ideology and agency accountability, are inevitably influenced by public attitudes – the 'moral panics' arising from fear and insecurity. Such fears, for example those experienced in relation to severe mental illness and dangerousness, can dominate both professional and agency thinking. Whilst it is important for professionals' decisions to hold public confidence, this should not be to the exclusion of other factors (Manthorpe *et al.*, 1995). By contrast, there is a view that a preoccupation with risk can be to the detriment of a wider consideration of need, with evidence (Farmer and Owen, 1995) that child protection conferences focus on controlling risk, obscuring the broader development and treatment needs of children and the severity of their parents' disadvantage.

The concept of risk

Decision-making in relation to the law cannot be considered without taking account of risk. This concept is the subject of some ambivalence. On the one hand risk is valued as associated with autonomy of choice and freedom (Brearley, 1982); on the other it is associated with an invitation to danger and negative outcomes (Carson, 1995). It is also notoriously difficult to measure, for not only is risk relative and situational (Fisher and Newton, 1985), it is also value-laden, in that some risks are deemed more acceptable than others, and in practice can arise from 'not doing' as well as from 'doing'. Any discussion of risk management usually incorporates notions of both protection and permission. Social work's role in managing risk has long been the subject of public scrutiny, with increasing emphasis on the need for more finely tuned risk assessments (SSI, 1995a) to produce better decisions about when to use statutory powers.

Brearley (1979b) makes a useful distinction between 'at-riskness' and 'risk-taking', pointing out that these are distinct entities and that social work is concerned with both. The determination of 'at-riskness' is a threefold process: the gathering of information about hazards currently experienced, whether 'predictive' or 'situational' (Brearley, 1979a); identification of the dangers posed by the hazards and the likelihood of the hazards resulting in the dangers. Thus someone who is frail through age (a predisposing hazard), or whose house is not heated in cold weather (a situational hazard) runs the danger of hypothermia. It is not uncommon for hazards and dangers to become confused, and for risk to be assumed because the hazard exists without proper identification of the likelihood of the danger occurring (Sheppard, 1990). Thus the danger of suicide could be assumed from the hazard of a medical diagnosis of depression. A further confusion lies in the analysis of cause and effect: a danger is perceived to be likely, and is assumed to stem from a hazard that is also identified, when in fact there is no causal link between the two. Thus 'risky social behaviour' (the danger) in someone who also has a mental disorder (the hazard) is likely to result in hospital admission despite the fact that the mental disorder is not causing the behaviour (Fisher *et al.*, 1984). Risk is thus assumed to be located within an individual whereas situational factors invariably exist which affect the likelihood, nature and extent of outcomes (Carson, 1990c).

It is not surprising that social workers have difficulty with the 'likelihood factor' of risk assessment. Building on actuarial models of risk assessment (using conclusions drawn from empirically established relationships, such as statistical likelihoods, predictive variables and weightings) as opposed to clinical judgement models (using individualised assessment based on personal knowledge of the unique variables in each case) (Carson, 1990d), statistical probabilities about the outcomes of certain courses of action have been used in medicine to formalise risk analysis into 'decision trees', in which the best course of action at key 'choice points' is determined by epidemiological data (Dowie, 1989a). The uncertain pathways between cause and effect in human behaviour, and the impossibility of controlling the variables which influence outcomes in the field of psychological harm or protection from abuse, make it difficult in social work to assign statistical probabilities to options in decision-making. Similar difficulties arise in the use of checklists and predictors pieced together from research which, whilst valuable in general terms, again are not predictive and do not guarantee specific outcomes. It is also tempting to treat outcomes that have occurred as more probable, with hindsight, than they were on best estimates at the time (Carson, 1990a).

Perceptions of 'at-riskness' are also affected by both personal and societal values. Stereotypical views of disabled people, for example, as vulnerable and dependent can result in less tolerance of risk and a defensive response (Knapp *et al.*, 1992). Personal interactions are also important components of judging 'at-riskness' – the quality of the relationship between the user and professional gives an important perspective on what risks are experienced, particularly with changes over time able to be tracked (Howlett, 1995).

The second component for consideration is 'risk-taking' – analysis of the consequences of available courses of action, involving consideration of the acceptability and desirability of potential outcomes. Social workers are often in the position of balancing potential risks in a hierarchy, in situations where action taken to prevent one danger may result in another (Brearley, 1979a, 1979b). It is broadly acknowledged that, when it comes to decisions about children (and arguably vulnerable adults also), no options are risk-free (SSI, 1992a). Carson (1988) makes the point that, rather than being engaged in 'risk-taking', social workers are involved in 'dilemma-management', situations where there are no harm-free options at all, and which present as emergencies where there is no time to decide. He advocates taking a more positive view of risk, framing decisions in terms of benefits to be gained rather than merely dangers to be avoided, and discounting from the equation benefits and dangers that would occur irrespective of intervention. He asks for outcomes to be weighted with a value, so that a few highly valued outcomes have the possibility of outweighing a larger number of less valued consequences. This concept of a balancing act is found in a court judgement which spells out the stages of decision-making. In *Re H* [1991] the judge described the process as one of gathering evidence, both factual and expert opinion, then, with the test of the child's welfare paramount, assessing the relative weight of both advantages and risks to a child of each possible course of action. Whilst this is one way of approaching the task, it adopts a 'snapshot' model of matters at a fixed point in time. Social work decisions commonly involve a more dynamic process, subsisting over time and involving a sequence of decisions (Carson, 1990d).

Official guidance on managing risk decisions (LASSL (94)4) attempts to incorporate both the sequential and the snapshot factors. It states that, whilst assessing risk is at best an inexact science, there are ways in which uncertainty can be reduced: gathering all relevant information, conducting a full assessment of risk, defining the situations known to present increased risk, and seeking expert help. Decisions in each case must be shown to have been taken after full and proper consideration of any evidence about the risks presented. Manthorpe *et al.* (1995) point out that acting in good faith may not be enough – legal liability for the consequences of a decision may still ensue. Carson (1995) confirms that a court would seek to establish whether the risk decision was of sufficient quality by reference to the information it was based on, the appropriate assessment of that information, and whether the decision would be supported by a body of professional opinion.

Breaking down the concept of risk into its component parts, it is possible to make a more systematic assessment of where the focus of social work attention might be in any given situation, and how legislation might be used to manage risk. Action may be taken to lessen vulnerability to predisposing hazards, to reduce the impact of situational hazards, to improve strengths and resources, to decrease the likelihood of dangers occurring, to minimise the impact of dangers or harms that have occurred, and/or to maximise benefits or change the values ascribed to outcomes. Legal duties may require harm to a child to be prioritised over harm to an adult, health and safety to be prioritised over civil liberties. A risk may be judged intolerable but there may be no power to do anything to avert it (Brearley, 1982). A risk may be clearly identified, but it may be argued that the individual has a right to run that risk (Counsel and Care, 1993). It will be important to match the response to the weight of evidence. Demonstrated danger will require curative action, probable danger would imply a preventive intervention, an identified or possible hazard would require further assessment (Sheppard, 1990). The identification of possible courses of action will also be assisted by clarity about whether the hazards stem from an individual's own actions or the actions of others, and whether the danger is to the individual or to others.

There must also be limits to social work's role in relation to risk. Social services departments are not responsible for universal public protection nor, because of the variable factors in people's lives, can they guarantee the protection of all their vulnerable service users, no matter how diligently they perform their professional responsibilities (ADSS, 1991). Nonetheless, a structured analysis of risk is an essential part of a decision-making framework and contributes to the considered and measured use of appropriate legal powers.

What the law says about decision-making

There is a body of case law which clarifies the law's position on local authority decision-making, and is thus relevant to social work practised in the statutory agency context. The primary emphasis is that decision-making should be reasonable and rational, based on a full examination of the facts and all the relevant factors, and reached according to guidance, such as Codes of Practice, where that exists (*R* v. *Kent County Council and Others, ex parte Bruce* [1986]; *R* v. *LB of Harrow, ex parte Deal* [1989]; *R* v. *North Yorkshire County Council, ex parte Hargreaves* [1994]; *R* v. *Islington LBC, ex parte Rixon* [1996]). Such decisions echo requirements in statute, such as that in section 13, MHA 1983, whereby an Approved Social Worker must consider all the circumstances of the case before deciding the most appropriate way of providing care and treatment to a patient.

Discretion must be exercised in every case. Operating blanket policies in community care would breach the duty to assess an *individual's* need for services (section 4, DPA 1986; section 47, NHSCCA 1990), and fetter discretion by neglecting issues relevant to an individual's case and thereby the possibility that this case may require departure from agreed policy or eligibility criteria. An example from child care is that a blanket policy of same-race placements for children is open to challenge through judicial review, on the basis that other factors may also be relevant in deciding a child's welfare.

Legal judgements have supported the principle of consultation with service users over decision-making on closure of provision.

Authorities must consult with users whilst proposals are still at a formative stage, clearly presenting reasons for the proposals. They must give users reasonable time to present their views and ensure that these are taken into account. Reasons must be given for decisions which must themselves be reasonable (*R* v. *Devon CC, ex parte Baker* [1995]; *R* v. *Durham CC, ex parte Curtis and Others* [1995]; *R* v. *LB of Barnet, ex parte B* [1994]).

Decisions on provision must again be rational, based on consideration of need and supported by adequate reasons (*R* v. *North Yorkshire County Council, ex parte Hargreaves* [1994]). When withdrawing or amending provision, adequate reasons must be given, together with an opportunity to comment. Regard must be paid to the effect of change on an individual before a final decision is made. Policy guidance must be followed (*R* v. *Rochdale MBC, ex parte Schemet* [1993]; *R* v. *Lancashire CC, ex parte Ingham and Whalley* [1995]).

The courts are entitled to interfere with local authority decisions only where the authority has exceeded or misused its powers, has misdirected itself in fact or in law, has exercised its discretion wrongly or for no good reason, or has acted perversely (*Smith and Others* v. *ILEA* [1978]; *Puhlhofer and Another* v. *LB of Hillingdon* [1986]). Courts are generally reluctant to interfere in the choices authorities have to make because they have no knowledge of competing claims on an authority's resources. Nor do they have access to the specialist knowledge required to determine what weight should be given to the factors involved in decision-making, and are in no position to express a view as to how an authority should deploy resources (*Re J (A Minor) (Wardship: Medical Treatment)* [1992]; *R* v. *RB of Kingston-upon-Thames, ex parte T* [1994]; *R* v. *Cambridge District Health Authority, ex parte B* [1995]). Courts can only consider the lawfulness of a decision at issue, and cannot arbitrate between conflicting medical opinions or competing claims on limited budgetary resources.

Local authority decisions may, of course, be challenged through the Commissioner for Local Administration (Ombudsman) on the basis of maladministration. This could cover bias, inattention to facts, delay, incompetence and arbitrariness. Maladministration has been established, for example, when an authority has not given a clear indication of likely delays in making an assessment or providing a service (396/J/82; 92/C/1403).

The components of a decision-making framework

Decision-making frameworks are commonly broken down into distinct categories of activity linked over chronological time (Specht and Vickery, 1977; Robinson, 1987; Woodcock, 1989; Pierson, 1990). Whilst the 'stages' carry differing names, they share common functions: investigation, analysis, hypothesising, examination of alternatives, weighing of consequences, consultation, planning, action, evaluation. Whilst analysis of the processes in this manner is helpful, it does not fully provide for the subtleties of the situations social workers face in applying the law, or for the multiplicity of influences upon the process. What follows is a framework that has three major component parts: structure, substance and principles.

Structure

The structure of the decision-making framework comprises a number of interconnected areas of enquiry which are prioritised in the course of making a decision. These are presented as a series of questions that practitioners may ask of people using services, of colleagues, of managers, of themselves, as a means of facilitating judgement.

WHAT?

What is the problem?

– What worries/concerns do I and others have?	– Look at the problem from different points in the system, not just the perspective of one person (DHSS, 1982).
– What evidence of the problem exists?	– Distinguish between fact and opinion.
– What interpretation do people place on the problem?	– People's subjective/internal experience is important (England, 1986). How these interpretations fit together clarifies positions and relationships within the system (Stratton *et al.*, 1990).

| – What might be happening here? | – Hypothesise from theory, feeling, observation and intuition. Seek patterns, using historical themes and information over time rather than considering events in isolation (Reder *et al.*, 1993). |
| – What further information do I need to clarify the problem? | – Check how this modifies/confirms hypotheses. |

What is the purpose?

– What do we want to achieve?	– Enhance coping? Rescue? Provide resources? Promote interpersonal change? Social change? Control?
– What are the broad objectives? What is the minimum goal?	– Damage limitation? Avert obvious dangers? Short-term safety? Long-term benefit? Reactive/proactive intervention?
– What would we like to be able to do? What do we think is feasible?	– Avoid nebulous phrases, identify concrete goals.

What needs/rights/risks exist?

– What needs does each person have?	– Are the needs, rights and risks of individuals in conflict? What part do various people play?
– What rights does each person have?	– Whose needs, rights, risks should be prioritised? Why?
– What risks does each person run/pose?	– Consider the practice dilemmas posed by the situation and where they arise from.

What is the legal context?

– What powers exist?	– Consider the range of legislation available.
– What duties exist?	– What must be done? What may be done?
– What are the grounds for intervention?	– What evidence exists for the legal grounds being fulfilled?

What is the agency context?

– What does my agency require/ allow me to do?	– The influence of policy and practice guidelines: advisory or mandatory. Has the agency made 'a decision always to make a certain decision in certain circumstances' (Dowie, 1989b)?

What resources?

– What means do we have of achieving objectives?	– Strengths (user, community, agency, professional system)
	– Resources
	– Legislation
– What solutions have been tried already?	– How far have they succeeded? Why? Why not? Were aims and methods agreed (Corden and Preston-Shoot, 1987)? Were workers/users clear?

WHEN?

– When must we intervene?	– To what extent do the circumstances of the situation match the grounds for intervention?
	– Is this an emergency?
	– Are the risks such that we must
	– overrule rights?
– When is the decision to be reviewed?	– Is there a legal requirement?
	– What does good practice demand?

WHO?

– Who makes the decision?	– Have consultation processes been used?
	– How is partnership with users to be practised?
	– Where in the organisational hierarchy is decision-making power located?
	– What is the status of decisions in supervision or consultation?

| | – Are case conference decisions binding on the agency? |
| – Who does what? | – Is everyone involved who should be involved? Are roles clearly understood? |

HOW?

– How are the goals to be achieved?	– The use of legal powers/duties? Non-statutory intervention? Contracts and written agreements?
– How is the law to be implemented?	– Statutory regulations? Agency guidelines? Professional codes? Are the tasks clear? Do we have the skills?
	– Are there requirements that influence how decisions are implemented (for example the timing of intervention so as to maximise legal evidence in the event of subsequent proceedings)?
– How will we know when the goals have been achieved?	– What evidence are we looking for? Who decides?

Substance

The substance of the decision-making framework comprises the accumulated knowledge, theory and wisdom derived from research and practice through which information arising from areas of enquiry will be filtered. Using a blend of theory and knowledge from a variety of sources assists in making sense of each individual situation (Curnock and Hardiker, 1979), though it is important to recognise that knowledge exists to inform understanding, not to dominate it (England, 1986). In situations where risk is inevitable, research knowledge avoids the danger of decision-making occurring in a vacuum. However, learning from research has been notoriously difficult to convey to practitioners, leading to more recent emphases upon methods of presentation and dissemination, such as operational briefs and practice checklists (White, 1992) to assist in its use in practice.

Checklists of childhood development (Fahlberg, 1981a; 1981b) are a good example of material to which practitioners have had recourse to help in formulating judgements about the seriousness and significance of information and observations gathered. They incorporate theories of child development, research findings and early warning signs, but can be misleading if applied rigidly; they may ignore family interaction, worker–family dynamics, financial disadvantage, power relations and situations of oppression, and potentially collude with narrow, individualised solutions. The Department of Health (1995a) stresses the importance of referring to evidence about what typically happens in families in attempting to establish the boundary between socially condoned treatment of children and that which may be defined as abusive. It acknowledges that thresholds for intervention are difficult to draw, and argues for more attention to be paid to outcome evidence on harm, as opposed to an isolated act or omission, in decisions taken. Bentovim *et al.* (1987) give a categorised series of indicators of the potential for successful rehabilitation (of abused children with their families), ranging from 'hopeful' (where parents/perpetrators acknowledge the abuse is wrong and take responsibility for working on problems), through 'doubtful' (where it is unclear whether abuse is acknowledged by all concerned and responsibility accepted), to 'hopeless' (where the child is blamed and scapegoated, abuse is not acknowledged, and protection cannot be counted upon). Checklists of characteristics in both parents and children have been produced to assist the identification of 'high risk' cases in child abuse (Greenland, 1987). Information on the outcomes of interventions, the characteristics of 'successful' and 'failed' child protection cases, has been usefully drawn together (D. Jones, 1991), as has evidence about the workings of the child protection system and the factors associated with protective outcomes (DoH, 1995a). These should inform professional activity. However, dangerousness remains notoriously difficult to predict, and the knowledge base remains limited (Parton, 1991).

There are examples, however, of checklists being given stronger emphasis in government guidelines which, while not having the force of legislation, are integral to its implementation. The Department of Health (DoH, 1988) incorporates a checklist approach when advising on factors which positively influence a decision to leave children with their families during a period of professional intervention. The

Mental Health Act Code of Practice (DoH, 1993c) clarifies provisions of the Mental Health Act 1983, and uses checklists to help practitioners decide when to invoke the law. With increasing awareness about the abuse of older people and other vulnerable adults, a similar trend of establishing checklists to anticipate risk has been discernible here (SSI, 1993b). Whilst useful to inform discussion and aid decision-making, such models can clearly not be taken as predictive and are no substitute for judgement.

Principles

The principles component of the decision-making framework involves consideration of the values underlying decisions, values that explain *why* certain decisions are taken, *why* certain needs or risks are prioritised, *why* interpretation of the law favours one intervention over another. Without principles, decision-making runs the risk of becoming pragmatic or opportunistic (Algie, 1976).

There is difficulty in 'defining and sustaining an appropriate professional role when deep emotions are involved and when ambivalence and conflict are integral to the situations within which social workers and sometimes others such as lawyers must work' (Stevenson, 1986). Professional principles underpin practice and illuminate the path to be taken. The principles that are prioritised influence the threshold of decision-making, having relevance at all stages in the framework – what? when? who? and how? A principle of 'respect for persons' may bring about a different decision from a principle of 'respect for life' in relation to involuntary admission to care from a risky situation (Brearley, 1982). A principle of prioritising responsibility to the persons most at risk in a situation (Bentovim *et al.*, 1987) may dictate the focus of intervention, but not necessarily the form; that would depend on where one stood in relation to other principles such as that of prioritising the 'least restrictive alternative' (BASW, 1977), or the 'least detrimental alternative' (Bentovim and Gilmour, 1981); what one considers detrimental depends on whether one prioritises the right to liberty over the right to treatment, permanency of placement over family ties. The principle of cost-effectiveness will produce a very different service from the principle of needs-led assessments. There is a danger in professional and organisational ideologies, assumptions and beliefs about what is right or wrong taking the place of knowledge, both in general and specific situations (DHSS, 1985). While we are not advocating that principles always lead decisions in a linear sense, clearly courses of action are informed by and in turn influence personal and organisational beliefs which should be brought into overt awareness during the decision-making process.

There are, however, some principles which are non-negotiable as a foundation for practice and with which the application of social work law must be consistent. The first is that an anti-oppressive stance must develop from the dual awareness of the way the law in itself discriminates against certain groups of people, and how social work practice can either condone and collude with that discrimination, or speak out and act against it. This is not just a question of 'being careful' in the way the law is applied to ensure that social control features are not used disproportionately against already disadvantaged groups. That is of course important, but even more so it is vital to challenge the myths and stereotypes that abound in the area of interface between the legal and social welfare systems, to use the law creatively to share the power that it bestows and to empower black people, women and people with disabilities against this oppression of the status quo.

The second is the issue of partnership, embodied in the Children Act 1989 and integral to its functioning, but also a key principle of services to people vulnerable through age, illness or disability. Partnership in planning for the delivery of services is indeed good practice, but there is a real challenge for practitioners acting in accordance with legal duties which require them in certain circumstances to override the wishes of individuals. How may partnership be construed in the context of compulsory admission to hospital, or of the best interests of someone deemed 'incapable' of consenting to medical treatment? These are not easy questions, but serve to illustrate how integral principles must be to any framework for decision-making, so that practitioners and managers debate and articulate the value bases of their judgements.

A decision-making framework must ultimately assist in identifying tangible options for action, and ensuring that the advantages and disadvantages of each option are systematically considered and taken into account. The acid test is whether at the end of the day social workers and their managers can account for *why* they did what they did, and whether their reasons can be supported by evidence that due care has been taken in the balancing act that often underlies the decision-making process.

Finally there is a need to heighten the emphasis on review. 'The more central social work becomes in the administration of any social policy, the greater the need to monitor its use of discretion' (Harris, 1982). Review is at two levels. At an individual level, decisions to invoke the law must be followed by evaluation of the outcomes, matching these against the original goals and priorities, ensuring that pursuing one set of objectives has not closed off awareness of the equal legitimacy of others, incorporating new information, monitoring the effects. At a wider level, agencies must monitor the kinds of decisions being made in similar sets of circumstances, examine how and when the law is being used, and problems and possibilities associated with its implementation, with a focus upon where it does not assist in promoting welfare as well as upon its benefits in doing so.

5

The Law Available to Social Workers

Since knowledge of the law alone is insufficient for effective practice, a decision-making framework and a critical appreciation of the context of social work law have been presented. Now the breadth of legal knowledge required may be articulated and applied. To facilitate retention of available knowledge, this chapter will anchor the law to case examples, connecting practice with legal remedies.

Case one

William is 80. He lives alone. Physically he is fit and regularly walks several miles. His memory is very poor and he is becoming increasingly disoriented. He sometimes gets lost and mislays money or keys. He was admitted to hospital twice recently with burns from sitting too close to the fire. He spends considerable time talking to photographs of his daughter, apparently assuming her to be his dead wife. He has begun to be aggressive towards her husband. His relatives are now reluctant to provide further support but William is refusing domiciliary and residential care. He will allow anyone into his home and has recently had money and possessions stolen. He will not throw away rubbish or rotten food. His capacity for self-care (continence, diet) is decreasing. There is growing concern about his health and conditions in the home.

What legislation might be helpful here?

Familiar practice dilemmas arise here. What risks should be supported and why, despite public anxiety about William's welfare? When does his right to choice give way to his right to protection if his judgement is impaired? Who should decide questions of services and protection, and on what criteria? What weight should be given to the needs of William, his carers and neighbours, when they conflict?

To determine what needs and rights exist, to decide objectives for intervention, those involved must be asked how they view the situation, and an evaluation must be made of what might be happening. If either William or his carers request this assessment, and William is disabled by virtue of being 'blind, deaf or dumb, or suffering from a mental disorder, or substantially and permanently handicapped by illness, injury or congenital deformity' (legal definitions, section 29, NAA 1948), then the local authority must consider William's needs for services under section 2, CSDPA 1970 (section 4, DPA 1986). The phrase 'substantially and permanently handicapped' should be interpreted widely, especially where there is uncertainty about duration. The reference to blind people also covers partially sighted people (LAC(93)10). When assessing his needs, the authority must consider the ability of any carer (excluding employees of statutory authorities) providing substantial care to continue providing such care (section 8, DPA 1986). Where neither William nor his carer request this assessment but it appears that he may need community care services, or if William is not disabled within the meaning of section 29 (NAA 1948), the local authority must assess and decide whether his needs call for service provision (section 47, NHSCCA 1990). For the assessment duty to be activated, all that is required is a possible need (Gordon, 1993). During this assessment the local authority must inform a district health or housing authority if he may require provisions which they control.

If and when the Disabled Persons Act 1986 is fully implemented, an authorised representative would be able to request an assessment (section 4) and local authorities would have to provide interpretation services for users and carers unable to communicate because of disability, to enable assessments to be completed (sections 3 and 8, DPA 1986). This is good practice anyway. So too would be providing a written statement specifying the needs the local authority will meet, the services it will provide and the basis on which the assessment has been made. The authority would be required to receive and consider further representations by users and their representatives, and to inform them of its decision and reasons for it (section 3, DPA 1986).

The needs of carers have now been more explicitly recognised in statute (Carers (Recognition and Services) Act 1995). Where a local authority conducts an assessment or reviews the needs of a disabled child (CA 1989) or of an adult such as William for community care services, and a carer provides or intends to provide a substantial amount of care on a regular basis, the carer may request an assessment of their needs. This assessment must be used in subsequent decision-making about whether the needs of the individual call for service provision. This duty, then, is activated by an assessment of a service user. If the service user refuses an assessment, carers may receive an assessment if they need community care services (section 47, NHSCCA 1990), if it is necessary to prevent illness (LAC(93)10; Schedule 8, NHSA 1977), or if they live with a child in need (section 17, CA 1989).

Young carers are covered by this Act and their particular needs have been emphasised (CI(95)12). Local authorities must link community care and children's services provisions, and ensure that young carers are regarded as children in need whose upbringing by their families should be promoted where appropriate. Assessment should take account of the preferences and circumstances of the young carer and his/her parent(s), and consider how to support the parent(s) whilst recognising the needs of the young carer.

A carer does not have to be living with the person cared for to receive an assessment, nor does the carer have to be the sole carer or a relative. The Act does not cover volunteers or people employed to provide care. Eligibility arises from providing, or intending to provide, a substantial amount of care on a regular basis. This is not defined by the Act, or subsequent section 7 (LASSA 1970) policy guidance (LAC(96)7), but is left to individual local authorities to determine. However, over-bureaucratic responses should be avoided and the Act's scope should be interpreted in an everyday sense. Thus, available practice guidance (LAC(96)7) refers to responsibility and supervision as well as practice tasks involving personal and physical assistance, and identifies what an assessment should cover.

Carers should be informed of their rights to an assessment and should be free to choose either a separate discussion or a joint assessment with the service user. The assessment and care plan should be recorded, and copies given, to promote a shared understanding of the process. Services should be clearly related to the assessed needs of both the user and carer. Local authorities should not assume that carers are willing to continue caring, or to care at the same level.

Where the authority is satisfied that it is necessary, an absolute duty exists (section 2, CSDPA 1970) to assist disabled people with domiciliary services; support to reduce the social and personal consequences of illness and disability; telephones; adaptations to accommodation; meals at home or elsewhere; recreational facilities, including radio, television and libraries; provision of, or assistance in taking advantage of, holidays and educational facilities. A duty exists to provide facilities for social rehabilitation and adjustment to disability, including assistance to overcome limitations of mobility or communication (LAC(93)10). A local authority cannot impose arbitrary financial or time ceilings on provision (*R* v. *Islington LBC, ex parte Hooper* [1994]) and must make provision for all section 2 services (*R* v. *LB of Ealing, ex parte Leaman* [1984]). A duty exists to provide residential accommodation to those who, because of age, illness, disability or other circumstances, require care and attention not otherwise available to them (section 21, NAA 1948). This duty may be delegated to private or voluntary organisations (section 26; *R* v. *Wandsworth LBC, ex parte Beckwith* [1996]). Users' ability to pay must be assessed (section 22) and their property (including animals) safeguarded (section 48).

Should the local authority complete an assessment and decide that residential accommodation should be provided for William, it must make arrangements for accommodation at the place of his choice if the preferred accommodation is suitable to his needs, is available, and if the authority would not be required to pay more than usual (LAC(92)27). Authorities cannot refuse on grounds of cost to provide accommodation chosen by an individual which they are already providing to others (*R* v. *Avon County Council, ex parte Hazell* [1993]).

Local authorities must charge service users for residential care provision (section 44, NHSCCA 1990). Concern is growing about the impact of charging – the fear and anxiety it creates for older people and their families, the growing prospect of evictions from homes in the independent sector. In relation to community care services, some services are exempt from charging (for example, after-care duties for people with mental health problems (section 117, MHA 1983)). Otherwise charging is optional but encouraged (section 17, HASSASSAA 1983). Where charges are levied they must be reasonable. Inability to pay should not mean the withdrawal of services.

Proper assessment of need is therefore the cornerstone of high quality care (DoH, 1990), with packages of care designed in line with individual needs and preferences. Assessment and the identification of need should be aimed at meeting an individual's wishes, and actively involve users whose views should be elicited and taken into account. When reconciling different perspectives between users, carers and/or other professionals, the assessing practitioner will need to have good reason for departing from the user's perspective. However, need is defined by the local authority rather than the service user (DoH, 1991j). Assessment should consider risk factors, health, finance, education/employment/leisure, accommodation, abilities, transport, personal care and social support needs, and be an exploration of needs rather than an application of eligibility criteria (DoH, 1990). When setting the standards of need to be met, discretion must be exercised reasonably (*R* v. *Gloucestershire County Council, ex parte Barry* [1997]). Assessment, the level of which is dependent on the issues to be addressed (DoH, 1991k), should be aimed at understanding an individual's needs and, subsequently, at agreeing priorities and objectives for intervention (DoH, 1991m). Need is defined as requirements to enable people to achieve, maintain or restore an acceptable level of social independence or quality of life (DoH, 1991j), where possible in their own home (DoH, 1990). Need includes psychological needs (*R* v. *Avon County Council, ex parte Hazell* [1993]) and possible future needs alongside immediate present needs (*R* v. *Mid Glamorgan County Council, ex parte Miles* [1993]). Need and service decisions are separate; need should be defined on an individual basis, as precisely as possible (DoH, 1991m; SSI, 1992b), thus recognising the individuality of need and the unique circumstances of each person's needs, and the importance of devising individualised rather than stereotyped responses to those needs.

Having decided that need calls for service provision, the local authority may determine the form this should take, weighing up all the circumstances including costs and resources (*R* v. *Lancashire County Council, ex parte RADAR and Another* [1996]). Care needs, for which services are provided, should be reviewed regularly, the purpose being to establish whether objectives specified in the care plan are being or have been met, and to increase, revise or withdraw services accordingly. Reviews should be needs-led and must take place *before* services can be withdrawn or considerably altered (*R* v. *Gloucestershire County Council, ex parte RADAR* [1995]). In relation to absolute duties, such as section 2, CSDPA 1970, resources may not be considered once authorities accept it is necessary to provide services (*R* v. *Gloucestershire County Council, ex parte Barry* [1997]). In relation to discretionary duties resources may be considered both at assessment and review (see Chapter 6).

Guidance (DoH, 1990) reinforces the requirement (section 20, RRA 1976) that decisions on providing services must be non-discriminatory and that service provision is made with due regard (section 71) to the need to eliminate discrimination and promote equality of opportunity. Thus William's racial origin, language and cultural needs must be considered in determining what services are provided. Services geared to the requirements of majority groups may not be appropriate (DoH, 1990) and special provision (section 35) may need to be made.

Local authorities must inform themselves of the number of people in their area who qualify under section 29, NAA 1948, and assess the need to make arrangements on their behalf (section 1, CSDPA 1970). Registers are the usual response here. These duties are fulfilled when services are offered. Users retain the right to refuse such provision.

Local authorities may promote the welfare of older people such as William and use voluntary organisations for this purpose (section 45, HSPHA 1968). This includes wardens, meals on wheels, day and domiciliary care, for which charges may be levied. A duty exists to provide home helps, meals and laundry services if required because of age, illness or handicap, and prevention, care and after-care services to people with physical and mental illness (NHSA 1977; MHA 1983). Intervention should be limited to that necessary to foster independence, prevent or minimise disability and illness, and promote individual strengths. It should be designed and reviewed in partnership with users and carers (DoH, 1990).

LAC(93)10 clarifies the powers and duties which authorities have in respect of provision of residential accommodation; prevention of mental illness, and care and after-care of people with mental disorders through the provision of centres, Approved Social Workers, social work provision, and domiciliary services; social work services for disabled people and older people, whether or not in residential care; facilities for rehabilitation; warden support. LAC(93)7 clarifies where responsibility resides between local authorities in respect of residential accommodation. Service provision should not be delayed because of uncertainty about a person's ordinary area of residence. The authority of the moment must meet a person's urgent needs. When an individual is placed in another authority's area, the individual remains the responsibility of the placing authority which may request the provision of support services. Clear agreements will be necessary about financing such arrangements and any changes to the care plan should be the subject of prior consultation between the authorities except in emergencies.

The Community Care (Direct Payments) Act 1996 now permits local authorities, having decided that a person requires community care services (section 47, NHSCCA 1990), to make a cash payment to that individual for the purpose of securing provision. The Act is permissive; it is for the authority to determine in what circumstances it will exercise such discretion. The Act allows the Secretary of State to make regulations imposing restrictions on those people who might be eligible, creating concern that some, for example learning disabled people, may be unreasonably excluded and that the principle of independent living will be undermined. There is also concern that the payments made will not reflect the true cost of services.

Social services departments may request assistance from a housing authority when assessing a person's needs for services (section 47(3)(b), NHSCCA 1990). The relevant duty owed to a mentally incapacitated person who is homeless is that contained in section 21, NAA 1948, and not in homeless persons provisions (HA 1996) (*R* v. *LB of Tower Hamlets, ex parte Begum* [1993]). Housing authorities may ask social services departments for assistance but are not obliged to do so. An applicant to a housing authority is therefore advised to request that authority to contact the social services department (*R* v. *Wirral MBC, ex parte B* [1994]). Housing need can easily be overlooked when assessing social care needs but housing authorities should play a full part in community care (LAC(92)12). This circular reinforces the importance of social services departments notifying housing authorities and inviting their assistance (with adaptations, equipment to assist safe, daily living, improvements and repairs) when a person appears to have a housing need. It encourages joint arrangements to deal with assessments, with the objective of restoring or maintaining where possible non-institutional living. Unmet need should inform community care planning.

Grants for renovation, improvements and facilities for disabled people, whether tenants or owner-occupiers, are available (Housing Grants, Construction and Regeneration Act 1996). Disabled Facilities Grants are mandatory in respect of access to a power source; or facilitating access to a dwelling, family rooms, toilet, cooking and washing facilities; or assisting a disabled person to care for others; or providing or improving heating (section 23(1)). In any other respect, a grant is discretionary (section 23(2)). A decision on an application must be made within six months. The work must be necessary and appropriate to meet the disabled person's needs (section 24(3)), and must be reasonable and practicable to carry out. The social services department may be asked to contribute to this assessment. The applicant, his or her spouse and others in the house will be means-tested (section 30). As of 1997 the grant ceiling is £20,000 but this may change (section 33). Payment of the grant may be delayed by the housing authority for up to twelve months (section 36).

Should William be admitted to hospital and be unable to return home, responsibility for him will depend on where the line is drawn between health care and social care. NHS services are free at the point of delivery. Local authorities may charge for community care services, and for residential care must charge. There have been concerns about bed blocking, unnecessary hospital stays, and inappropriate hospital discharges or placements in residential as opposed to nursing care.

The development of a policy on continuing care has not been straightforward. However, guidance (LAC(95)5) details what services the NHS must fund in relation to older people, including those with a mental illness, people with dementia, children, and adults with health-care needs arising from illness or accident. These include services of assessment, medical and nursing care, rehabilitation and recovery, palliative health care, and health authority support in nursing homes, residential care or community care packages. NHS-funded care will be appropriate if a person has an ongoing and regular need for specialist clinical supervision because of the complexity, intensity, frequency or nature of their medical or nursing needs, if a period of rehabilitation or recovery is required, or if, after acute or inpatient palliative care, they are likely to die in a short time.

Health authorities and social services departments must agree procedures for discharging patients from NHS care and eligibility criteria for continuing health care. Service users and carers must be involved in discharge planning, including being provided with information about eligibility criteria and care package options to enable them to make informed decisions. Patients should only be discharged after a multidisciplinary assessment which takes account of user and carer views. Written discharge information should be provided, including details of any continuing care arranged for them and of the cost to the patient of care options after discharge. Patients have the right to refuse discharge to nursing home or residential care provision. In these circumstances they may be discharged into the community with an appropriate care package.

The guidance calls for the integration of NHS and local authority procedures, and for collaboration in establishing unified assessment procedures, but it does not address adequately the challenges and barriers to multidisciplinary collaboration which undermine the effectiveness of the 'seamless' service (see Braye and Preston-Shoot, 1995). Further guidance has provided details of a review procedure (LAC(95)17), the aim of which is to provide an adequate safeguard for patients assessed as ready for discharge from inpatient care who believe that eligibility criteria for continuing inpatient care, whether in a hospital or nursing home, have been incorrectly applied. This procedure is separate from complaints procedures, which should be used for challenging the content of the eligibility criteria and any care package offered. It is also separate from procedures which must be established to resolve disputes between health and local authorities about responsibility for funding care in individual cases.

Moving from enabling to protective intervention objectives, the law provides little assistance in safeguarding older people's welfare. If William is mentally disordered within the meaning of section 1, MHA 1983, he could be compulsorily admitted to psychiatric hospital for assessment (section 2/4) or, if he has one of four more specific conditions, for treatment (section 3) (see case three). The only other power of removal is under section 47, NAA 1948. Criticised in earlier chapters, this section is available in respect of people of any age but is normally used with older people, suggesting ageism. There is no guarantee that the person will be represented in, or attend, legal proceedings, or be aware of their right to appeal. Section 47 permits removal of people who are (a) suffering from grave disease or, being aged, infirm or physically incapacitated, are living in insanitary conditions *and* (b) unable to devote to themselves or are not receiving from others proper care and attention, *when* it is in their interests or to prevent nuisance or injury to the health of others. The local authority applies to a court with a recommendation from the Community Physician. The person must be given one week's notice. Detention, renewable, may last three months. Immediate removal is allowed, for three weeks, on application to a magistrate supported by two medical recommendations, including one from the Community Physician.

An alternative strategy could be guardianship (MHA 1983). Application may be made by an ASW or the nearest relative, supported by two medical recommendations, to the local authority for the appointment of a guardian (section 7, MHA 1983). The grounds are that he has a specific diagnosis of mental illness, mental impairment, severe mental impairment or psychopathic disorder, of a nature or degree warranting reception into guardianship, and that this is necessary for his welfare or the protection of others. Accurate diagnosis of William's mental state is thus crucial to whether guardianship could be used. An order lasts six months, renewable for six months and thereafter at yearly intervals. The nearest relative can object to the application, or discharge the 'patient', and application may be made to the Mental Health Review Tribunal. Guardianship is essentially a *relationship* in which the guardian can choose to exercise three essential powers: to require the person to reside at a specified place; to require the person to attend at specified places for medical treatment, occupation, education or training; and to require access to the person to be given to a doctor or ASW. In practice, even if these powers were deemed a useful contribution to William's welfare, they are of limited use if he resists, for there is no accompanying power physically to enforce the requirements, other than to return him to where he is required to live if he physically absconds from there.

Provisions also exist to protect individuals' financial affairs, although these may be insufficient to prevent financial abuse. Mentally competent people may appoint agents to collect benefits or, via third party mandates, to undertake more detailed financial transactions. The Department of Social Security will allow appointees to collect benefits on behalf of people unable to manage their own affairs, when satisfied of their suitability, but it does not usually monitor the arrangements unless someone complains that the benefits are being misused. Individuals may give power of attorney to others, written authority to act on their behalf. A donor must be mentally capable when giving the power, which lapses when the donor becomes mentally incapable unless given under the Enduring Power of Attorney Act 1985. Here the power endures after the donor becomes mentally incapable providing it is registered with the Court of Protection at this point and neither the donor nor nearest relatives object. The Court of Protection must be satisfied that the donor is mentally incapable and must consider any objections which are lodged. The Court of Protection, on application from someone concerned, may appoint a receiver to act according to the court's instructions in administering a person's affairs, if medical diagnosis confirms incapacity by virtue of mental disorder.

Concerns remain, however, about the adequacy of these 'safeguards': the vague legal and medical terminology used, especially concerning the point of mental incapacity; the subject's ability to make representations or object; and the duress to which they can be exposed prior to orders or once these have been made (Greengross, 1986).

Thus current legislation gives limited means of protecting William from abuse, exploitation or self-neglect without major infringement of his civil liberties. There is recognition of the need for legislative reform. Proposals from the Law Commission (1995) include:

- a duty on social services departments to investigate where a vulnerable person is suffering or is likely to suffer significant harm;
- new crisis intervention powers to enable either the removal of the vulnerable person or specific protective assistance to them (an assessment order, temporary protection order, power of entry, power to apply for an entry warrant – similar to orders available under the Children Act 1989);
- non-molestation or exclusion orders against named individuals;
- amendments to guardianship, extending the powers of the guardian, removing the nearest relative's right of veto, and widening the eligibility criteria;
- introducing a continuing power of attorney which will extend to matters relating to personal welfare, health care, property and affairs;

- extending the powers of the Court of Protection to give it jurisdiction over matters of welfare and health; and
- new tribunals or panels to consider protective actions, perhaps with judicial involvement at some level of decision-making.

Currently, however, if William refuses services and does not fulfil the criteria for removal under section 47 (NAA 1948) or the MHA 1983, the law can do little to alleviate his situation. At the very least, however, practitioners can push for developments in policy to allow multidisciplinary decision-making, with police involvement to consider the use of criminal law, as in child protection, to be extended into the field of adult services. There is evidence that this is happening with the development of policies on vulnerable adults covering all forms of abuse and emphasising the importance of information collection, multidisciplinary case meetings, and coordinated action.

Case two

Martin is physically disabled, uses a wheelchair and requires 24-hour care. He requires assistance with all daily living tasks and personal care. He uses a specially constructed letter and symbol board to communicate. He lives with his parents. Both Martin and his parents wish to explore the possibility of him living (semi-) independently. He is 15.

What legislation has a bearing on this case?

1. The Education Act 1993 and Education (Special Educational Needs) Regulations 1994 require children with special educational needs to be educated in ordinary schools where possible. There are duties on local education authorities to:

- identify and assess all children with (or if aged between two and five, likely to have) special educational needs, to make a statement of these needs and to arrange provision to meet them (sections 160, 165, 175);
- comply with a parental request for an assessment (section 172) if one has not been undertaken within six months;

- involve parents fully in the assessment, including providing information and reports;
- meet all, not merely some, of the needs identified (*R* v. *Secretary of State for Education and Science, ex parte E* [1992]); parents may appeal to a Special Educational Needs Tribunal if a statement does not match the assessment of the child's needs;
- detail each and every special educational need identified in an assessment and the provision necessary to meet them; authorities are not bound to make the best provision but provision that will work (*R* v. *Surrey County Council, ex parte H* [1984]); provision should be cost-effective but consistent with a child's assessed needs (DFE, 1994); statements should clearly specify what the education authority considers should be provided *(R* v. *Cumbria County Council, ex parte P* [1995]);
- accept parental preference for a particular school (Schedule 10(3)) unless this would be unsuitable for the child's age, ability, aptitude or special educational needs, or incompatible with the education of other children or with the use of resources;
- inform relevant nursing and social services officials, when assessing a child, to ensure relevant information is available;
- disclose to social services departments the statement of a child's special educational needs to enable obligations under the Disabled Persons Act 1986 (sections 5 and 6) and under the Children Act 1989 (sections 22(3), 85(4), 86(3) and 87(3)) to be met; and
- review statements annually and when there are significant changes in a child's circumstances.

Local education authorities are empowered to assess children aged under two on parental request. No duty to make provision arises here. They must also seek to meet the needs of children who are not statemented but who have special needs. Health authorities must inform parents and local education authorities when they consider a child under five to have special educational needs (section 176). Special educational needs include any kind of learning difficulty significantly greater than that experienced by most similarly aged children, or disability preventing a child from using ordinary educational facilities effectively, and requiring special educational provision to be made (section 156(2)). This will include dyslexia, emotional and behavioural disorders, physical disabilities and sensory impairment.

Local education authorities may request assistance from district health authorities and social services departments who must comply unless this would be inconsistent with their duties and functions, or they consider that help is unnecessary (section 166). They must have regard to the provisions of the Code of Practice (DFE, 1994), to which a tribunal may refer in relation to any questions arising on appeal. The Code of Practice recommends that assessment should take place in a setting where the child and family feel comfortable, and that all services should have information about procedures for identifying special educational needs. Regulations lay down time limits for deciding whether to assess a child, completing the assessment, providing copies of the proposed statement to parents following assessment, and completing the statement. The process should be completed within 26 weeks. Some exceptions to this are allowed. Regulations also specify who should be present at reviews.

Parents may appeal to a tribunal when a statement is made or amended, including where an authority ceases to maintain it, or if an education authority decides not to (re-) assess, or to issue or amend a statement. The decision of the tribunal is binding. It must give reasons for its decisions and may order an education authority to act. Other than for advice, legal aid is not available. Only parents may appeal to the tribunal, not children (*S* v. *Special Educational Needs Tribunal and the City of Westminster* [1996]).

2. Disabled Persons Act 1986. Sections 4 and 8, covered in case one, apply here. Two other duties exist under this Act. First (section 5), local education authorities must ascertain from social services departments whether statemented children are disabled (section 29, NAA 1948 defines 'disabled') at the first review of the statement after the fourteenth birthday. The LEA must notify the SSD between twelve and eight months before a disabled child is due to leave full-time education. Unless the person or, if under 16 the parent, objects the SSD must then assess the person's needs for services – residential or day care (NAA 1948) and welfare services (CSDPA 1970). Where possible this assessment should be completed prior to the leaving date, even when the LEA gave shorter notice, to enable relevant provisions to be made. When a person decides not to leave full-time education the LEA must inform the SSD, whereupon

assessment is suspended until subsequent notification by the LEA or, where appropriate, a college of further education (LAC(93)12) of a leaving date. Second (section 6), LEAs must review dates when disabled children are expected to leave full-time education.

Social services departments can assist disabled people to take advantage of education facilities (CSDPA 1970). Students in further and higher education may be eligible for grants for non-medical helpers, major items of equipment, and minor items of equipment, in order to facilitate their attendance at and completion of programmes of study (LAC(93)12).

3. Children Act 1989. The definition of children in need includes disabled children (section 17). Local authorities must, therefore, provide a range and level of services appropriate to their needs, to safeguard and promote their welfare and, where possible, upbringing by their families (section 17). These services should aim to 'minimise the effect on children of their disabilities and give them opportunities to lead lives as near normal as possible' (Schedule 2(6)). Services include advice and counselling; occupational, social, cultural and recreational activities; home help; travelling assistance to take advantage of services; holidays (Schedule 2(8)); day care for children in need aged under five and not in school (section 18); registers (Schedule 2(2)) and family centres (Schedule 2(9)). A duty exists to have regard to different racial groups to which children in need belong (Schedule 2(11)) and, where such children are accommodated by local authorities, to place them where practicable and consistent with their welfare near home (section 23 (7)). Social services departments may request help from education, housing and health authorities (section 27, CA 1989) who must comply if the request is compatible with their obligations.

Once Martin is 16, he may request accommodation by the local authority (section 20(11)). As a young person his views are increasingly important but not necessarily determinative. Transition services for disabled young people need a higher priority, and guidance (CI(95)27) encourages social services departments to work together with education and health authorities in developing joint policies and commissioning strategies for moves from residential care or the parental home into suitable accommodation with support services then negotiated on an individual basis.

4. NHS and Community Care Act 1990 and Carers (Recognition and Services) Act 1995. The duties and principles outlined in case one also apply here.

The law provides a framework for what must happen and when. For the principle of partnership, which underpins it, the duty to provide information about services (section 9, DPA 1986; Schedule 2(1), CA 1989; section 46, NHSCCA 1990) is crucial. However the picture has been somewhat dismal (SSI, 1990b; Croall, 1991; K. Jones, 1991): resource shortfalls creating serious problems in implementing legislation; difficulties in coordinating an inter-agency approach; wide variations in numbers of children being statemented and types of needs considered eligible; parental views given insufficient weight; inadequate information about procedures and provisions.

Agencies should provide an equal opportunity, anti-oppressive continuum of care. The practitioner's contribution consists of producing with Martin and his carers an assessment of needs (physical, emotional, practical, housing, financial, educational, employment and mobility) and maximising Martin's control over his life decisions. Maintaining inter-agency links and 'feeding' shortfalls of provision into agency planning processes are key tasks too.

However practitioners will sit uncomfortably astride the needs v. resources, humanitarianism v. economics practice dilemmas, for, whilst practice demonstrates clearly that resource-led assessments are uneconomic and frequently ineffective, guidance (DoH, 1989c) stresses that needs must be met within available resources. Authorities must decide criteria of need reasonably and might be acting *ultra vires* if not providing services to meet assessed needs because of insufficient funds (see Chapter 6). Nonetheless social workers must act vigilantly against restrictive criteria of need and definitions of statutory duties, and any erosion of social work's values.

Case three

Amy is aged 49, living with her two teenage children and partner Jim in a council flat. She has had inpatient psychiatric treatment, after her second child was born and again following an overdose when her marriage was ending. Since redundancy from her job a year ago she has been feeling low again. She has had medication from her general practitioner who has requested social work involvement to help with 'family problems' that are affecting her mental health. An urgent call is now received from Jim saying Amy is very distressed. He asks for someone to come and talk to her about going into hospital.

The initial response here is governed by the Mental Health Act 1983. The local authority must direct an ASW as soon as practicable to consider making application for the patient's admission to hospital where requested by the patient's nearest relative (section 13(4)). *Is Amy a patient?* A patient is 'someone suffering or appearing to be suffering from mental disorder' (section 145(1)), meaning mental illness, arrested or incomplete development of mind, psychopathic disorder and any other disorder or disability of mind (section 1(2)); given her doctor's concern, Amy could well be covered by this wide definition. *Is Jim her nearest relative?* Section 26(1) lists who qualifies as nearest relative. Top of the list is 'husband' or 'wife'. This includes a heterosexual cohabitee of more than six months' standing, providing the patient is permanently separated from the marital partner (section 26(6)). Thus Jim may well be Amy's nearest relative. *Does his phone call constitute a request?* The Act does not specify how a request must be made. The Code of Practice (DoH, 1993c) recommends that local authorities issue practice guidance. The phone call could constitute 'a request'. *Who should go?* Although mental health issues may be encountered by any social worker, in this case the response must be by an Approved Social Worker appointed under section 114 of the Act. If the ASW decides, having investigated the request, not to make application for hospital admission, she must inform the nearest relative of the reasons in writing.

An ASW visits the flat and meets Jim, who says Amy has 'gone over the top', thrown a knife at him and locked herself in the flat with her pills, saying she will take them all. He is locked out on the landing and has phoned the police. *How can the ASW gain access to Amy?*

An occupier of the premises can permit entry. Thus, unless Amy has exclusive rights of occupation, Jim could break down his own door or authorise someone else to do so. Where an occupier is unavailable, or unwilling, the police have powers of forcible entry (PACE 1984) to save life and limb and/or to prevent the commission of a crime. Without this justification, the ASW must apply to a magistrate for a warrant (section 135, MHA 1983) empowering a police constable to enter, by force if necessary, accompanied by an ASW and a doctor, and remove Amy to a place of safety. The police hold further emergency powers (section 136) to remove to a place of safety someone who is in a place to which the public have access and who appears to be mentally disordered and in immediate need of care and control, if this is necessary in their interests or for the protection of others. This does not apply to Amy as she is in a private dwelling.

Amy allows access to the social worker and a long discussion reveals that she is indeed very distressed. She feels her life has no meaning and there is little point in being alive. Physically she looks undernourished and unwell and has observable bruises. She says Jim caused these: he has always been violent, worse recently. She threw the knife at him because he threatened her and she suddenly snapped. When the doctor arrives she talks with Amy and considers she is depressed and needing hospitalisation. Amy refuses to go.

There are responsibilities here under mental health legislation. In addition, while not possessing specific duties or powers in relation to domestic violence to adults, social workers are in a key position to give support and advice about recourse to the law, and indeed within an anti-oppressive practice model should do so.

Mental health

Amy could be admitted to psychiatric hospital compulsorily (MHA 1983). This could be admission for assessment (section 2) or for treatment (section 3). The grounds for section 2 are that she is suffering from a mental disorder of a nature or degree that warrants her detention in hospital for assessment (including medical treatment) and that she ought to be detained in the interests of her own health or safety or for the protection of others. Note that it is sufficient that she has an unspecified 'mental disorder' – a wide catch-all phrase (see case five). Detention is for 28 days. It may not be renewed but may be followed by a treatment order. The patient may appeal to a Mental Health Review Tribunal for review of the detention within 14 days.

The grounds for section 3 are that she is suffering from one of four specific disorders (mental illness, mental impairment, severe mental impairment or psychopathic disorder – see case five) of a nature or degree which makes it appropriate for her to receive treatment in a hospital; that in the case of mental impairment and psychopathic disorder the condition is treatable; that treatment is necessary for her health or safety or for the protection of others; that treatment cannot otherwise be given. Detention is for six months and is renewable. The patient may apply to an MHRT for review of the detention. The Code of Practice (DoH, 1993c) recommends reserving the use of section 3 to situations where the patient is known to the clinical team, having had recent assessment and diagnosis.

Application for admission under section 2 or 3 is made to the hospital on relevant forms and must be accompanied by two medical recommendations: one by a doctor approved as having special experience in the diagnosis and treatment of mental disorder and the other, if the first doctor does not have previous acquaintance with the patient, should be by a doctor who does. In respect of section 2 admissions, if there is urgent necessity and complying with the requirements would cause undesirable delay, section 4 allows for an application to be supported by only one medical recommendation, given if practicable by a doctor who knows the patient.

Either an ASW or the nearest relative may make the application. It is the duty of an ASW (section 13(1)) to make the application where she is satisfied that one should be made and, having regard to relatives' wishes and other relevant circumstances, that it should be made by her. The ASW is 'usually the right applicant, bearing in mind professional training, knowledge of the legislation and of local resources, together with the potential adverse effect that a nearest relative's application might have on their relationship with the patient' (DoH, 1993c). If the NR does make the application, the local authority must after the event provide a social worker (not necessarily an ASW) to make a social circumstances report to the hospital. If the ASW makes the application she must, before doing so, interview the patient 'in a suitable manner' and determine that detention in hospital is in all the circumstances of the case the most appropriate way of providing the care and medical treatment needed (section 13(2)). For section 3 admissions, as with guardianship (see case five), the ASW must consult if practicable with the NR and cannot proceed if they object (section 11(4)), unless they are replaced by County Court (section 29, see case five). An NR, unless replaced, can discharge a patient from section 3 and appeal to an MHRT if blocked from doing so. For section 2 there is no duty to consult, but the NR must be advised of the admission, and of their power to discharge the patient, within a reasonable time (section 11(3)).

The effect of an application for admission is that Amy could be taken to psychiatric hospital, reasonable force being used if she resisted (section 137(2)), and given medical treatment (see case five for discussion of consent to treatment). Clearly the MHA 1983 provides a very individualised solution, based on a medical model of mental health. However the ASW may only make an application if it is 'in all the circumstances . . . the most appropriate way of providing . . . care and treatment' (section 13(2)). This implies careful and comprehensive assessment of the complex web of social interactions which affect and are affected by mental health problems, and active consideration of alternative courses of action. All the general welfare legislation (see case one) applies to Amy as of course do the provisions of the Children Act 1989 in respect of her children (see case four). She would be a disabled person within the meaning of section 29, NAA 1948.

Domestic violence

Both criminal and civil remedies are available. The police have powers of arrest (section 5(3), PACE 1984) where there is a need to prevent injury or protect a child or other vulnerable person. Under the Offences Against the Person Act 1861 there are offences of common law assault, assault occasioning actual bodily harm, unlawful wounding and assault occasioning grievous bodily harm. Only common assault is not an arrestable offence, and the law provides here for private prosecution or action for damages through civil courts. The use of arrest and prosecution by the police in cases of domestic violence is increasing, but is by no means yet the remedy of automatic recourse. If a prosecution is made, the injured party can be compelled to give evidence (section 80, PACE 1984): women who are fearful of doing so are afforded some protection by provision in the Criminal Justice Act 1988 for written evidence.

Civil remedies are primarily under two pieces of legislation:

Family Law Act 1996	*Domestic Proceedings and Magistrates' Court Act 1978*
Available to both married and unmarried partners, with provisions also covering children for whom adults have parental responsibility or are parents. The orders are also available to divorcees, former cohabitees and relatives. Young people may apply with leave if of sufficient understanding	Available only to married partners

County Court	*Magistrates Court*
Has discretion to make:	Has discretion to make:

County Court

Has discretion to make:

- non-molestation orders (to include violence, threats and harassment), as part of or without other family proceedings, including on the court's own motion in family proceedings
- occupation orders, whether or not the applicant has an existing right to occupy the house. Such orders can enforce a person's right to remain, or can regulate occupation by prohibiting, suspending or restricting a person's right to occupy. The order can exclude a person from part or all of a house, and from a defined geographical area. The application is considered by reference to the respective conduct of the parties, their housing needs, their financial and housing resources, the time since they ceased to live together and the time they have lived together, the likely effect on the health, safety or well-being of the parties or children, and the welfare and needs of any children. Courts must make

Magistrates Court

Has discretion to make:

- personal protection orders (to cover violence and threats of violence only)
- exclusion orders, to exclude one party from the home (but not the surrounding area) only if
  : violence has occurred

OR
  : threats of violence and actual violence to a third party

OR
  : breach of personal protection order

AND
  : there is real danger of injury

an occupation order if the applicant or child is likely to suffer significant harm, unless the respondent or child would suffer significant harm as a result of the order being made which would be greater than the harm likely to be suffered as a result of the respondent's behaviour if an order is not made

- exclusion orders, to exclude one party from the home and/or from the surrounding area
- injunctions to require one party to allow the other back into the home

There is no need for actual or threatened physical violence to be proven. The orders can be for a specified period or until further notice	There must have been violence or threats of violence, not other forms of molestation

Ex parte hearing in an emergency. Under the Family Law Act 1996 this is available when there is a risk of significant harm to the applicant or a child, or where an applicant would otherwise be likely to be deterred from pursuing an application.

Breaking an injunction constitutes contempt of court. The applicant has to advise the court and request a warrant for arrest be issued.

The respondent can be ordered to court and cautioned, fined or imprisoned.

Powers of arrest can be attached to the original injunction if actual injury has occurred and is likely to do so again (DPMCA 1978) or if the respondent has used or threatened to use violence to the applicant or a child and, in *ex parte* orders, where there is also a risk of significant harm (FLA 1996), allowing arrest without warrant if the injunction is broken. Under the Family Law Act 1996, no power of arrest can be attached if the court accepts an undertaking which is acceptable as if a court order.

The Family Law Act 1996 plugs one loophole exposed when the Court of Appeal ruled that a prohibited steps order (section 8, CA 1989) cannot be used to oust a parent (*Nottinghamshire County Council* v. *P* [1993]). A court may now add to an emergency protection order or an interim care order an exclusion requirement if it is likely that a child will cease to (be likely to) suffer significant harm or, in the case of an EPO, it is likely that enquiries will cease to be frustrated. Another person must be able to care for the child and consent to the order being made. A court may attach a power of arrest or accept an undertaking. The exclusion requirement ceases to have effect if the authority subsequently removes the child from home for a continuous period of more than 24 hours. Exclusion can mean from the house and/or a defined geographical area.

Partners who are not living together are not protected by any of this legislation unless the actions took place before separation and they have been married or cohabitants (section 62(3), FLA 1996). For non-cohabiting partners the only recourse is through assault and trespass law (Mama, 1989). Other related legislation is the Housing Act 1996 and the Child Support Act 1991 (see case four). Using the legislation to gain protection is a complex process and many women have experienced difficulties (McCann, 1985). Current immigration legislation compounds the difficulties for black women, who leave a violent relationship only to find they can be deported if their immigration status is not secure (Mama, 1989).

There is also considerable controversy about the position in law of women who have endured domestic violence and kill their partners in self-defence. For a defence of provocation to succeed, so that a murder charge is changed to manslaughter, the provocation had to have resulted in sudden and temporary loss of control. Women who had been provoked through violence but who through fear or unequal strength waited before retaliating until, for example, their partner is asleep, have had pleas of provocation refused, unlike men, who kill without apparent premeditation and successfully plead provocation through 'nagging' or infidelity (Edwards, 1985b).

However, the law has softened its treatment of such women and widened the definition of provocation by allowing a slow build-up and cumulative strands of potentially provocative conduct over time to be analysed for their significance (*R* v. *Humphreys* [1995]). The longer the delay and the greater the deliberation, the more difficult it will be to establish the defence of provocation (*R* v. *Ahluwalia* [1992]). 'Battered women's syndrome' and post-traumatic stress are now recognised as relevant characteristics but, as provocation requires temporary or sudden loss of control at the time, the court must ask whether a reasonable woman with battered women's syndrome would have reacted to provocative conduct in this way (*R* v. *Thornton (No. 2)* [1996]).

Case four

Mary met her husband while he was working in Nigeria, her country of origin. Joshua, their son, is three. Since arriving in England 18 months ago Mary has been aggressive towards her husband and son, painting herself and Joshua white, periodically refusing to eat, afraid of poisoned food, and locking herself away. Her husband wants a divorce but remains at home because of concerns about Mary's behaviour and Joshua's development and safety. What legislation is relevant here?

Divorce

The sole ground is that the marriage has irretrievably broken down. A divorce order will be granted if this ground is proved *and*:

- a statement to that effect is appropriately made by one or both parties (section 6, FLA 1996);
- the period for reflection and consideration (nine months) has ended (section 7);
- the party making the statement has attended an information meeting prior to making the statement (section 8);
- the court is satisfied with the future arrangements concerning finance and children agreed by the parties during the period of reflection (section 9);
- granting the divorce would not involve substantial financial or other hardship to a party or a child (section 10);
- one year has elapsed since the end of the period of reflection and consideration.

The court may direct, on its own motion or on application, each party to attend, separately or together, a meeting to allow an explanation of the facilities available for mediation and to provide parties with an opportunity to agree to participate (section 13, FLA

1996). The court can waive the section 9 requirements if the applicant can demonstrate that he or she took reasonable steps to reach an agreement but was frustrated by the behaviour of the respondent, difficulty of making contact, ill-health or disability where further delay would be detrimental to the welfare of a child or prejudicial to the application, or if an occupation order or non-molestation order has been made and delay, to reach an agreement, would be detrimental to a child or prejudicial to the application (Schedule 1, FLA 1996).

Legal aid is not available for undefended divorces but may be paid for mediation services and may enable people to obtain advice. A solicitor is not necessary but advisable. The petitioner, in cases involving violence, may ask the court to withhold his or her address from the respondent.

In determining property and finance questions legal advice is essential. Courts may make financial orders in favour of a party or a child, once a statement has been made or an application for divorce received, or after an order has been made. Courts may order periodical or lump sum payments, including interim orders (Schedule 2, FLA 1996), and may make occupation orders which regulate where parties to a marriage or cohabitation are to live (section 33). A child's needs are only one consideration here, alongside the housing needs and financial resources of those involved, the likely effect of an order on the health, safety and well-being of the parties and children, and the conduct of the parties.

In determining maintenance for children, courts will consider a parent's income, earning capacity, property and other resources; each person's financial needs, obligations and responsibilities; the child's financial needs, income and resources; any physical or mental disability of the child; and the manner in which the child was being, or was expected to be, educated or trained (Schedule 1(4) CA 1989). Orders can also be made against non-parents, when courts will additionally consider the responsibility they had assumed for maintaining a child. Lump sum and periodical payments, settlement or transfer of property may be ordered.

The court's wide powers do not guarantee payment of maintenance. The Child Support Act 1991, addressing concern about defaulters, created a Child Support Agency to assess, review, collect and enforce maintenance payments. Mary could request such assistance but could be 'fined' (section 46) through benefit reductions for failing to provide details of Joshua's father (section 6) unless able to demonstrate evidence of risk to herself or Joshua of significant harm or distress. The coercive intention and economic motivation here is clear: government ministers have opined that fear of violence is insufficient.

Concerning Joshua within the divorce process, as in all proceedings the court would only make an order if so doing would be better than making no order at all (section 1(5), CA 1989). The court must consider, in light of the arrangements proposed by the parties to divorce for the upbringing and welfare of children involved, if it should exercise any powers under the Children Act 1989 (section 11(1), FLA 1996). The court may delay a divorce order while it considers the case (section 11(2)). The welfare of the child is paramount here, and the court must have particular regard to risk; the wishes and feelings of a child in light of their age, understanding and circumstances in which they have been expressed; the conduct of the parties in relation to a child's upbringing; and the principle that usually a child's welfare is best served by maintenance of a relationship with family members. If unhappy with any proposed arrangements, the court *could*:

1. order a welfare report (section 7, CA 1989); there is no obligation to follow a report's recommendation but courts should give reasons when departing from them (Bainham, 1990);
2. direct the local authority to investigate Joshua's circumstances (section 37) where it believes a care or supervision order may be appropriate; the usual time for this assessment will be eight weeks. Where the authority decides not to apply for an order, it must inform the court of its reasons, any services or actions proposed, and any decision to review the case subsequently;
3. regulate parental responsibility by making one or more section 8 orders:
    (a) a residence order, resolving where Joshua will live;
    (b) a contact order, allowing Joshua to visit, stay with and have contact with his other parent;
    (c) a prohibited steps order, limiting the exercise of parental responsibility in specified areas;
    (d) a specific issue order, namely directions on specific actual or potential questions; or

4. make a family assistance order (section 16), requiring the local authority to advise, assist and, if appropriate, befriend those named in the order whose consent (other than the child) is required and whose circumstances must be exceptional. The maximum duration of this order is six months.

Shared residence orders are possible in circumstances where there would be a positive benefit to a child (*A* v. *A (Minors) (Shared Residence Order)* [1994]; *Re H (Shared Residence)* [1994]). Parents, with or without parental responsibility, guardians, and those with a residence order, may apply for any section 8 order. Additionally, those who have cared for a child for more than three years may apply for a residence order or contact order. Others require leave to apply for section 8 orders (section 10, CA 1989). Leave will depend on the nature of the application, the person's connection with the child, any risk to the child's life, and the local authority's plans if the child is being looked after. If the child is in the care of the local authority, the court can only make a residence order. In such a situation, when questions about medical treatment arise, wardship must be used. A child must seek leave to apply for a section 8 order. Leave will be granted if the child has sufficient understanding and if the case has merit (that is, if the case might reasonably be expected to succeed). A child's understanding is assessed in relation to the issues raised by the case (*Re S (A Minor) (Representation)* [1993]; *Re SC (A Minor) (Leave to Seek a Residence Order* [1994]).

The court *must*:

1. give paramount consideration to the child's welfare (section 1(1)), determined by consideration of (section 1(3)) Joshua's wishes and feelings; his physical, emotional and educational needs; the likely effect on him of any change in his circumstances; his age, sex, background and relevant characteristics; any harm he has suffered or may suffer; the capabilities of his parents and relevant others in meeting his needs; the powers available to the court. Although the child's wishes and feelings head the welfare checklist, they do not have priority over other matters therein (*Re W (A Minor) (Medical Treatment: Court's Jurisdiction)* [1993]). A satisfactory status quo could, for example, overrule a natural mother's claims (Hodson, 1990);
2. avoid delay (section 1(2));

3. appoint a guardian *ad litem*, and specify the issues for investigation, unless this is not necessary in order to safeguard Joshua's
   interests (section 41). The guardian *ad litem* has a statutory right
   of access to information (section 41(2)), must have regard to the
   welfare checklist and the need to reduce delay. He or she must
   assess the child's needs and provide the court with a reasoned
   and coherent view of the child's situation, the options available,
   and a clear recommendation of what appears to be in the child's
   best interests (DoH, 1992b). This includes assessing the local
   authority's application and care plan. It is an active role as
   representative of the child and adviser to the court on all
   relevant matters, such as the timetable for proceedings.

Whatever order the court makes, Joshua's parents can still
exercise independently their parental responsibility providing (section 2(8)) this is not incompatible with the order. This could
obviously create difficulties.

Joshua's parents may apply for section 8 orders without divorce
proceedings. If cohabiting rather than married, Joshua's father
would only acquire parental responsibility if it was ordered by a
court or given to him by Mary (section 4(1)). A court should not
withhold parental responsibility in order to exact financial dues (*Re
H (Parental Responsibility: Maintenance)* [1996]). The court should
consider the degree of commitment shown to the child, the degree of
attachment between child and father, and the reason for the
application (*Re G (A Minor) (Parental Responsibility Order)*
[1994]). Section 8 orders can be used subsequently to control any
abuse of the exercise of parental responsibility adverse to the child's
welfare. A committed father should have the status of parenthood
(*Re S (A Minor) (Parental Responsibility)* [1995]). Anyone with
parental responsibility, or Joshua with leave, could apply for this to
be rescinded. Parental responsibility granted by a mother should not
be terminated by a court except in serious circumstances, using as a
guide whether the court would be likely to make a parental
responsibility order if an application were to be made by *this* person
(*Re P* [1995]). If without parental responsibility, Joshua's father
could still apply for a section 8 order. The court, if making a
residence order in his favour, would also make a parental responsibility order (section 12). If a step-parent, he could apply for a
residence or contact order (section 10(5)).

Child care/protection

Mary's mental health (see cases one and three) and Joshua's development and safety require assessment. Additional to the guiding principles when applying child-care legislation (DoH, 1989a) (see Chapter 6), the provisions of the Race Relations Act 1976 also apply in respect of discrimination in services and the promotion of equal opportunities (see case one).

If a local authority believes that Joshua is suffering, or is likely to suffer, significant harm, enquiries must be made to determine whether action should be taken to safeguard or promote his welfare (section 47, CA 1989). Reasonable steps must be taken to gain access to Joshua. If access is denied an emergency protection or other order must be sought unless his welfare can be safeguarded satisfactorily without doing so.

Joshua may be judged a child in need: unlikely to achieve or maintain a reasonable standard of health or development, or with that standard likely to be significantly or further impaired without service provision. Social workers must, therefore, safeguard and promote his welfare, involving where possible upbringing by his family, by providing appropriate services, including cash in exceptional circumstances, to Joshua and his family (section 17, CA 1989, see case two). Authorities must not define this duty restrictively (DoH, 1991b) but take reasonable steps to prevent ill-treatment and neglect, and reduce the need for care proceedings.

The authority must provide Joshua with suitable accommodation if his parents are prevented, temporarily or permanently, from providing it, having ascertained and considered Joshua's wishes as far as practicable (section 20). Contact between them must be promoted if practicable and consistent with Joshua's welfare (Schedule 2(15)), including assistance with travel expenses. If either parent objected and was willing and able to provide accommodation, or arrange such provision, the authority could only provide accommodation if someone with a residence order agreed. Either parent, unless one has a residence order when the right is limited to them, could remove Joshua subsequently.

If services are offered and refused, or fail to safeguard and promote Joshua's welfare, or the degree of risk appears serious, or assessment is frustrated, protective measures may be sought. Local authorities must demonstrate the necessity for such orders, providing evidence that service provision has failed or would be likely to do so (DoH, 1991d). To satisfy this requirement, investigation should precede application (sections 17 and 47). Courts must regard Joshua's welfare as paramount and be satisfied that making an order is better than not. Courts should avoid delay since this might prejudice the child's welfare (section 1(2), CA 1989). However, cases have established the principle of positive, planned and purposeful delay where the complexity of the case or the need for further assessments create the need for additional time in order to determine if an order is necessary (*R* v. *South East Hampshire Family Proceedings Court, ex parte D* [1994]; *Re A and W* [1992]; *Re C (Minor) (Care Proceedings)* [1992]). The protective measures which are available under the Children Act 1989 are:

1. Prohibited steps or specific issue order (section 8) if Joshua is not subject to a care order.
2. Child assessment order (section 43): where significant harm is suspected but Joshua is not at immediate risk, or no firm evidence exists of actual or likely significant harm (DoH, 1991d), and where efforts have failed to secure parental cooperation and assessment of health and development would clarify his needs. Children of sufficient understanding may decline examination or assessment, which should be sensitive to gender, race and culture (DoH, 1991d). The order lasts seven days and may specify assessment away from home. Those able to do so must produce the child for assessment.
3. Emergency protection order (section 44). The court must be satisfied that Joshua is likely to suffer significant harm or that, pursuing enquiries, social workers have had access refused unreasonably and it is required urgently, given reason to believe he is suffering or likely to suffer significant harm. If heard *ex parte* the child, a parent, or anyone with parental responsibility or with whom Joshua was living beforehand may seek discharge after 72 hours. There is no appeal. Joshua must be produced or his whereabouts disclosed. The applicant is given parental responsibility but its exercise is limited to measures necessary to safeguard Joshua's welfare. He may be removed to accommodation but must be returned if it is safe to do so. He may be removed again if necessary. Contact with parents and others

should be reasonable unless the court makes a specific order. Joshua, if of sufficient understanding, may refuse any examination or assessment ordered by the court. The order may be extended once, seven days further (maximum), at an *inter partes* hearing if significant harm would be likely otherwise. A power to enter and search specified premises may be given, also a warrant authorising the police to assist (section 48). The court must be notified of the outcome here.

The police also have powers of protection (section 46) where a child is suffering significant harm. They may remove a child to, or prevent their removal from a place of safety. The power extends for 72 hours during which they must inform the social services department which will assume responsibility for the child's welfare, and notify the parents.

4. Care or supervision order (section 31):

   (a) if the court is satisfied that Joshua is suffering or likely to suffer significant harm, attributable to the care given, or likely to be given if an order is not made, not being what is reasonable to expect a parent to give. The date determining this is that on which the local authority put arrangements in place to protect the child (*Re M (A Minor) (Care Order: Threshold Conditions* [1994]). If the need subsequently ceases for such arrangements, the court cannot look back to a time when they were necessary. To establish the likelihood of significant harm, the proof is the balance of probability where likely means real or substantial possibility (*Re H and R (Child Sexual Abuse: Standard of Proof)* [1996]);

   (b) only if no better way exists to safeguard or promote Joshua's welfare, for example if services had failed to remedy his circumstances (DoH, 1991d);

   (c) parents retain parental responsibility; the local authority acquires it when a care order is made, with the power to restrict, when necessary to safeguard or promote Joshua's welfare, the way in which parents exercise their responsibility (section 33);

   (d) courts must consider arrangements proposed by social workers (section 34(11)); reasonable contact must be allowed. In urgent situations an authority may refuse contact for up to seven days; courts must determine contact (section 34(5)), including termination on application by local authority or child;

(e)   an authority may not change Joshua's surname or religion, consent to adoption, appoint a guardian, or remove him from the country without permission for longer than one month;

(f)   interim orders are allowable when reasonable grounds exist for believing that requirements for care orders are met (section 38). Here courts will have to balance the various risks (for example, the risk of harm and the risk of disruption to attachments), will consider written advice from the guardian *ad litem*, and must ensure an early full hearing, transferring the case to another court where necessary. The court will leave disputed facts to a full hearing, restricting any evidence and cross-examination to essential issues at this stage where a change in the child's position is being contemplated. Changing the child's residence at this point should only be rarely done but the court may add safeguards (*Hampshire County Council* v. *S* [1993]). Courts should give reasons for decisions on interim care orders. Courts may also issue directions about examinations and assessment which children of sufficient understanding may refuse;

(g)   supervision orders require practitioners to advise, assist and befriend children, to take reasonable steps to enforce the order, and to consider whether variation or discharge should be sought. Orders are made for one year, renewable to a maximum of three years; they may include specified activities or directions, not exceeding 90 days, or requirements for medical and psychiatric examination, possible here only if the child consents (Schedule 3); a child may be required to live in a particular place and to present themselves to a specified person. An order cannot be enforced by the court but breakdown could be used as evidence in further proceedings;

(h)   a child, local authority, or person with parental responsibility may apply for variation or discharge (section 39); others must seek a residence order which would automatically discharge care and supervision orders (section 91(1)); applications for discharge, variation or contact, without leave of the court, may not be made within six months of previous applications (section 91(15)(17)).

In determining whether to make a care order or supervision order, the court will assess future risks by scrutinising past events and the need for the local authority to hold parental responsibility from which a duty arises to safeguard the child's welfare (section 72, CA 1989). It will consider the need to require compliance from the parents as compared with relying solely on their agreement, and the possible need to remove a child no longer safe (*Re S(J) (A Minor) (Care or Supervision Order)* [1993]).

After a care order is made the court has no continuing role (*Re B (Minors) (Care: Contact: Local Authority's Plans)* [1993]). Nor can the court impose conditions, with the result that the court will carefully scrutinise the local authority's care plan and will refuse to make an order when dissatisfied with it (*Re T (A Minor) (Care Order: Condition)* [1994]).

If Joshua is accommodated by the local authority or subject to a care order, the authority must:

1. safeguard and promote his welfare; consider his religion, racial origin, cultural and linguistic background; ascertain and consider his wishes, those of his parents and relevant others with or without parental responsibility, prior to decision-making; and use where reasonable services available for children cared for by their own parents (section 22);
2. so far as possible place Joshua near home and with family, relations or friends unless inconsistent with his welfare or impractical (section 23);
3. establish representations and complaints procedures, and reviews within regulated timescales (DoH, 1991a) which allow full participation and comparison of plans with duties under the Act (section 26).

In all child-care/protection activities, practitioners must obtain legal advice about which orders to seek, whether the grounds are satisfied, and the evidence to present. Multidisciplinary cooperation (see Chapter 6) in sharing information and decision-making is required (sections 27 and 47).

Unless the child's interests indicate otherwise there is a strong presumption throughout the Children Act 1989 in favour of contact, to enable a child to retain a sense of identity and to promote their physical and emotional development (DoH, 1994a). The question will be whether there are any cogent reasons why contact should be denied (*Re H (Minors) (Access)* [1992]). These might include persistent refusal by a child, harm or distress caused by contact, or persistent undermining by a parent of long-term planning for the child (DoH, 1992b; *Re M (Contact: Welfare Test)* [1995]). The principle of contact is balanced against the child's long-term welfare. Contact must not be allowed to destabilise arrangements for the child. For children in care, the local authority must justify its plan where contact is excluded, but plans to terminate contact should not be overturned on the remote possibility of rehabilitation in the future (*Re B (Minors) (Care: Contact: Local Authority's Plans)* [1993]). Local authorities should be clear about the purpose of contact, ensure that staff are skilled in managing it, and facilitate parents to attend. Contact should be reviewed regularly (DoH, 1994a).

Grandparents must seek leave for a section 8 order for contact, and the granting of leave does not create a right to contact (*Re A (Section 8 Order: Grandparent Application)* [1995]). Conditions may be attached to a contact order for indirect contact (*Re O (Contact: Imposition of Conditions)* [1995]). Applications for section 8 orders may be restricted in exceptional circumstances (section 91(14)), such as where there is a risk to the child of emotional and psychological distress (*Re G and M (Child Orders: Restricting Applications)* [1995]). Agreements between parents should only be set aside by a court in exceptional circumstances (*S v. E (A Minor) (Contact)* [1993]). Courts are very reluctant to allow a hostile parent to prevent contact (*Re D (A minor) (Contact: Mother's Hostility)* [1993]; *Re W (A Minor) (Contact)* [1994]), although they will conduct a balancing exercise between the benefits of contact and the harm which might result to the objecting parent's health and/or to a reluctant child.

Housing

Housing departments must assess cases where applicants are homeless or threatened within 28 days with homelessness, to establish if they are eligible for assistance and, if so, what duty is owed (section 184, HA 1996). Housing departments must give reasons for their decisions, and have a duty to provide advisory services (section 179). If a person appears to be homeless, eligible for assistance and in priority need, the housing department has a duty to provide accommodation pending any final decision concerning their duties and irrespective of any possibility of referral to another authority (section 188). Applicants must have the mental capacity to understand and respond to the offer of accommodation and to undertake the responsibilities involved (*R* v. *LB of Tower Hamlets, ex parte Begum* [1993]).

Mary (say) would be homeless if:

1. unmarried: not entitled to occupy accommodation, if neither (joint) owner nor tenant;
2. married: entitled to live in the matrimonial home (FLA 1996) but locked out or likely to be subjected to actual or threatened violence (section 177, HA 1996);
3. it is not reasonable for her to occupy the accommodation, together with any other person who normally resides or might be reasonably expected to reside with her (section 175(3) and section 176, HA 1996).

The authority might seek to insist that other legal provisions are used to gain entry or prevent violence. Previous history or degree of violence, and the inadequacy of the law on violence should be stressed here.

Authorities must provide suitable accommodation for homeless people, and those reasonably expected to live with them, if in priority need, homeless unintentionally and with a local connection. This duty is initially for two years (section 193), after which authorities may continue to provide such accommodation, but are not obliged to do so, if the person is in priority need, there is no other suitable accommodation, and the individual requests it, with a review every two years (section 194(2)). This brings statute in line with case law which had established that a housing authority could discharge its duty in stages (*R* v. *LB of Brent, ex parte Macwan* [1994]), and that the duty is to provide suitable accommodation which does not necessarily mean permanence (*R* v. *LB of Brent, ex parte Awua* [1995]). The impact of this provision, particularly on children, could undermine their sense of stability and security. Finally, where other suitable accommodation is available, the duty of the housing authority towards those for whom it would otherwise have a housing duty will be to provide advice and assistance to enable the applicant to acquire accommodation (section 197). This does not affect their interim duties to provide accommodation for those in priority need pending a final decision (section 188).

If people have a priority need but are homeless intentionally, temporary accommodation only is provided, for a period considered reasonable to enable the applicant to make other arrangements, together with advice and assistance in securing accommodation (section 190(2)). If they are homeless but not a priority need the authority must provide only advice and assistance as they consider appropriate to assist the applicant secure accommodation, whether or not homeless unintentionally (sections 190(3) and 192). An unreasonable refusal of an offer of accommodation may discharge the authority from its duties (section 193(5)).

Priority need covers pregnancy; disaster; dependent children, even if living elsewhere because of violence or homelessness (*R* v. *Lewisham LBC, ex parte C* [1992]); vulnerability of self or another reasonably expected to live with the applicant, owing to age, disability (including mental illness) or special reasons. Vulnerability means being less able to fend for oneself so that injury or detriment will result, where the less vulnerable person would cope without harmful effect (*R* v. *Waveney DC, ex parte Bowers* [1982]). Intentional homelessness means deliberate actions or omissions, in consequence of which the applicant has ceased to occupy accommodation which it was reasonable to occupy, or is threatened with homelessness. Domestic violence and an act or omission in good faith because of unawareness of a relevant fact fall outside definitions of intentional homelessness. Unintentional homelessness may result from harassment, the effect on health of local crime and violence, and from inadequate resources/poverty where an applicant maintains children at the expense of rent and arrears (*R* v. *Wandsworth LBC, ex parte Hawthorne* [1995]). Authorities can pass applicants on to others if applicants have a local connection there (section 198) and would not be exposed to domestic violence. A local connection is defined (section 199) as a place where the applicant is/ was normally resident or employed, or a place with family associations. Once an applicant is notified of an authority's intention to refer on, that authority is no longer under a duty to provide accommodation (section 200). If they are entitled to accommodation the authority must help applicants protect property if a danger of loss or damage exists and applicants are unable to make suitable arrangements. This duty includes a power to retrieve (sections 211 and 212). Where the housing authority requests it (section 213), another housing authority or a social services department must co-operate in so far as is reasonable.

Applicants have the right to request a review of an authority's decisions in a case (section 202) within 21 days. If the review finds against them, they may then appeal on a point of law, again within 21 days, to the county court. Whilst an application is subject to review or appeal, the authority may provide accommodation.

Children are not eligible to apply for housing using homeless persons provisions when their parents have been found intentionally homeless (*R* v. *Bexley LBC, ex parte B (A Minor) [1993]; R* v. *Oldham MBC, ex parte G (A Minor)* [1993]). However, social services departments and housing departments should not engage in buck-passing. Indeed, the former may provide financial assistance (section 17(6), CA 1989) in order to secure accommodation for children in need and their families where a housing authority has found a family to be intentionally homeless (*R* v. *Northavon DC, ex parte Smith* [1994]).

Immigration

Marital breakdown may have far-reaching consequences for Mary. Entitlement to income support and housing (section 185, HA 1996), indeed the right of abode in Britain, varies according to citizenship and immigration status. Only people who are British citizens under the 1981 Nationality Act, Commonwealth citizens with an established right of abode and Irish citizens are free to enter and settle in the UK. If Mary does not have this status she will have been subject to immigration control under the 1971 Immigration Act, and her leave to stay made dependent upon the continuation of her marriage. If her husband is not a British citizen, he may have been required to give an undertaking that Mary and Joshua could be supported without recourse to public funds and Mary may have difficulty obtaining benefits and services. If she has not already been given indefinite leave to stay in Britain she may now be denied it. This is an area where specialist advice is essential.

Case five

Janet is 25. She has a learning disability and lives with her parents. She attends a day centre where she is developing skills in self-care. The centre is part of a care in the community scheme, and Janet has met a group of friends whom she visits in their shared accommodation. Staff have encouraged this, feeling it helps Janet be less isolated. Her parents have complained that she has been returning home with dishevelled clothing and has started to show sexualised behaviour. On one occasion they went to collect her and found her in bed with one of the young men in the house. Since then, Janet has come to the centre with bruising on her arms, saying her father has been cross. The parents have now stopped her attendance until staff guarantee she will not visit her friends. The family doctor has said contraception is impractical and has referred Janet for sterilisation. Janet wants to see her friends but does not want to make her parents cross.

The issues here centre upon the theme of autonomy v. paternalism in decision-making about Janet's life: who has the right to make what decisions, and why? It will be important to determine the purpose of using available legislation: to increase Janet's autonomy from her parents? To protect her from ill-treatment? To facilitate a sexual relationship? To protect her from sexual abuse? To prevent pregnancy? To secure her further education and training?

The proposed sterilisation raises questions of consent to medical treatment. The basic principle of common law is that any intervention requires real consent, based on adequate information and given without duress or undue influence. To be deemed capable of giving real consent, the person must understand in broad terms what is involved. This will be based on knowledge of the purpose, nature, likely effects and risks of treatment, including the likelihood of success and alternative options. Capacity is being capable of understanding, not actual understanding. The quality of the decision is irrelevant to the capacity to make it. A person may be incompetent if they fail to understand what is involved, if they deny or misperceive reality, or if they are unable or refuse to understand the nature of their situation. An 'irrational' decision based on a value position must be distinguished from a decision based on wrong facts or delusions. However, a person with a mental illness does not necessarily lack the competence to understand what is involved in a proposed treatment (*Re C* [1993]; *Re T (Adult: Refusal of Medical Treatment)* [1992]). The Mental Health Act 1983 Code of Practice (DoH, 1993c) gives further guidance on the determination of capacity.

There are exceptions to the need for consent:

- emergency treatment immediately necessary to preserve life and health;
- inevitable everyday life contacts within acceptable standards of conduct;
- the person does not have capacity to consent;
- where statute permits.

Treatment may be given to a person who is not capable of consenting provided it is in her best interests, that is necessary to save life or ensure improvement or prevent deterioration in physical or mental health, and is in accordance with practice accepted as proper by a responsible and competent body of relevant medical opinion. In the case of sterilisation, however, application should be made to the High Court to establish that the sterilisation is indeed in the person's best interests, and for a declaration that it is therefore lawful. Application may be made by anyone who has care of the person, or the doctor proposing to treat. In the case of a minor, the courts must similarly be asked to sanction sterilisation, application here being made for a specific issues order (section 8, CA 1989), by anyone with a right or leave to apply, unless the child were in care, in which case the local authority would have recourse to the inherent jurisdiction of the High Court (section 100(3), CA 1989), which is still available for decisions which are highly contentious or outside the normal scope of decision-making (DoH, 1991d).

Thus, in Janet's case, it is crucial to determine whether she has capacity to consent to the proposed sterilisation. If she does not, the judge will require evidence of permanent incapacity, that pregnancy is a real danger, that she will experience greater substantial trauma or psychological damage if pregnancy occurs than through sterilisation, that she is incapable of caring for a child and that there is no less intrusive means of achieving the objective (Official Solicitor, 1989).

A connected issue is that under the Sexual Offences Act 1956 it is an offence for a man to have sexual intercourse with a woman knowing her to be 'of arrested or incomplete development of mind, which includes severe impairment of intelligence and social functioning'. Staff encouragement, or merely allowing it to happen, could be deemed 'aiding and abetting' such an offence. Thus it may be crucial to determine the degree of severity of Janet's mental disability, though in practice this legislation, intended to protect from abuse or exploitation, runs counter to developments in awareness of the sexual rights of people with learning difficulties. It will still be important, however, to establish that Janet's participation is voluntary and that she is not being abused, and to provide counselling and advice where appropriate.

Consent may also be dispensed with by statute, notably the Mental Health Act 1983. Section 63 allows detained patients in hospital (other than on very short-term orders – sections 4, 5, 135, 136, 35 and 37(4)) to be treated for *mental disorder* without their consent, unless the treatment is:

- section 57: psychosurgery or the surgical implantation of hormones for suppression of male sex drive, which can only be given if the patient, understanding the nature, purpose and likely effects of the treatment, has consented *and* a second opinion appointed doctor considers it therapeutically warranted;
- section 58: medication beyond three months or ECT, which can only be given if the patient consents *or* an SOAD considers it therapeutically warranted.

This does not, however, apply in Janet's case, as she is not in hospital and the proposed sterilisation is not a treatment for mental disorder.

Thus legislation provides a foundation, albeit paternalistic and medically dominated, to underpin the complex and difficult ethics of decision-making about highly personal matters.

Turning to the issue of Janet's relationship with her parents, the law is notoriously silent on the protection of vulnerable adults (see case one). In respect of her father, private or criminal prosecution under the Offences Against the Person Act 1861 might be possible.

It is an offence 'to ill-treat . . . a mentally disordered patient who is . . . in his custody or care' (section 127, MHA 1983). An ASW, having reasonable cause to believe that a mentally disordered patient is not under proper care, may at all reasonable times enter and inspect any premises, other than hospitals, in which the patient is living (section 115). The ASW may not use force but obstructing an ASW without reasonable cause, refusing to allow an inspection or interview, is an offence (section 129). It would be possible (section 135) to enter the house and take Janet to a place of safety with a view to making an application for hospitalisation or guardianship, or other arrangements for her care (see case three for details). It is debatable, however, whether hospitalisation would be right or fair to Janet, in the absence of any indication that she needs psychiatric assessment or treatment.

Guardianship would provide a less restrictive legal remedy (see case one for discussion of grounds and powers). In this case, guardianship could provide a framework for Janet's continuation at the day centre and thus her further lifeskills training, including sexuality, or even for a move of home. Whichever of her parents is her nearest relative (the elder) could object to the making of an order, or could discharge Janet from guardianship. Application could, however, be made to the county court replacing the NR if their objection to the order is unreasonable or, in applying for discharge, they are not paying due regard to Janet's welfare (section 29).

The major problem of guardianship for Janet lies in the restrictions upon who may be subject to such an order. Where do people with learning difficulties fit into the classifications of mental disorder (section 1, MHA 1983)? The catch-all definition 'mental disorder' clearly includes 'arrested or incomplete development of mind'. Thus any of the sections for which 'mental disorder' is one of the grounds (for example, sections 2, 4, 5, 135, 136 – short-term admissions for assessment) may be used for people with learning difficulties. The grounds for section 3 admission to hospital for treatment or section 7 application for guardianship require more specific conditions: 'mental illness, mental impairment, severe mental impairment or psychopathic disorder'. Mental impairment is defined as 'a state of arrested or incomplete development of mind which includes significant impairment of intelligence and social functioning and is associated with abnormally aggressive or seriously irresponsible conduct'. A guardianship order can only be made in respect of Janet (in the absence of any 'mental illness') if her behaviour fits the stringent criteria of mental impairment. As with the majority of people with learning difficulties, she may well be excluded from eligibility.

All the legislation in relation to disabled people (case one) applies here. The legislation does not provide simple solutions and, if used, would not be without consequences for the relationships of those involved. It is likely that practitioners would, as always, rely on familiar skills of negotiation between the conflicting interests involved. The implementation of sections 1 and 2 of the Disabled Persons Act 1986 allowing for a representative to ascertain and voice Janet's wishes would be an important improvement. It must be remembered that ultimately there will be many areas of her life about which she is quite capable of deciding, including where she lives, how she spends her time, her sexual relationships and contraceptive needs, and that these decisions remain her right.

Case six

Following serious non-accidental injury, for which his mother was responsible, Sam, now aged two, was made the subject of a care order. Sam's father does not have parental responsibility. In line with case law, he was notified of the care proceedings as exceptional circumstances to withhold this did not exist (*Re X (Care: Notice of Proceedings*) [1996]). He did not contest the authority's application for a care order, nor the subsequent termination of contact. Sam has lived with foster parents since he was nine months old. The local authority's care plan ruled out rehabilitation and contact has been terminated between Sam and his parents. What options now exist?

Prior to placement, or as soon as possible afterwards, a written plan must be compiled in consultation with Sam, his parents and other relevant people and agencies. It should be reviewed four weeks and three months after placement, and at subsequent six-monthly reviews. Amendments should be notified to relevant people in writing. For children on court orders, partnership and agreement with parents should be sought if possible. Planning, to avoid drift, must assess and consider Sam's needs, contact arrangements, his parents' capacity to meet his needs, race, culture, religion and language, and the appropriateness of the placement. It must determine, after full consideration of the wishes and feelings of Sam and his parents, objectives to secure Sam's welfare (section 22(4), CA 1989; DoH, 1989a, 1991a). The court, prior to making a care order, must consider and invite comment upon arrangements proposed or made by the authority (section 34(11), CA 1989). If the court is not satisfied that the care plan meets the interests of the child, or if it has not been prepared in accordance with guidance (DoH, 1991a), it could refuse to make a care order (*Re J (Minors) (Care: Care Plan)* [1994]). If there are likely to be difficulties in implementing the plan, the court will proceed providing the authority is aware of how to respond to potential problems.

Placement with parents, relatives or friends should be considered first where practicable and consistent with Sam's welfare (section 23(6)). Where one parent cannot look after a child and where another parent, with or without parental responsibility, is willing and fit to look after the child, this option should be exercised rather than adoption. At this stage the question is not one of balancing the merits of this parent versus adoption (*Re O (A Minor) (Custody: Adoption)* [1992]). Parents should be involved in decision-making about Sam's future. Reasonable contact must be allowed (section 34) unless defined or terminated by a court. If the authority applies for variation or termination of contact, it must notify in writing those affected, giving reasons (DoH, 1991a). It may not be sufficient for the local authority to apply for termination of contact on the basis that there is no likelihood of finding suitable adopters who would entertain open adoption (*Re E (A Minor) (Care Order: Contact)* [1994]). Contact may be of value in supporting the child's identity and in facilitating the child's commitment to a new family knowing that this has the approval of the birth parent(s) (*Re B (Minors) (Care: Contact: Local Authority's Plans)* [1993]).

Where rehabilitation is excluded:

1. parents may apply for a residence order (section 8) which, if granted, would discharge the care order;
2. relatives may apply for section 8 orders having obtained leave; courts will decide questions of leave by considering the applicants' connection with Sam, the order sought, the risk of disruption and harm to Sam's life and, since he is in care, the

authority's plans and the feelings and wishes of Sam's parents (section 10(9), CA 1989);

3. after a three-year placement, or earlier with the authority's consent (section 9(3)), the foster parents may apply for a residence order;

4. the foster parents may apply to adopt Sam.

Courts will use the welfare checklist (section 1(3), CA 1989) to determine what section 8 or contact order to make. In adoption proceedings, courts may make any section 8 order as an alternative or addition to an adoption order if better for the child (DoH, 1991d). In adoption, courts must have regard to all the circumstances, first consideration being given to the need to safeguard and promote the child's welfare throughout childhood. The child's wishes and feelings about adoption should be ascertained and considered, as far as practicable given age and understanding (section 6, AA 1976).

So far as practicable the adoption agency must have regard to any wishes of the birth parents about the child's religious upbringing (section 7). Other things being equal, placement with a family sharing the same ethnic origin and religion is likely to best meet a child's needs (CI(96)4; DoH, 1991a). Children should not be allowed to drift within the care system because local authorities exclude placements with families who do not share a child's heritage but who could offer a suitable home and help a child understand their racial and cultural identity. Thus, a court will balance ethnic origin as a placement factor against attachment to current (foster) carers and whether to move the child would cause psychological damage (*Re P (A Minor) (Adoption)* [1990]; *Re JK (Adoption: Transracial Placement)* [1991]).

Adoption law is currently being reviewed, particularly the question of open adoption. The present system, closed adoption, transfers parental responsibility to the adoptive parents. An open system could allow for continued contact with and inheritance rights from the birth family. Although inconsistently used by courts (Triseliotis, 1991), an adoption order may include such terms and conditions as a court decides (section 12(6), AA 1976), including contact with birth family members. Prior agreement of the parties is usual, although some form of contact may be allowed against the wishes of the adopters, for example to ensure that a child has knowledge of his or her cultural heritage (*Re O (Transracial Adoption: Contact)*

[1995]). No order should be made where contact has already been agreed between adoptive and birth parents (*Re T (Adoption: Contact)* [1995]). Proposed arrangements must serve the best interests of the adopted child and should not threaten a successful adoption (CI(96)4). Before placing for adoption, the agency should discuss the question of contact, and the forms it might take, with the child, family and prospective adopters. There is currently no presumption of contact.

A review of adoption law has been prompted by the need to clarify the links between the Adoption Act 1976 and the Children Act 1989, especially concerning contact between children and their birth parents, and the emphasis now on partnership with parents which contrasts with the practice of 'forced' adoptions of children once care orders had been made. A child cannot be a party in adoption proceedings, unlike in Children Act proceedings, whilst the emphasis in the Children Act 1989 on race, culture, religion and language makes it important to clarify these matters in relation to adoption, for instance concerning cultures where adoption is not known. Current adoption law does not reflect contemporary concerns or changing practice based on the benefits to be gained from openness, the importance of information and contact for identity development, and the changing age of children available for adoption (Redding, 1991b).

Proposals for reform (DoH, 1993e) include:

- that the child's welfare will be the paramount consideration throughout;
- a welfare checklist for agencies and courts to assess a child's interests;
- children over twelve having the right to decide if adoption should proceed, and all children being eligible for party status in adoption proceedings;
- freeing orders replaced by a placement order, granted by the court, which would give parental responsibility to prospective adopters but not remove it from others, and which would permit placement without agreement of the birth parents;
- simplifying procedures for dispensing with consent of birth parents;
- alternatives to step-parent adoptions – a parental responsibility agreement whereby the birth parent and new spouse are jointly

able to exercise parental responsibility without links being severed with the child's other birth parent, with the courts involved only if the non-resident birth parent did not consent; and a new guardianship order, intended to allow carers to obtain legal recognition of their role, where links with birth parents would not be severed but where only a court could dissolve the order, thus providing a clear and permanent status for carers;

- for step-parents who prefer adoption, a simplified procedure so that the birth parent is not obliged to adopt his/her own child;
- consideration of older applicants, and a complaints procedure for rejected applicants;
- birth parents allowed to make section 8 (CA 1989) applications with a court's permission;
- contact between an adopted child and his/her birth family having due regard to the wishes, feelings and welfare of the child. Complete severance of contact should occur if there are clear and significant advantages to this.

The proposals are unlikely to make the child's ethnic background the decisive factor in an adoption, despite the importance of identity development and the positive emphasis in the Children Act 1989 on race, culture, religion and language. Ethnic background will be considered alongside the ability of adoptive parents to help and support a child through life. The proposals are unlikely to lift the ban on adoption by unmarried couples, including therefore by gay men and lesbians. Adoption applications by single individuals will require 'particular careful matching' (DoH, 1993e).

In Sam's case, an adoption process would involve the following:

1. SSD Adoption Panel considers whether adoption is in his best interests and whether he should be freed for adoption;
2. Panel considers whether prospective adopters are suitable to be adoptive parents, generally and for Sam.

Both these processes require social work and health assessments. In respect of adopters, agencies must consider the qualities which they have to offer. Older prospective adopters may be suitable (CI(96)4); selection and preparation programmes should be sensitively managed.

3. Application for Sam to be freed for adoption:

Parents consent freely, unconditionally, with full understanding.	Parents do not consent.
↓	↓
	If Sam was not in care by court order, this would be necessary first.
↓	↓

SSD may apply for freeing order; medical and social work reports provide details of Sam, his parents, the prospective adopters, and SSD's involvement. If Sam's parents are unmarried, a freeing order in respect of Sam's father may be made only if he does not intend to apply for a parental responsibility order (section 4, CA 1989) or a residence order (section 8) or, if he did so apply, it would probably be refused (Schedule 10(6); *Re H and Another (Minors) (Adoption: Putative Father's Rights)* [1989]).

↓	↓
	Application to dispense with consent, the available grounds (section 16(2), AA 1976) being that parents (a) cannot be found (b) are incapable of giving consent (c) are withholding consent unreasonably (d) have abandoned or neglected Sam (e) have failed without reasonable cause to discharge their parental responsibilities

(f) have persistently
ill-treated Sam
(g) have seriously
ill-treated Sam and
rehabilitation is unlikely
(Hoggett, 1987).

The adoption agency must take all reasonable steps to find a parent
or guardian (*Re F (An Infant)* [1970]). Where a parent withholds
consent and the court must decide whether to dispense with their
consent on the grounds that it is being withheld unreasonably, the
question is whether a reasonable parent in the circumstances of the
case could withhold agreement. It is not a question of whether the
decision is right or wrong. The court must not substitute its own
judgement for that of the parent. A reasonable parent would
consider the child's long-term welfare and the advantages of adoption, as well as his or her own feelings (*Re W (An Infant)* [1971]; *Re
L (A Minor)* [1990]). A reasonable parent would recognise the
benefit of adoption to a child and should not allow a grievance
against the local authority to interfere with this. However, a parent
should also have a proper opportunity to show that continued
contact would benefit the child, and the local authority must not
be unreasonable concerning contact and the timing of a freeing
application (*Re E (Minors) (Adoption: Parents' Consent)* [1990]; *Re
C (Minors)* [1991]; *Re B (A Minor) (Adoption: Parental Agreement)* [1990]). The welfare of the child overrides a parent's wish to
keep the 'door open' (*Re L (A Minor)* [1989]). A parent whose
consent is required is a parent with parental responsibility (section
16, AA 1976; *Re M (An Infant)* [1955]). If a father does not have
parental responsibility, the local authority may decide whether or
not to include him in the adoption process, and whether or not to
name him and interview him (*Re L (A Minor) (Adoption: Procedure)* [1991]).

↓   ↓

Reporting officer confirms   Guardian *ad litem* appointed
consent freely given.   to investigate and report to
                                     court.

Hearing.

Court decision, using section 6 criteria (see above). If freed, parental responsibility resides solely with SSD.

↓

Parents may decide against further involvement in Sam's future. Otherwise they must be told after one year whether Sam has been placed or adopted (section 19). If not, they can apply for the freeing order to be revoked (section 6 criteria would be used again) with parental responsibility consequently returned to them. They must be notified thereafter whenever a placement begins, ends or concludes with adoption. Parents may apply for revocation of the freeing order if no adoption order has been made after twelve months and if the child does not have his/her home with the people with whom he/she has been placed for adoption (*R* v. *Derbyshire County Council, ex parte T* [1989]).

↓

Application to adopt. Joint applicants must be married. Where a single person submits an application, careful attention must be paid to their home circumstances (CI(96)4). Where an unmarried applicant (in this case a foster parent) is living with a cohabitee and is therefore obliged to apply alone for an adoption order, the court may also make a joint residence order to give the cohabitee parental responsibility (*Re AB (Adoption: Joint Residence)* [1996]).

↓

Report by SSD on suitability and desirability of adoption. Child and applicants must be seen

together in their home. This is a schedule 2
(Adoption Rules 1984) report. It covers the
child's placement history, health, and parentage.
Where an unmarried father does not know of
the child's existence, and since the schedule 2
report requires that the local authority sets out
the wishes and feelings of each birth parent
concerning adoption, the father's wishes should
be ascertained, and any matters arising dealt
with now, unless his becoming aware of the
child's existence would be more detrimental to
the long-term welfare of the child (*Re P
(Adoption) (Natural Father's Rights)* [1994]).

↓

If adoption granted, Sam may apply for access
to his birth records when he is 18. He may also
then enter his name on the Adoption Contact
Register. When he registers his relatives' details
will be passed to him if they have also registered
(Schedule 10(21), CA 1989). The right to such
information is not absolute and may be
withheld where there is a significant risk to
safety or of a serious crime being committed (*R
v. Registrar General, ex parte Smith* [1990]).

An order made by consent can be set aside when events have
demonstrated that it had been made in circumstances that consti-
tuted a classic mistake. Such occasions will be exceptional, for
example where a father consented to a step-parent adoption without
knowing that the mother had terminal cancer. The order was set
aside when she died (*Re M (Minors)* [1990]). However, it has also
been held that an adoption order, regularly made, cannot be set
aside despite the presence of a fundamental mistake of fact on which
it was based, in this case a person whose birth father was an Arab
being adopted by a Jewish family and brought up as a Jew (*Re B
(Adoption Order: Jurisdiction to Set Aside)* [1995]).

A young person may, however, seek leave to apply for a residence
order (section 8, CA 1989), to live with members of her birth family
rather than with her adoptive parents (*Re C (A Minor)* [1993]).

Good practice requires (SSI, 1993g) good recording; full information for adopters awaiting adoption, for adopters and birth parents on plans for the child, for adopters and for the child on the background; and post-adoption support.

Case seven

Wayne, aged 16, is at the police station, suspected of having committed motoring offences. The police have requested that a social worker attends as an 'appropriate adult'. What legislation applies here?

Appropriate adult provisions apply to juveniles, people with learning difficulties or mental illness, and anyone who appears unable to understand the significance of questioning. Parents (unless the child objects or has admitted to them, or they are a victim, co-accused, or witness), guardians, social workers or other responsible adults independent of the police may act as appropriate adults. A social worker may act if parents refuse, cannot be contacted or are unavailable, or if a parent is mentally disordered. For Wayne to receive an adequate service, the appropriate adult *must* understand the role (Blackwell, 1990). Training is essential.

Wayne may be detained without charge for 24 hours, extendable by a superintendent or above to 36 hours if the investigation concerns a serious arrestable offence, and by magistrates to a maximum of 96 hours (PACE 1984). Wayne must not be interviewed or make a statement without an appropriate adult present unless any delay would involve immediate risk of harm to people or property, and then only until that risk has been averted.

Before interviewing, the police must attempt to inform the person responsible for Wayne's welfare of the detention (section 57, PACE 1984). Wayne's right to inform someone of his detention and to legal advice before questioning may be withheld for up to 36 hours if this would alert others, interfere with evidence collection, or risk physical injury to others and the investigation concerns a serious arrestable offence. Wayne has a right to read the codes of practice governing detention. The appropriate adult should discuss these rights with Wayne privately and call a (duty) solicitor if appropriate. The appropriate adult should also (*Childright*, 1991):

1. ascertain if Wayne is detained and the reasons – if not, he is free to leave;
2. note the time of arrest and the request to attend;
3. actively participate to ensure that interviews are fair and to facilitate communication between Wayne and the police;
4. ensure that no informal statements were made;
5. identify the custody officer who makes decisions about detention and charge, is independent of the investigation, and reviews detention after six hours and every nine hours subsequently, deciding whether or not to charge Wayne. The appropriate adult should be present when these decisions are taken;
6. be present when Wayne is cautioned or charged and ensure his understanding;
7. read the written statement of the interview and discuss errors;
8. (if a social worker) not consent to treatment, the taking of samples or fingerprinting unless Wayne is in care by court order, but to be present during intimate or strip searches, unless he objects and the appropriate adult agrees, or when Wayne is asked to consent to any identification procedure (sections 54–9, CJPOA 1994).

In court, evidence obtained unfairly may be excluded (section 78, PACE 1984). The prosecution must prove that evidence or confessions were not obtained unreasonably (section 76).

Once charged, Wayne must be released on bail, whatever his attitude or offence, unless he has no certain address, or evidence exists that he might not attend court, or release would interfere with investigations, or detention is necessary for his protection or to prevent injury to others or property loss/damage. Equally, bail may be refused to prevent him from committing an offence or because it would be in his own interests. Conditions may be placed on the granting of bail. If bail is refused, the custody officer must record reasons for Wayne's detention. He must be transferred to local authority accommodation (Schedule 13(52), CA 1989) unless weather, industrial action or time of day prevents this, or for young people over 12 (section 24, CJPOA 1994) because secure accommodation is unavailable and available accommodation would not protect the public from serious harm (section 59, CJA 1991). Serious harm refers to violent or sexual offences causing physical and/or psychological injury. Wayne must not be placed in a cell unless it is impracticable to supervise him elsewhere in the police station.

After charge, the police may give a formal caution in the presence of a parent or guardian providing the offence is admitted. Cautions should not be given for the most serious indictable offences, and only one caution should usually be given unless a subsequent offence is trivial and sufficient time has passed since the previous caution (six months if under 14, one year if older). The victim should be informed, but not for the purpose of enabling them to influence the decision whether or not to caution (Home Office Circular 18/94). Parents should provide informed consent. This circular, arguably, stifles the spirit of diversion, seeking as it does a reduction in cautioning. It is somewhat sceptical about a multi-agency approach, leaving decision-making to the police who must be satisfied that a caution is likely to be effective, is in the public interest, and is for a minor offence.

At court, a parent or guardian, or social worker if Wayne is in care or provided with local authority accommodation, must attend (CJA 1991, section 56). The local authority has a duty, unless it believes it unnecessary, to investigate and provide a report to court (section 9, CAYP 1969). When requested by a court, a report must be provided, available also to parents, defence solicitors and the child if age and understanding warrants this.

Wayne may decline to answer questions out of court and is a non-compellable witness in his own defence (section 35(4), CJPOA 1994). However, the prosecution and the court may now comment on his failure to answer questions or give evidence. Inferences may be drawn if Wayne, when under caution or charged, fails to mention facts which he then relies on at trial; or refuses to answer questions and give evidence at trial (unless he is under 14 and/or it appears to the court that his physical or mental condition makes it undesirable for him to give evidence (section 35)); or refuses to account for the possession of objects or marks, or his presence at a particular place (sections 34–7, CJPOA 1994).

Wayne is over 14 and, therefore, fully responsible for his actions. If he was aged between 10 and 13, a court would have to be satisfied that he had committed an offence and knew it was wrong (*C (A Minor)* v. *DPP* [1995]). This may be derived from interviews, from the child's conduct and age, and from the nature of the act.

Various sentences are available:

1. absolute discharge, a conviction for the purposes of determining offence seriousness;
2. conditional discharge, for a maximum of three years. If Wayne re-offends, he will also be sentenced for present offences;
3. deferred sentence (for a maximum of six months) (PCCA 1973), if Wayne consents and a change in circumstances is imminent;
4. fines, to maximum of £250 (10–13 years) or £1000 (over 14); parents may be held responsible for payment (section 57, CJA 1991), but the power to require the local authority to pay the fines of young people for whom they had parental responsibility has been abolished (Schedule 9(42), CJPOA 1994);
5. where the young person is under 16 binding over parent/guardian for a maximum of three years; this maximum period is shortened if the young person would reach 18 in a period shorter than three years (section 58, CJA 1991); consent (with fines for unreasonable refusal) of parent/guardian is required; they may be required to take proper care and exercise proper control, and to ensure that the young person complies with the requirements of any community sentence which is imposed (Schedule 9(50), CJPOA 1994);
6. compensation orders: where a local authority holds parental responsibility, they can be ordered to pay compensation if their actions, being unreasonable and short of the standard expected, have contributed to the offences taking place (*D (A Minor)* v. *DPP* [1995]; *Bedfordshire County Council* v. *DPP* [1995]);
7. supervision orders, for a maximum of three years, with or without specified activities and conditions imposed by court or supervisor for a maximum of 90 days; a breach may result in fine or attendance centre order, or resentence or custody if the supervision order contained specific activities (Schedule 7, CJA 1991); for young people of or over the age of 16, a probation order, combined order or curfew order may be made (see case eight);
8. attendance centre, for up to 24 hours (CJA 1982), or 36 hours for young people over 16 (section 67(1), CJA 1991), following a pre-sentence report; such an order is only made in special

circumstances following a previous custody sentence; if breached, resentence follows;

9. community service, once aged 16, for between 40 and 240 hours, with consent (PCCA 1973; section 10, CJA 1991); resentence if breached;

10. secure training order, for young people over 12 and under 15 (section 1, CJPOA 1994), who are convicted of an imprisonable offence which is so serious that only a custodial sentence can be justified or where, in the case of a violent or sexual offence, custody is justified to protect the public from harm. The young person must have been convicted of at least three imprisonable offences, whether now or previously, and be in breach of a supervision order or convicted whilst subject to such an order; the total order may last between six months and two years, with equal periods spent in detention and under supervision by a probation officer or social worker; breach of the supervision part of the order may result in either a fine or detention in a secure training centre not exceeding the shorter of three months or the remainder of the period of the order (section 4);

11. custody, for offenders over 15, for serious imprisonable offences, where the tariff has failed or the offender is unwilling to use it, or to protect the public from harm (CJA 1982); except for certain grave offences, the term must not exceed one year (section 63(4), CJA 1991); these grave offences (section 53(2), CAYP 1933) have been extended to include indecent assault, death by dangerous driving and death by careless driving due to alcohol or drugs, and now apply to young people aged over 10 (section 16, CJPOA 1994).

Pre-sentence reports will be required before passing a custodial or a community sentence except where the offence is triable only on indictment and where the court has considered a previous report (Schedule 9(40), CJPOA 1994).

Courts cannot now make care orders in criminal proceedings (section 90(2), CA 1989) but may add a residence requirement to supervision orders (Schedule 12(23), CA 1989), to live for up to six months in accommodation provided by or for the local authority. Courts may stipulate people with whom Wayne must not live. Courts must satisfy several conditions here:

1. consultations with local authority;
2. a previous supervision order with a residence or specified activities requirement;
3. the offence was committed during this order, is serious and, for adults, would have been punishable with imprisonment;
4. the offence is related to the circumstances in which Wayne is living;
5. a pre-sentence report is available, also legal representation unless refused by Wayne.

The residence requirement should not be punitive but rather aimed to assist Wayne work through problems and stop reoffending (DoH, 1991d).

A court will depart from a presumption of bail in respect of an indictable only or triable either way offence committed whilst on bail, or when a condition of bail is broken, or where there is a risk of absconding, offending or interference with justice. A court may impose conditions to bail if risks exist but these are not so substantial as to deny bail. Conditions should be exact, effective and enforceable. Prior to sentencing Wayne could be remanded to local authority accommodation (Schedule 12(26), CA 1989), and arrested if he breaches the conditions of his remand (section 23, CJPOA 1994). Wayne's parents would retain parental responsibility. The court may specify with whom Wayne should not be placed. It may make a security requirement, giving reasons, that Wayne be kept in local authority accommodation (section 60, CJA 1991): being over 12 (section 20, CJPOA 1994), charged with or convicted of violent, sexual or other offences imprisonable for at least 14 years; or having a history of absconding and offending when remanded; *and* to protect the public from serious harm.

A child looked after by the local authority may be placed in secure accommodation if there is a history of absconding, the person is likely to abscond and suffer significant harm or, if not in secure accommodation, is likely to injure themselves or others (section 25, CA 1989). This power may be exercised for up to 72 hours without court authority. Otherwise, a court order is necessary, for up to three months on first application and six months thereafter (Children (Secure Accommodation) Regulations 1991). A child bailed on condition that they reside where the local authority directs can be made subject to a secure accommodation order (*Re C (A Minor)*

(Secure Accommodation Order: Bail) [1994]). The welfare checklist (section 1(3), CA 1989) does not apply but the matters contained therein are not irrelevant (*Hereford and Worcester County Council* v. *S* [1993]).

Wayne would then qualify for advice and assistance from the local authority (section 24, CA 1989) to promote his welfare when he ceases to be looked after. This includes preparation in financial and practical skills; assistance with education, training or employment; and inter-agency cooperation, especially with housing departments (DoH, 1991i). In practice this should involve participation in decision-making about care plans, access for Wayne to advocates and organisations of young people in or leaving care, and work which focuses on personal development (identity, self-esteem, practical skills, education potential), maintaining significant links, and respect for diversity (race, gender and sexuality). The local authority has a duty to promote Wayne's welfare after leaving care, and has a power to assist him financially in respect of his education, training and employment beyond the age of 21. There is a duty to provide accommodation up to the age of 21 if he is in need and his welfare would otherwise be prejudiced. In other circumstances this duty becomes a power.

Concerns exist that local authorities are failing in their duties to young people leaving care, particularly in respect of accommodation, reviews, and a failure to provide a coordinated housing and social services department response to young people who should be regarded as children in need because of their potential or actual vulnerability (McCluskey, 1994).

Local authorities must take reasonable steps to encourage children not to commit criminal offences and to avoid the need to place children in secure accommodation (Schedule 2(7), CA 1989). Those involved in administering criminal justice must avoid discriminating against people on grounds of race, sex or other grounds (section 95(1)(b), CJA 1991). NACRO (1992) has issued guidance, for example on pre-sentence reports.

Case eight

Toby is 27. He is unemployed and lives with his mother. This relationship has become very strained following several incidents when he physically assaulted her. Following the most recent assault, Toby became very drunk and attacked people in the local public house. He has previous convictions for criminal damage, theft and assault.

Toby has a diagnosis of schizophrenia. He frequently enters hospital on an informal basis but never stays longer than a few days before discharging himself. He has been compulsorily admitted on four occasions. While on medication his symptoms do not trouble him, but he becomes physically and verbally aggressive without it. At these times he experiences hallucinations and becomes suicidal.

Toby is enmeshed in the criminal justice system and particularly the conflicting imperative of welfare versus justice which permeates it and dominates debates about the role of the probation service. He is caught too in the mental health system and especially in images of race and violence which are powerful influences on psychiatric and judicial responses (see Chapter 2).

Debates about the purposes of the criminal justice system, including probation, and about sentencing options are not immune from political ideologies and economic considerations. They are fuelled by critiques both of the effectiveness of welfare and of punishment approaches to offending behaviour. What is usually missing, however, is reflection on the (in)adequacy of services to support young offenders and disabled offenders. Individuals are portrayed as deviant, requiring punishment and control. Structural inequalities and the (dis)organisation of services receive less attention – for example, poverty as an outcome of welfare rights reform, and unsatisfactory placement and service provision decisions governed by resources rather than needs-led assessments. The myth is that the law is all that is needed.

Toby is unemployed and has mental health problems. He may soon be homeless. Like many offenders he is caught in structural inequalities and material disadvantage. Focusing on welfare or justice, Toby or his outside world, to the exclusion of the other, will prove simplistic and ineffective. Case seven covered the role of the appropriate adult during questioning at police stations, applicable here owing to Toby's mental ill-health. Appropriate adults are not always called in such cases. Case four covered the law relating to homelessness. Given his disability Toby could be in priority need. Case seven highlighted the requirement on people in the criminal justice system to avoid discrimination. Case one covered the law relating to community care services to which, as a disabled person (section 29, NAA 1948) Toby would be eligible.

Where possible, mentally disordered people should be diverted away from the criminal justice system (HO 66/90). However, to be cautioned Toby must admit the offence, understand the implications of a caution and be able to agree to it. The presumption is not to prosecute mentally ill, mentally impaired or severely physically ill offenders (HO 18/94) unless justified by the seriousness of the offence. If prosecuted, the offence with which Toby is charged will determine in which court he appears. Summary, or least serious, offences are dealt with by magistrates. Serious criminal, indictable offences, such as murder, manslaughter, robbery or grievous bodily harm, must be tried in Crown Court. Toby was charged with actual bodily harm (Offences Against the Person Act 1861). Like his previous charges of theft and criminal damage over £5000 (section 46, CJPOA 1994), this is an either way offence. Venue for trial is decided by magistrates on the basis of submissions by prosecution and defence lawyers, the nature of the offence and whether sentences open to the Magistrates' Court are sufficient, and, where magistrates consider a summary trial possible, the defendant's option to choose this or trial by jury in Crown Court. Previous convictions or the offender's circumstances are not included at this point.

Toby's mental health circumstances are relevant at several points at which the criminal justice process is intertwined with the mental health system. Police powers (section 136, MHA 1983), to remove to a place of safety someone who is in a place to which the public have access, and who appears to be mentally disordered and in immediate need of care and control, were covered in case three. Toby could have been taken directly from the public house under these powers to hospital.

Even once in the criminal justice system prosecution could be dropped, or Toby could be found 'unfit to plead' – unable to understand the charge and trial, enter a plea, instruct a defence, or follow evidence (Criminal Procedure (Insanity) Act 1964). The consequence used to be detention in hospital with the same status as a patient on a restriction order of unlimited duration, unless he was discharged by the Home Secretary or transferred back to the penal system for trial, or discharged by a Mental Health Review Tribunal (Hoggett, 1990). The serious injustice, that a mentally disordered offender could be held for longer than either the offence or the mental condition warranted, was rectified by the Criminal Procedure (Insanity and Unfitness to Plead) Act 1991. This provides for a trial of the facts to determine whether the jury is satisfied that the accused did the act beyond reasonable doubt. It then offers courts wide options ranging from absolute discharge, through supervision, treatment and guardianship orders, to hospitalisation (with restrictions if necessary (section 41, MHA 1983)). Where supervision or treatment orders are made, these may be for a maximum of two years on medical advice that compulsory detention in hospital is not needed and that release poses no unacceptable risks to public safety. An ASW supervises the individual. In the event of non-cooperation, the police should be warned and action under the Mental Health Act 1983 considered (LASSL(91)12).

During criminal proceedings, if charged with an imprisonable offence, Toby should be allowed bail (Bail Act 1976) unless it is likely that he would fail to surrender to custody or appear in court, commit further offences, interfere with witnesses or otherwise obstruct the course of justice, or that detention is necessary to prevent harm to himself or others, or that bail would render it impracticable for enquiries to be made and reports completed. Bail will not be allowed if he is charged with or has been convicted previously of homicide or rape (section 25, CJPOA 1994), or if accused or convicted of committing an offence triable on indictment or either way whilst on bail (section 26). Conditions may be attached to bail by the police or courts, such as residence in a bail hostel (courts only) (section 49, PCCA 1973) or making oneself available for enquiries to be made, where necessary to prevent absconding, interfering with witnesses or obstructing justice (section 27, CJPOA 1994). If magistrates refuse bail they must give reasons (section 5, Bail Act 1976). Application may then be made to a Crown Court judge.

In court, Toby will be covered by provisions which allow inferences to be drawn from a failure to answer questions (see case seven), although as a mentally ill person inferences should not be drawn from any failure to give evidence (section 35, CJPOA 1994).

Toby could be remanded to psychiatric hospital for reports on his mental condition (section 35, MHA 1983), if the alleged offence is one punishable by imprisonment (unless the sentence is fixed in law) and one doctor gives evidence that there is reason to believe he has a mental illness, mental impairment, severe mental impairment or psychopathic disorder and a psychiatric report is impracticable if bail is given. Detention is for a maximum of 28 days at a time, renewable up to twelve weeks. Under section 36, MHA 1983, alleged offenders can be remanded to hospital by Crown Court for treatment if two medical reports confirm they are suffering from mental illness or impairment of a nature or degree warranting such detention. Again detention is for 28 days maximum at a time, up to twelve weeks.

It is possible for the court to find the accused incapable of criminal intent and return a verdict of 'not guilty by reason of insanity' on the basis that they suffer from a 'disease of mind' which led to a 'defect of reason' such that they did not know the nature of what they did, or did not know it was wrong. The Court's powers here are as in a finding of 'unfit to plead'. In a case of murder the concept of 'diminished responsibility' may, under the Homicide Act 1957, reduce the conviction to one of manslaughter, thus allowing any of the disposals for that offence rather than the mandatory life sentence for murder.

To assist courts in determining the most suitable method of dealing with offenders, that is, to consider the seriousness of the offence and a disposal suitable for the offender, probation officers and social workers have a duty to compile pre-sentence reports when requested (Schedule 3(8), PCCA 1973). However, courts may decide that a custodial sentence (section 1(2), CJA 1991) or community sentence is justified without regard to a pre-sentence report, irrespective of the type of offence (Schedule 9(40), CJPOA 1994). Considering pre-sentence reports is good practice, however, in order to ensure balanced reflection on all the options and on any available information concerning mitigating and aggravating factors. Courts must obtain and consider medical reports (section 4, CJA 1991) when offenders are, or appear to be, mentally disordered before passing custodial sentences other than those fixed by law. Here courts must consider the likely effects of a custodial sentence on the offender's mental health and on any treatment available for it.

The framework for pre-sentence reports is contained within National Standards (Home Office, 1995) and includes a requirement that they be completed within fifteen working days. At least two interviews are recommended. Report writers must balance in their recommendations realism and appropriateness, considering the likely outcomes in relation to future offending, risks, needs and the seriousness of the offence. They should consider all relevant information about the offender and their circumstances. They should analyse the offence, including mitigating (for example provocation, duress, mental incapacity, ignorance) and aggravating factors (premeditation, abuse of trust, victim's vulnerability, force), together with the offender's attitude to the offence and its consequences. Personal and social information may be included if relevant to the person's behaviour. Responses to previous convictions and sentences, together with mitigating factors not relevant to the offence (for instance, character), will be relevant.

If convicted, to what could Toby be sentenced? Once again psychiatry and criminal justice are sometimes intertwined, as in probation orders with psychiatric treatment conditions. Here psychiatry and criminal justice are 'partners', implying collaboration in a shared project of rehabilitation and readjustment. Sometimes, however, they stand opposite each other as distinct alternatives (Allen, 1986). A hospital order precludes imposition of penal sentence, the offender becoming the responsibility of the psychiatric system.

If Toby is convicted of an offence punishable by imprisonment (or, in the case of Magistrates, if the court is satisfied Toby committed the offence) the court may order detention in psychiatric hospital or under guardianship if Toby is suffering from mental illness, mental impairment, severe mental impairment or psychopathic disorder and if, taking into account the nature of the offence, Toby's antecedents and other available options, the court deems this to be the most suitable disposal (section 37, MHA 1983). Two medical recommendations must satisfy the court that the disorder is of a nature or degree that warrants hospitalisation (and that for mental impairment and psychopathy the treatability clause is satisfied) or guardianship.

A person so hospitalised may receive compulsory treatment as in section 3, may not be discharged by the nearest relative but may apply to the Mental Health Review Tribunal. Discharge is determined by the responsible medical officer or MHRT unless restricted. Section 41 allows the Crown Court to impose restrictions on discharge of a hospital order if it is necessary to protect the public from serious harm. Discharge is then regulated by the Secretary of State or, in certain circumstances, by the MHRT.

If the court is considering the suitability of a hospital order, it may make an interim order for twelve weeks renewable for periods of 28 days up to six months maximum (section 38, MHA 1983). The other possibilities are the following:

1. Deferred sentence – a postponement, to which Toby must consent, where there are specific reasons, such as a change in circumstances or desired behaviours which cannot be made part of a probation order, and which can be specified as clear objectives by a court.
2. Absolute discharge (see case seven).
3. Conditional discharge for a specified period to a three-year maximum, with no further sentence if Toby does not commit further offences within this time.
4. Fine, with deductions possible from income support (section 24, CJA 1991). The amount is related to the circumstances and seriousness of the offence and the offender's ability to pay (sections 18 and 19, CJA 1991; section 65, CJA 1993).
5. Compensation order, limited to a maximum of £5000 in Magistrates' Courts. Courts are encouraged to make and to provide reasons for not making such orders.

Various community sentences follow, made if the seriousness of the offence(s) warrants them and if they are suitable for the offender (section 6, CJA 1991).

6. Probation order, for a minimum of six months and a maximum of three years, with Toby's consent. Now a sentence in its own right (section 8, CJA 1991), with the objectives of securing the offender's rehabilitation and/or protecting the public from harm or preventing the commission of further offences, the order may be made with requirements additional to the obligations to be of good behaviour, lead an industrious life, inform the probation officer of changes of address or employment, comply with reporting instructions and receive visits at home (Schedule 1, CJA 1991):
   (a) residence, for a specified period, in an approved hostel or other institution;
   (b) attending specified places;

    (c)   participating for a maximum of 60 days or refraining from participating in specified activities;

    (d)   attending a probation centre, for a maximum of 60 days;

    (e)   submitting for a specified period to treatment (by or under the direction of a medical practitioner or psychologist (Schedule 9(10), CJPOA 1994), either resident or non-resident, for a mental condition where a duly qualified medical practitioner approved under section 12 (MHA 1983) provides evidence that an offender's mental condition requires and may be susceptible to treatment but is not such as to warrant a hospital order;

    (f)   treatment for drug or alcohol dependency, for a specified period, resident or non-resident at a specified place.

The 60-day time limit in (c) and (d) above does not apply to offenders convicted of sexual offences but the required number of days must be specified by the court. The specified period in (a), (e) and (f) may be the whole period of the probation order.

7.   Community service order, with Toby's consent and following consideration of a pre-sentence report which, *inter alia*, confirms his suitability for such work and its availability. The specified period is between 40 and 240 hours, to be completed in one year. The order is available for offenders convicted of an imprisonable offence. Toby could, but does not have to be, sentenced to custody for refusing to consent to this order or any community sentence order being made (section 1(3), CJA 1991) which requires consent.

8.   Combined order (section 11, CJA 1991), a pre-sentence report having been considered, bringing together probation and community service.

9.   Curfew order (section 12, CJA 1991), for specified periods at specified places, with Toby's consent. Electronic monitoring (section 13) may be an added enforcement requirement.

Failure to comply with the terms of a community sentence may be dealt with by fine, to a maximum of £1000; by community service order, to a maximum 60 hours and not exceeding 240 hours if consecutive with another such order; by revocation and resentence. If Toby committed further offences, the community sentence order could be revoked and he could be resentenced (Schedule 2, CJA

1991). Regard to the extent that Toby has complied with the original order must be given in each circumstance.

10. Custody, where the offence is so serious that only a custodial sentence is justified or, in respect of violent or sexual offences, it is necessary to protect the public from serious harm (physical or psychological, death or serious personal injury) from *this* offender (section 1, CJA 1991). These thresholds do not apply when custody is determined by law or an offender has refused to consent to a community sentence. The court must consider the facts and circumstances of the particular case rather than the legal category into which the offence falls (*R* v. *Bradbourn* [1985]). When giving reasons the court must specify the particular features of the offence which make it so serious that only custody is justified. The minimum and maximum custodial sentence available to magistrates is five days and six months respectively, with consecutive orders possible to a maximum of one year. Besides pre-sentence reports (see above), sentencers must consider all information relevant to the circumstances of the offence (section 3(3), CJA 1991) including any previous convictions and any failure to respond to previous sentences (section 66(6), CJA 1993). This may include diminished culpability based on provocation, reduced or impaired mental capacity, and duress (Wasik and Taylor, 1991), whilst an offence committed on bail is an aggravating factor when considering seriousness. The reasons for a custodial sentence must be explained to an offender. This includes suspended sentences. When Crown Court suspends a prison term of more than six months' duration, it may make a suspended sentence supervision order for a specified period not exceeding the suspended term (PCCA 1973). Its requirements are similar to those of a probation order.

It is important to be familiar with how the Court of Appeal has interpreted offence seriousness and appropriate sentencing (see NACRO 1992a, 1992b; Gilyeat, 1994).

If Toby is detained under section 3 or section 37 (MHA 1983), social services and the district health authority have a duty to provide after-care services (section 117, MHA 1983). Otherwise the local authority has a power to provide preventive, care and after-care services to people with physical and mental illness (NHSA 1977). This may include social work support; training, rehabilitation, recreational and occupation facilities; meals; and accommodation.

For patients over 16 detained under sections 3, 37 or 47 (MHA 1983), they may be released subject to a supervised discharge order (MH(PIC)A 1995) to ensure that they receive after-care services. The patient must have one of the four categories of mental disorder (section 1, MHA 1983), must present substantial risk of harm to their own or other people's health or safety, or be at risk of being seriously exploited if after-are services are not provided, and supervision must be likely to ensure that the patient receives services. Application is made by a responsible medical officer, usually the consultant, after consultation with the patient, care team, nearest relative, and social services department. Consultation with the nearest relative may not take place if the patient objects, there is no propensity to violence or dangerous behaviour, and the responsible medical officer agrees. The application must be supported by a doctor and ASW, and be accompanied by statements from a supervisor and doctor in the community agreeing to involvement, details of services to be provided and any requirements to be imposed on the patient. These requirements may be that the person resides at a specified place, attends at specified places and times for medical treatment, occupation, education and training, and gives access to the supervisor, medical practitioner, ASW and anyone else authorised by the supervisor. The person may be conveyed by the supervisor, or anyone authorised by them, to the place where they are required to reside and/or attend. The supervisor, who may be any member of the care team, is responsible for monitoring discharge arrangements and the after-care plan, ensuring patient compliance, liaison and coordination of the care team's work, reviews, and using their power to convey where necessary. The patient must be informed orally and in writing of the supervised discharge order, its effects, and their right of appeal to the MHRT.

The order should be reviewed when a patient refuses or neglects to comply. This may result in modification of the care plan or requirements, or in readmission to hospital (LAC(96)8). If the person is readmitted as an informal patient or under section 2 (MHA 1983), the supervised discharge order is suspended. If the readmission is under section 3 (MHA 1983), the order is terminated.

Modifications to the order or care plan require consultation involving those listed above. Supervised discharge orders are for six months, renewable for a further six months, and then annually, after examination by the responsible community medical officer and providing the original criteria for the making of an order still apply. Again, consultations are required as detailed above. An order may be ended after consultation (see above), or by an MHRT, or if the person is admitted to guardianship (section 7, MHA 1983) or to hospital under section 3 (MHA 1983), or if the person is sentenced to custody for longer than six months. After-care (section 117, MHA 1983) continues after the end of a supervised discharge order until the health authority and social services department agree that such services are no longer required.

Guidance (LAC(96)8) requires that supervised discharge orders incorporate the key principles of the Care Programme Approach (LASSL(90)11) and reflect the guidance on the discharge of mentally disordered people (LASSL(94)4). Those subject to supervised discharge orders should be included on supervision registers as they present substantial risk of harm to themselves or others (HSG(94)5). Accordingly, there should be a risk assessment prior to discharge and the care plan should be based on an assessment of need. When nearest relatives are consulted this should focus, *inter alia*, on the patient's history, seriousness of any violence, and responses to treatment. A key worker should monitor the care plan. Guardianship (MHA 1983) remains an option but supervised discharge orders have an advantage of allocating clear roles to the supervisor and responsible community medical officer, and of building in reviews of after-care arrangements. An inter-agency agreement is required on risk assessment procedures, consultation on proposals for, and reviews of supervised discharge orders in respect of, individual patients, and when to use powers to convey.

Guidance on registers (HSG(94)5) provide for a register of patients who are, or are likely to be at risk of serious violence, suicide or self-neglect. The person should be informed orally and in writing of why they have been registered and to whom disclosures may be made, unless there are clinical reasons why this information would harm their health. Reviews held every six months under the Care Programme Approach should consider whether registration remains appropriate, on which the patient, via an advocate if necessary, should be invited to comment. The register should include personal details, legal status, key worker and care team details, and the elements of the care plan.

The Care Programme Approach (LASSL(90)11) requires the health authority and social services department to agree policies to ensure that people receive health and social care services through systematic arrangements for deciding whether or not a person can be treated in the community, and then implementing agreed service provision. Guidance on risk assessment (LASSL(94)4) recommends that patients should only be discharged when and if they are ready to leave hospital, when the risk to themselves or others is minimal and can be managed effectively, and when they will receive necessary support through a systematic assessment of need and a care plan. Finally, the Mental Illness Specific Grant (LAC(94)6) invites local authorities to support applications for funding to improve social care services to people with a mental illness who are in need of specialist psychiatric care. These services should be linked into the Care Programme Approach. It remains questionable as to whether these various provisions will break down the fragmentation of services and facilitate multidisciplinary working, resource acquisition, service coordination and the circulation of information – factors which have featured in enquiries into tragedies involving mental health service users.

6

The Law on Social Work Practice

This chapter considers the law *on* social work practice: legislation, government regulations, circulars and codes of practice. Much of what makes social work practice effective is not legislated for. Sometimes social work research and practice influence and are in advance of regulation and guidance. However an increasing amount of official guidance regulates standards of practice, forging a significant interrelationship between regulation and practice, between the law and social work values and concerns.

Legislation expresses duties and powers that determine how local authorities must or may act. Some duties are absolute, not dependent on the exercise of professional judgement. Others are discretionary, arising from the exercise of professional judgement and/or shaped by how an authority determines the duty is to be implemented by reference to appropriateness and necessity. Legislation is then interpreted, with decisions in the House of Lords and Court of Appeal binding on lower courts. Regulations, guidance and codes of practice connect these duties and powers to principles for practice, clarifying how legislation is to be understood and implemented. Their status has been clarified (DoH, 1989a). Regulations have the full force of legislation. They may include duties (directions), powers (approvals) and restrictions. Government circulars and guidance, when issued under section 7 of the Local Authority Social Services Act 1970, have regulatory status, must be followed, and may be quoted in complaints procedures, Ombudsman investigations, and judicial review proceedings, as when directions on choice of accommodation (LAC(92)27) were quoted in a successful challenge to a local authority's decision on a placement for a learning-disabled young man (*R* v. *Avon County Council, ex parte Hazell* [1993]). The law can be elaborated and extended through circulars, as when the

Secretary of State for Health made approvals and directions concerning local authority responsibilities for welfare services and residential accommodation for adults needing care and services (LAC(93)10). Other guidance not issued under section 7 is intended to promote rather than 'legislate for' good practice. However, authorities must pay regard to this guidance also when performing statutory functions (*R* v. *Islington LBC, ex parte Rixon* [1996]).

There is no legal duty to comply with codes of practice. Rather they represent principles of good practice. For example, although not legally required, the assessment and action records, designed to measure children's progress and assess the quality of care they receive when looked after by local authorities, have been widely adopted as part of reviews (Parker *et al.*, 1991). Again, if police officers breach the codes of practice to the Police and Criminal Evidence Act 1984, courts may decide nonetheless to accept the evidence so obtained (*Childright*, 1991). Failure to follow the codes may be used as evidence in legal or internal disciplinary proceedings, but, since they may be ignored and since non-compliance does not necessarily give rise to any civil or criminal liability (Haley and Swift, 1988), principles can easily be compromised. Therefore the degree to which the codes can ensure good practice is questionable. It remains for disadvantaged and disempowered individuals, who may be unaware of their rights under the codes and who may not have the resources, to seek redress.

The exercise in discretion leaves much room for local variations in response. An authority's resource balance sheet will be influential, as will values. For instance, access to records (Braye *et al.*, 1988) may be characterised by a bureaucratic approach (emphasising procedures and accountability to the authority), a professional approach (emphasising what contributes to effective practice), or a political approach (emphasising, for example, service user rights or resources). The bureaucratic approach tends to govern the exercise of discretion by local authorities.

Conflicting imperatives and practice dilemmas may be identified in regulations and guidance, as with legislation, leaving practitioners confused about how to proceed. This arises, partly, because pronouncements about how social workers should approach their tasks are often a reaction to particular circumstances, about which there is no consensus. Thus Mr Justice Brown, evaluating the actions of social workers in Rochdale, opined that, where ritual or satanic

---

Exercise 6.1

Researching guidance as a method of locating practice

Take one key piece of social work law literature, such as a local authority circular, code of practice, or inquiry report investigating practice. Summarise the document chosen, identifying the key points and their implications for practice. Prepare a presentation for colleagues, identifying the importance of the material read. Finally, take a case with which you are working and discuss with a colleague how the material read may be integrated into your work.

---

abuse is suspected, children should not be removed until expert advice has been sought. Listening to expert police advice about dawn raids has, however, been heavily criticised. Partnership with parents is strongly emphasised, and yet is built on to previous exhortations to maintain a healthy scepticism about information given by parents and to guard against deception (Beckford Report, 1985).

Further difficulties arise because guidance often does not prioritise policy objectives and because it would appear unlawful to ignore one element of guidance in reaching a decision. A local authority which acted lawfully in interpreting section 7 (LASSA 1970) guidance in respect of corporal punishment of children by childminders (DoH, 1991b) found its actions overturned because it gave too much weight to this one component of guidance (*Sutton LBC* v. *Davis* [1994]). Guidance in one area should be read in the overall context of guidance – in this instance about day-care provision. Otherwise, giving disproportionate and inflexible importance to one issue would render impossible a correct balancing exercise and a reasonable decision based on the merits of the case. A similar balancing exercise must be undertaken when following community care guidance which requires a proper assessment of need and a move away from resource-led decisions, but which also demands value for money and setting provision levels against what is affordable (DoH, 1990). When, however, is a proper assessment of need undermined by the importance attached to (a lack of) resources?

As with legislation, guidance does not construct a seamless service. Responsibilities may be held by several agencies, with lack of clarity about how a range of needs will be coordinated in a comprehensive assessment and package of care. People with a mental illness, for example, are covered by the Care Programme Approach (LASSL(90)11), supervision registers (HSG(94)5) and discharge arrangements (LASSL(94)4).

Non-compliance by local authorities with directions and regulations emerges consistently. For example, inspections have found:

1. a lack of published statements about the purpose and function of residential care that were understood by children, and a lack of information for service users, especially about complaints procedures (SSI, 1993a);
2. a failure by local authorities to meet regulations on short-term care schemes, reviews and child-care plans in respect of services to disabled children (SSI, 1994a);
3. a failure of case conference minutes to contain formal statements about unresolved child protection issues that make an inter-agency plan necessary, and to clarify how the child protection plan relates to the risks identified (DoH, 1995a);
4. a failure to follow guidance about the suitability of residential care placements for young people (DoH, 1991i), creating risks for the young people inappropriately placed and for staff who themselves appear unaware of the guidance.

Ombudsman investigations have found maladministration. For instance, local authorities in relation to their duties to children with special educational needs have delayed issuing statements and have tailored them to what they could afford rather than to the child's needs, in clear contravention of guidance (91/C/2428; 92/C/2729 and 2833/4). Research reports and judicial review decisions have found that agencies are failing to assess need in a structured way, to provide services to people whose needs have been assessed as requiring them, to provide sufficient assistance, to provide help within a reasonable time period, to conduct regular reviews or to provide written plans. Agencies do not always report deficits in service provision, or consult with users and carers and take their views into account, or manage complaints procedures fairly (Rickford, 1992; *R* v. *Avon County Council, ex parte Hazell* [1993]; *R* v. *North Yorkshire County Council, ex parte Hargreaves* [1994]; Age Concern, 1995; RADAR, 1995).

Moreover legislation and regulatory guidance will only be as effective as the conditions for practice provided for social services staff. Concerns about the timing of and funding for major changes are regularly reported in the media. The impact of cuts in services on morale, risks, quality of work provided, and case outcomes has been highlighted (Fox Report, 1990; SSI, 1990a; Ritchie *et al.*, 1994), yet social services staff continue to be exhorted to improve their practice. This is especially worrying since adherence to good practice *lessens* the closer one approaches operational reality (Booth *et al.*, 1990), with professional staff more easily identifying practice which *should* arise rather than believing that such practices *can* be implemented in their work. Several truths remain unpalatable: that resources are required to underpin good practice, that no regulations can be foolproof, and that redress is difficult to achieve.

Resources

There is no absolute right for an individual to receive a service or treatment. Rather health and local authorities have powers and duties. Duties are sometimes owed to particular groups, such as children in need, and known as target duties. Sometimes duties refer to individuals who might qualify for a service. Stronger than target duties and, therefore, possibly easier to enforce, local authority decisions must be related to each individual to whom the duty is owed.

Local authorities regularly express concern that additional duties do not attract additional funding, and that identifying need might have serious consequences for their resources and legal position. Resource constraints are, for example:

1. creating a restrictive rather than broad interpretation of family support to children in need (section 17, CA 1989), despite guidance which cautions against employing narrow definitions (DoH, 1991b; Aldgate *et al.*, 1994; Colton *et al.*, 1995);

2. limiting responses, other than at crisis points, to the needs of disabled children and their families (SSI, 1994a);
3. limiting investment for quality in residential care for looked-after children (SSI, 1993a);
4. resulting in inexperienced practitioners handling child protection situations alone. The failure to provide sufficient experienced staff results in low thresholds for action, important issues are overlooked, and family members are not engaged (DoH, 1995a);
5. limiting assistance to people who need community care services, with many who would previously have received help no longer eligible (Faulkner, 1994; Marchant, 1995);
6. limiting local authorities' use of guardianship (MHA 1983) (DoH, 1994b) and their ability to provide sufficient staff, key workers, appropriate placements and after-care plans for people with mental illness (Ritchie *et al.*, 1994).

The net effect is that standards promoted in guidance are eroded. The UN Committee on the Rights of the Child has expressed concern about the adequacy of measures taken to ensure the economic, social and cultural rights of children, and about insufficient expenditure allocated to the social sector (*Childright*, 1995d). Practitioners are indeed gatekeepers to an inadequate system (Jones and Novak, 1993). The ideology of curtailing welfare expenditure is sometimes quite explicit. The Mental Health Act 1983 Code of Practice (DoH, 1993c) states that people to whom the Act applies should have their needs fully taken into account though, within available resources, it may not always be practicable to meet them. Services for learning-disabled people (LAC(92)15) should ensure support in a setting which affords most scope for individual development and well-being, in so far as resources allow. Only rarely is service user anxiety acknowledged about the likely availability or continuity of provision.

What is the legal position on services and resources? Local authorities are required to have sufficient staff to enable their social services functions to be exercised (section 6, LASSA 1970). This is a target duty and the discretion in local authority decision-making here may prove difficult to contest. Ombudsman investigations have, however, referred to this duty in cases involving delay. In relation to absolute duties provision cannot be fettered by resource considerations (DoH, 1990; SSI, 1992b; Clements, 1992; 1993; *R* v. *LB of Brent, ex parte Connery* [1990]). The financial situation is not relevant where there is an absolute duty to do something. Appropriate funds have to be found to enable that duty to be fulfilled.

In relation to discretionary duties owed to the general population or specific groups, courts are reluctant to interfere in an authority's exercise of discretion and are likely to accept that financial restrictions are legitimate and proper factors to take into account, for instance in respect of children in need (*R* v. *RB of Kingston-upon-Thames, ex parte T* [1994]; *Re J (A Minor) (Specific Issues Order)* [1995]; *Re C* [1996]), or health care provision (*Re J (A Minor) (Wardship: Medical Treatment)* [1992]; *R* v. *Cambridge District Health Authority, ex parte B* [1995]). This is providing that the authority's actions are neither perverse nor unreasonable (*Puhlhofer and Another* v. *LB of Hillingdon* [1986]) and that authorities have not exceeded or misused their powers, misdirected themselves in law or fact, or exercised discretion wrongly or for no good reason. Thus, eligibility criteria may be set but must be fair, reasonable and non-discriminatory (DoH, 1990), and not set so narrowly that the discretion to assess and provide services where it appears necessary excludes those who might need provision. All issues relating to an individual case must be considered in order to establish whether agreed eligibility criteria should be departed from.

In relation to discretionary duties owed to individuals, it may prove harder for local authorities to take resources into consideration with reference to decisions about assessment and service provision. This is because such decisions should recognise a person's individuality and should not be based on predetermined or stereotypical notions of need and appropriate provision (LAC(92)15). The level of response should be related to the extent of the need (SSI, 1992b), where need is a basic or essential requirement and a question of assessment, necessity and levels of satisfaction *(R* v. *Gloucestershire County Council, ex parte Barry* [1997]). Nor can resources be used as a reason for failing to follow section 7 (LASSA 1970) guidance, for example concerning reviews and reassessment of the need for provision (*R* v. *Gloucestershire County Council, ex parte RADAR* [1995]). However, resources may be considered when deciding *how* to meet assessed needs, either when need is first established or on review and reassessment, providing all issues relevant to the case are evaluated (*R* v. *Lancashire County Council, ex parte RADAR and Another* [1996]).

In *Berkshire County Council* v. *C and others* [1993] the court held that it may give mandatory directions in care proceedings (section 38(6), CA 1989) when a local authority has indicated that it is unable to allocate work due to lack of resources, providing that the court takes account of available information and the financial implications of its direction. In *R* v. *Secretary of State for Education and Science, ex parte E* [1992] it was held that local education authorities must make provision for each and every special educational need identified in a statement which itself must set out all a child's needs and the provision for each, not merely some. On occasion, then, courts are not reticent to weigh resources against other factors, and to challenge how authorities allocate resources and resolve the difficult judgements facing them.

The Ombudsman has found maladministration in how authorities have approached assessment of need and have defined appropriateness of provision in relation to need. The Ombudsman has been reluctant to accept that a shortage of funds is an answer to complaints about delay or a failure to meet a duty (91/C/0565; 91/C/1972; 92/A/1173 and 4108; 92/A/1374; 92/C/1400; 93/A/2071 and 2536) and has criticised the strict application of policies when this has inhibited a proper assessment of need. Even when the Ombudsman has been sympathetic to an authority's position, recognising that priority has to be given to those in greatest need, it has found maladministration when an authority has not given a clear indication of likely delays in making an assessment or providing a service (396/J/82; 92/C/1403).

Antidiscriminatory policies and practice

Social workers must be competent in taking action to counter discrimination and inequality, and in integrating antidiscriminatory values and practices into the social work process. They must be able to question personal attitudes and identify the sources and impact of inequality and injustice (CCETSW, 1995).

This key commitment within social work practice finds some support in legislation and regulations. Section 71 of the Race Relations Act 1976 imposes a duty on local authorities to make appropriate arrangements to secure that their functions are performed with due regard for the need to eliminate unlawful direct and indirect racial discrimination, and to promote equality of opportunity and good relations between people of different racial groups. Section 20 makes it unlawful for anyone concerned with providing goods, facilities or services to the public to discriminate by refusing or deliberately omitting to provide them or by the quality, manner or terms in which they are provided. Accordingly failing to provide appropriate services is evidence of discrimination and institutional racism (B. Ahmad, 1990). Section 35 allows actions which enable the special needs of particular racial groups to be met as regards education, training and welfare, where a special need can be shown, by preferential allocation or restriction of access to such groups.

Subsequent legislation and guidance begins to seriously address good practice in relation to race and culture. Underpinning community care is the recognition (DoH, 1989c) that people from varying cultural backgrounds have different care needs, and that community care must take account of the circumstances of minority communities and be planned in consultation with them. Further guidance (DoH, 1990) acknowledges that the requirements of the majority are not always appropriate. Accordingly, when preparing community care plans (section 46, NHSCCA 1990), health and local authorities should ensure that the needs of black and minority ethnic communities are included in the consultation process: identifying care needs; assessing available services; highlighting services required in response to care needs. In care management assessment procedures must be accessible to all potential users and carers, and service provision must be non-discriminatory. Further non-regulatory guidance (DoH, 1991g; SSI, 1993b) is more specific. It states that policies and practice should ensure that people have their cultural, ethnic, religious, sexual and emotional needs recognised and respected. Departments should develop their equal opportunity policies to ensure that everyone has equal opportunity regardless of race, gender, disability or age. Information provided should take account of special needs, different languages and cultural backgrounds.

Exercise 6.2

Combining the requirements of the Children Act 1989 and the
Race Relations Act 1976, what are the implications for policy
and procedures in day and substitute care (nurseries, family
centres, private sector provision, childminders, foster carers)
in respect of:

1. access to services (to include information, publicity, admissions criteria);
2. staffing; and
3. environment, programme, relationships and behaviour?

Take an authority known to you and research the following
questions:

1. How far do residential, domiciliary and day care services
   reflect the requirements of black and minority ethnic
   communities?
2. Are local authorities, when registering and inspecting
   homes for older people under the Registered Homes Act
   1984, following guidance (DoH, 1989d) and enquiring
   about arrangements to enable residents to follow customs
   and practices related to their cultural and racial background, and to ascertain the wishes and needs of residents
   and to meet these wherever possible?
3. What provisions are made regarding language, worship
   and diet? What staff recruitment policies are pursued?
   What training and monitoring of staff attitudes is undertaken?
4. Do complaints procedures ensure that those investigating
   any complaint reflect the gender and racial background of
   the complainant?

The track record of local authorities in developing appropriate
antidiscriminatory policies and services is hardly impressive. Needs-
led assessment appears to be influenced by white eurocentric norms,
applying Western concepts of well-being (Mirza, 1991). Assimila-

tionist and culturalist policies form the basis of needs assessment in white organisations (Ahmad-Aziz *et al.*, 1992), based on myths and stereotyping (Gunaratnam, 1993) and leading to inappropriate services which ignore the needs of black people and their communities (NAREA, undated). Guidance says little about funding of the voluntary sector to ensure its survival, yet this is where many black projects exist. The emphasis on value for money leads to standardisation which invariably means what is suitable for the majority group.

The Mental Health Act Code of Practice (DoH, 1993c) refers to the principle that people should receive respect for and consideration of their diverse social, cultural, religious and ethnic backgrounds, but concern continues about the over-representation of black people in measures which exert social control and under-representation in supportive, facilitative service provision (Barnes *et al.*, 1990; Fernando, 1991).

Similarly, section 95, CJA 1991, requires those administering justice to avoid discrimination against people on grounds of race. National Standards (Home Office, 1995) require that work should be free from discrimination. A racial motive to a crime has been held to justify, in the absence of a specific offence of racial violence, a higher sentence. It is an aggravating factor when weighing seriousness (*R* v. *Ribbans, Duggan and Ridley* [1994]). However, Afro-Caribbean people are more likely to be stopped or arrested by the police, are less likely to receive probation orders or bail, and are over-represented in the prison population (Home Office, 1992).

The Children Act 1989, and the regulatory guidance issued subsequently, affirm antidiscriminatory practice. Building on the principle (DoH, 1989a) that agency services and practices must not reflect or reinforce discrimination, the Act includes:

1. race, culture and religion as characteristics which courts should consider in determining children's welfare (section 1(3)(d));
2. religious persuasion, racial origin, cultural and linguistic background to which local authorities must give due consideration in making decisions about children being looked after by them (section 22(5));
3. a duty to consider racial groups to which children in need belong and, in respect of day and foster care, to have regard to different racial groups (Schedule 2(11)).

Similar duties exist in relation to voluntary organisations (section 61(3)(c)), registered children's homes (section 64 (3)(c)), and cancellation of registration of those providing day care and childminding (section 74(6)) where seriously inadequate care includes lack of attention to children's race, culture, language and religion.

Regulatory guidance refers to:

1. valuing children's religious, cultural, racial and linguistic identity (DoH, 1991b); and
2. ensuring the availability of experience and expertise to assess children's needs, including ethnic origins, religion and special needs (DoH, 1991a).

Thus the law endorses antidiscriminatory practice. Lack of resources will not excuse discriminatory practice. Resources must reflect the profile of the communities served.

Criteria are required to judge seriously inadequate day care (Lane, 1990). Refusing to care for black children is illegal under the Race Relations Act 1976, and would indicate unsuitability to care for any child on the basis that positive recognition of all racial groups is an integral part of child care in a multiracial society. Inadequate diet and racist remarks are clear examples, but how will registration criteria, review and monitoring procedures tackle more subtle attitudes?

What is due consideration? To what extent are questions of race, culture and religion to be determinative? Bandana Ahmad (1990) argues that due consideration of such questions must be taken to mean paramount. However the law balances the importance of race against other matters, such as attachment to present carers, in deciding a child's welfare (*Re P (A Minor) (Adoption)* [1990]). A blanket policy may be open to challenge through judicial review (Freeman, 1990). Accordingly placement regulations (DoH, 1991a) endorse same-race placements as most likely to meet a child's needs and to safeguard their welfare, 'other things being equal'. This obscures rather than endorses social work definitions of good practice.

Generally there are no grounds for complacency. Action is available in the county court to individuals who believe they have been discriminated against but cost and the track record of courts in understanding the needs and experiences of black people are major deterrents. Robbins (1990), reviewing local authorities' child-care policy statements, found that discrimination was mentioned only in approximately one-third. Whilst some authorities clearly regarded policies against discrimination on grounds of race, gender, class or disability as fundamental, the variable approach to confronting individual and institutional racism is a matter of concern. Similarly, concern exists that guidance on assessment (DoH, 1988) is euro-centric (Phillips, 1990; Parton, 1991). Social services have, as yet, made little progress towards meeting the needs of black and minority ethnic communities, and promoting equality (Macdonald, 1991). Thus, a report on services for disabled children (SSI, 1994a) found that none of the authorities surveyed were consulting with representatives from black and minority ethnic groups when planning services. A study of residential care (SSI, 1993a) found that the needs and experiences of many black children were not being valued or acknowledged. Many black families, involved with child protection services, do not have access to much needed family support services (DoH, 1995a).

The Sex Discrimination Act 1975 (amended 1986) parallels the Race Relations Act 1976 in making it unlawful to discriminate on sex grounds in employment, education and the provision of goods, facilities and services. Sex is included in section 95 (CJA 1991). Regulatory (DoH, 1991b, 1991c) and other guidance in relation to children (DoH, 1989a) refers to equal opportunities, including the importance of practice avoiding gender stereotyping. However, the policy guidance on community care (DoH, 1990a) is silent on promoting equality for women, reflecting dominant images of gender roles in relation to caring. Grimwood and Popplestone (1993) demonstrate the assumptions of a heterosexual, gender-neutral context which inform the policy background, ignoring the power dynamics within families and the pressure on women to construe their own needs as identical to those of other family members. Gender assumptions influence decisions on service delivery (Graham, 1993) and result in a failure to focus services on people with the most intense needs (Bebbington and Davies, 1993). Fisher (1994) argues that assumptions about gender and care need to be fundamentally reexamined and services then based on negotiations.

In relation to disability, the range of services which may be provided under the Children Act 1989 and the Chronically Sick and Disabled Persons Act 1970 do little to challenge discrimination because they do not challenge restrictive attitudes and the able-bodied assumptions and orientation of social arrangements. They emphasise individualised needs and resources, rather than rights. Professionals dominate the definition of need and decision-making about services. One report (SSI, 1990b), critical of local authorities' implementation of the Disabled Persons Act 1986, recommended that social services departments give priority to considering the special needs of minority ethnic and cultural groups in order to discharge effectively their duties under sections 5 and 6.

Local authorities are required to provide services to children with disabilities which are designed to minimise the effects of the child's disability and to give children the opportunity to lead lives that are as normal as possible (Schedule 2 (9), CA 1989). Guidance (DoH, 1991n) lists the principles for such work: the welfare of the child is paramount; access for all children to the same range of services; disabled children are children first; partnership; and recognition of the importance of parents and families. Accommodation for disabled children should be as suitable as possible for their needs (section 23(8), CA 1989). A register of disabled children should be kept to assist with future planning of services (Schedule 2(2), CA 1989).

The Disability Discrimination Act 1995 makes it unlawful to discriminate in connection with employment, access to buildings, and the provision of goods, facilities and services. It contains measures to assist disabled pupils and students, and access standards for transport. However, the legislation lacks a commission with powers of enforcement, and its provisions are vague, weak and not comprehensive in terms of groups of disabled people or areas of daily living covered. It is unlikely to promote integration into economic and social life, or to assist disabled people in community participation and presence. It is unlikely to free disabled people from constraints which affect their lives, especially since service provision legislation is narrowly focused on particular types of care-based services.

Social work's conception of inequality also embraces sexuality, age and class. There is no comparable duty to that in the Race Relations Act in respect of these inequalities. Indeed, in relation to sexuality, the reverse is apparent. Section 28 of the Local Government Act 1988 views homosexual partnerships as 'pretended family relationships' and prohibits local authorities from promoting them. The Human Fertilisation and Embryology Act 1990 (section 13(5)) invokes the law in questions of fitness to parent when requiring that treatment must take account of the welfare of the child, including the need of that child for a father. Whilst people in same-gender relationships are not to be disqualified from adoption or fostering (DoH, 1991a), the guidance still refers to the chosen way of life of some adults rendering them unable to provide a *suitable environment* for the care of children. Whilst some cases view fairly positively the contribution which lesbians and gay men may make to the care of children (*Re C (A Minor) (Residence Order: Lesbian Co-Parents)* [1994]), the ideal environment is still seen as male/female, or the closest to that 'ideal' (*C* v. *C (A Minor) (Custody: Appeal)* [1991]). Homosexuality can still be seen as something from which children should be protected (*S* v. *S (Custody of Children)* [1980]). Whilst the evidence supporting heterosexual partnerships as the 'ideal' family unit is hardly overwhelming, this view of 'normality' continues to obscure the quality relationships which gay men and lesbian women can offer children. In deciding questions of residence, courts will look at the totality of relevant facts, including any evidence that contact with lesbians or gay men is likely to corrupt; relevant research; and the impact for the child of living in the community (*Re P (A Minor) (Custody)* [1983], *B* v. *B (Minors) (Custody, Care and Control)* [1991]).

Regulatory guidance (DoH, 1991i) covering preparation of young people for leaving care, when discussing sexual relationships, requires that the needs and concerns of 'gay young men and women' must be recognised and approached sympathetically. This potentially conflicts with duties described above. It falls considerably short of positive social work practice (Macdonald, 1991): ensuring availability of information and literature; challenging heterosexist behaviour and language; promoting clear messages about the validity of being lesbian, gay or heterosexual; identifying staff who can talk to young people about their sexual identity in confidence.

Whilst legislation and guidance may be closer now to social work's commitment to antidiscriminatory practice, the disjunctions highlighted above leave practitioners with a dilemma: to whom do they owe allegiance, and what action should they take when they believe that agencies are acting in discriminatory ways? Possible responses are discussed in Chapter 7.

Accountability and responsibility

The emphasis in social work training on competence in knowledge, values and skills for practice (CCETSW, 1995) introduces professional accountability for standards, if only at qualification, but the absence of a universally adopted and enforceable code of ethics, and a General Social Services Council, together with the variable availability and quality of supervision and post-qualifying training, leaves service users vulnerable to poor and unethical practice. It leaves practitioners exposed when negotiating ethical issues in practice, and when confronting conflicts between individual, organisational, professional and social values, or clashes between the rights and wishes of different individuals. Judicial review, complaints procedures and the local government ombudsman (Commissioner for Local Administration) may all inquire and provide redress. However, given the questions of liberty, violence, risk and compulsion faced daily by social workers, given the abuses of power known to occur within welfare services and the power imbalance between service providers and users, it is questionable whether such post-event protection is sufficient.

The introduction of National Standards, for instance for the supervision of offenders in the community (Home Office, 1995), may be seen as an attempt to promote accountability by making clear requirements and the framework within which professional judgement is to be exercised. Pre-sentence reports, for example, must be impartial, balanced and accurate. Critics argue, however, that such standards have a negative effect by elevating coercion and removing discretion from practitioners (Blaug, 1995; Ward, 1996). This approach, they argue, hinders good workers whilst not assisting (or effectively regulating) weak practitioners.

A general legal principle is that practitioners should follow the standard of the reasonable professional who is skilled in that profession (Dimond, 1995). Where professionals depart from accepted practice for good reasons, these should be recorded fully. However the Mental Health Act 1983 is unique in requiring practitioners to possess 'an appropriate competence' (section 114) to act as Approved Social Workers. No such requirement exists elsewhere. The Act also refers to *how* they should act: in good faith and with reasonable care. However this accountability to users is weakened in several ways. Whilst the Mental Health Act Code of Practice (DoH,

1993c) delineates the responsibilities of practitioners and agencies, the needs of people to whom the Act applies can only be met as resources allow. Mental Health Review Tribunals only have the power to consider whether or not detention should continue, not the legality of the original decision or the manner in which it was made. To question that, individuals must seek leave for civil and/or criminal proceedings (section 139), use complaints procedures or seek judicial review. Cases, for example, have been brought where the nearest relative has not been consulted, or involved or removed (section 29, MHA 1983) correctly, and concerning the repeat use of section 2 and failure to observe the distinction between section 2 and section 3 in the Code of Practice (DoH, 1993c) (*R* v. *The Managers of South Western Hospital, ex parte M* [1994]; *Re S-C (Mental Patient: Habeas Corpus)* [1995]; *R* v. *Wilson and Another, ex parte Williamson* [1995]).

Older and disabled people face similar constraints. Local authorities are expected (DoH, 1989c) to discharge their community care responsibilities for assessment, design and delivery of services, monitoring quality and effectiveness, and establishing complaints procedures, efficiently and effectively. Subsequent guidance (DoH, 1990) refers to users and carers feeling that the assessment process is aimed at meeting their wishes. This consensual view is not disturbed by reference to risk or compulsory powers, or to the dilemmas which arise when financial constraints are influential in determining the type and level of services to be provided. Nor is there any questioning of whether the services available (CSDPA 1970) coincide with what older and disabled people regard as relevant. Indeed guidance has recommended (CI(92)34) that authorities should record users' wishes and preferences, rather than needs, and should detail unmet need generally rather than relating them specifically to individuals. This guidance is designed to limit the duty to meet assessed need with services and to facilitate revision of community care plans, but makes it more difficult for users to challenge assessments. Evidence suggests that authorities are not recording unmet need, or are not making such records available to users (Ellis, 1993). Additionally, the purchaser/provider split contributes to confusion, and increases the difficulty for users to enforce accountability, by diffusing responsibility and obscuring any tensions between bureaucratic and professional cultures (Cornwell, 1992/93). Despite the rhetoric of choice and involvement, who really controls the assessment process? Government reviews, indeed, have found inadequate or non-existent monitoring of the assessment process (DoH, 1993a). The poor quality of monitoring information raises questions about the ability of local authorities to accurately identify demand and evaluate the effectiveness of policies and services.

Principles of good practice in child care (DoH, 1988, 1989a) refer to the rights of children and adults, especially regarding the manner in which help is offered and interventions conducted. These rights – to information, involvement in decision-making, careful assessment prior to decision-making, clear explanations of local authority powers and reasons for concern, and to reviews and complaints procedures – are embodied in the Children Act 1989 and regulatory guidance which underpins it. This should strengthen accountability. However phraseology such as 'due consideration' and 'as they [local authorities] consider appropriate' raises the spectre of attitudes and resources, and questions the degree of involvement really being offered. Needs and opinions, as defined or expressed by service users, can still be ignored, even though in other respects the Act and regulatory guidance do specify how social workers and local authorities must act in implementing their duties and powers. Much depends, ultimately, on the attitudes and values of agencies and employees; on their skills in partnership, use of authority, assessment, direct work and supervision; and on whether their resource base facilitates good practice.

Inspection and regulation

One means of ensuring accountability is through inspection and regulation of service provision, and a detailed policy for following up results. Section 48 (NHSCCA 1990) requires local authorities to establish arm's length inspection units – independent of normal local authority management structures and directly accountable to directors of social services – to inspect standards of community care services, including residential homes in the public, private and voluntary sectors, for older and disabled people. The duty is to evaluate the quality of care provided and the quality of life experienced. Local authority chief executives are required (LAC(94)16) to present annual reports to councillors, based on an assessment of the work of inspection units and the social services department's response to reports on the services it manages.

The scope of the Registered Homes Act 1984 has been extended by the Registered Homes (Amendment) Act 1991 to small homes having fewer than four residents, but this legislation still applies only to homes in the independent sector. The Residential Care Homes (Amendment) Regulations 1991 require that applicants for registration must disclose criminal convictions to the registering authority and that police checks are completed. Guidelines for standards in residential care exist (DoH, 1989d) and the Social Services Inspectorate is developing standards as part of quality assurance visits.

Standards in homes have risen (Day *et al.*, 1995) and targets for inspections have generally been matched or exceeded (SSI, 1993e). However concerns remain about the adequacy and scope of monitoring and inspection, and about the emphasis on procedures rather than on whether people are enabled to live in the community and to exercise greater choice from flexible and innovative services (Henwood and Wistow, 1995). Specific concerns have been raised concerning:

1. the difficulty for inspection units coping with increased workloads, inadequate communication between inspectors and service managers to discuss matters arising from inspections, and insufficient emphasis on the views of service users (SSI, 1993e);
2. the failure to regulate private domiciliary care agencies, and inadequate regulation of independent organisations providing community care for mentally ill people;
3. variations in standards demanded by units of providers and a failure to use reports as an information tool for (prospective) users (SSI, 1993e; Day *et al.,* 1995).
4. a lack of well-defined service standards contributing to monitoring difficulties and poor quality control (SSI, 1993c).

There is no statutory duty here to review the cases of individual users. Moreover, the consequences of regulation violation, together with the infrequency of visits, appear insufficiently serious to deter bad practice.

The Children Act 1989 provides for the registration, annual review of registration, and twice-yearly inspection of private children's homes (DoH, 1991i; Children's Homes Regulations 1991).

Local authorities must inspect their own homes (LAC(92)14). They must register day services for children under eight (schedule 14, CA 1989), inspect them annually, and impose where appropriate requirements concerned with numbers, safety and records. They must assess (section 76(4)) a person's fitness to care and to be in the proximity of children being cared for in premises. The local authority has the burden of proof to demonstrate lack of fitness and may cancel registration for inadequate care or breach of requirements. They must coordinate the review of all childminding and day care provision, whether or not directly provided by the local authority, for the level, pattern and range of care available (section 19, CA 1989). They must inspect the welfare of children in independent boarding schools (DoH, 1991c).

However, the frequency of inspections of boarding schools has been reduced to once every four years (LAC(95)1). There is no national monitoring of whether health authorities inform local authorities of disabled children accommodated for more than three months, as required by law. Children's homes with fewer than four residents are not inspected and there is little evidence of investigation of such homes – for staffing, accommodation, and police checks – prior to placement as required by placement regulations (LAC(93)16; Clark, 1995; Hamilton, 1995). The Social Services Inspectorate (1993a) has stressed the need to establish management structures that monitor standards and the performance of independent children's homes. It bemoans the absence of knowledge about current practice.

Utting (1991) has criticised the inadequacy of current regulations and guidance on inspection. High-profile cases involving deaths of children being cared for raise similar questions. The Ombudsman has criticised delays in registering new childminders (92/A/2412).

Complaints and representation

Both the Children Act 1989 (section 26) and the NHS and Community Care Act 1990 (section 50) establish complaints procedures. These represent another avenue for ensuring local authority accountability for decisions. Additionally, the Mental Health Act Commission may investigate complaints, on clinical judgement and non-clinical matters, from or on behalf of detained patients (section 120, MHA 1983; Dimond, 1995). The significance of these procedures has been enhanced by courts criticising the use of judicial review to challenge local authority decisions when a more appropriate remedy exists – by virtue of speed, a mandate to consider the matter afresh and to exercise an independent judgement on the merits of the facts, and the power to make recommendations to which an authority must pay due regard. Judicial review is then reserved for a challenge to the use made by an authority of a complaints panel's findings, or for an authoritative resolution of a legal issue (*R* v. *Durham CC, ex parte Curtis and Others* [1995]; *R* v. *RB of Kingston-upon-Thames, ex parte T* [1994]; *R* v. *LB of Barnet, ex parte B* [1994]; *R* v. *Cambridge District Health Authority, ex parte B* [1995]). Modifications by an authority to a panel's recommendations will not necessarily be unreasonable (*R* v. *North Yorkshire County Council, ex parte Hargreaves* [1994]).

The procedures which local authorities must establish are governed by regulations (Complaints Procedure Directions, 1990; Children Act Representations Procedure (Children) Regulations, 1991) and guidance (DoH, 1991l). There are three stages to the procedure – an informal or problem-solving stage, a formal stage, and a review stage. One important difference between the procedures is that an independent person must be involved at the formal stage in Children Act complaints but only at the review stage in community care complaints. The number of independent people on the review panel of three persons is for the local authority to determine.

Users' and carers' knowledge of complaints procedures is poor. Procedures have been insufficiently advertised and appear inaccessible (DoH, 1993a; Jackson, 1993). People are not routinely informed about them when they first become involved with social workers (Buckley *et al.*, 1995). This lack of information inhibits a challenge to decisions (Warner, 1995). Progress in implementing the requirements has been variable, particularly in recording numbers of complaints, using the results to influence policy and service delivery, adhering to timescales, circulating information to users and carers, and consulting with staff (DoH, 1993b). Local authorities vary in how they define a complaint (Rowe and Kent, 1992; Dean and Hartley, 1995). Advocacy arrangements are poorly developed and there is an over-reliance on formal procedures for resolving disagreements (Jackson, 1993; DoH, 1993b). Simons (1995) found that users and carers lacked information about the informal stage, appeared uninformed that they could proceed straight to the formal stage, and required assistance to frame their concerns and access the procedures. There was widespread under-recording. Users reported dissatisfaction with the response of staff at the informal stage, highlighting defensiveness and the difficulty in establishing a culture where the right to complain is accepted.

The reasons why users do not complain are complex and varied. Some may be sceptical of the benefits to be gained or daunted by the procedures once these are known. Equally, users are often anxious about the potential adverse consequences of complaining or perceive that they are not encouraged to express views. Ellis (1993), for instance, found that people who are knowledgeable and claim their rights are seen by practitioners as fussy and demanding. A culture shift is required if people are to feel empowered to overcome a reluctance to complain. The provision of procedures alone is insufficient.

Judicial review decisions (*R* v. *Kent County Council and Others, ex parte Bruce* [1986]; *R* v. *Norfolk County Council, ex parte M* [1989]; *R* v. *London Borough of Harrow, ex parte Deal* [1990]) have established that local authorities must not act irrationally or manifestly fail to discharge their responsibilities. They have a duty to act fairly. However users must first seek leave for a review, for which they may not have all the available evidence. Moreover judicial review is only concerned with the decision-making process and its legality; with procedural propriety and reasonableness, not with the merits of the case. It is not, therefore, a reappraisal of the case. Users may find the review upholds their complaint but that the local authority makes the same decision again via correct procedures. Some other shortcomings in complaints procedures were highlighted in Chapter 3.

Additionally, it is possible to complain to the Commissioner for Local Administration, the local Ombudsman, having exhausted other local authority avenues first. The Ombudsman may investigate maladministration – unreasonable delay, failure to comply with legal requirements, failure to investigate an issue properly, failure to take appropriate action, failure to provide adequate information or explanation. The Ombudsman's enquiries are not restricted, as in judicial review, to the legality of an authority's actions, but focus more broadly on the administration of the case. The Ombudsman has been critical of the operation by local authorities of complaints procedures, particularly citing deficiencies in gathering facts, recording meetings, conveying decisions, giving reasons and using clear criteria for decisions (90/A/2675; 92/A/3725). The Ombudsman may prove useful since investigations have set standards to which reference can be made, namely: that shortage of funds and staff is not an answer to complaints about delay or failing to meet duties; that any delay must be reasonable and practice competent; that there should be high standards of decision-making, demonstrating fairness, absence of bias, and due regard for procedures. However, even if the Ombudsman finds in favour of the complainant, this official has no power to enforce any recommendations suggested to rectify injustice arising out of discrimination, incompetence, delay or other maladministration (Cooper, 1990). The process is also lengthy.

Finally, individuals may sue an authority for compensation to cover injury or damage that has been suffered as a result of negligence, incompetence or failure to implement adequately a statutory duty. Legal advice is essential here (Cooper, 1990). However the House of Lords has limited this avenue of redress by holding that, in relation to child protection services, there is no private duty of care to an individual child and that it is not for courts to interfere in the exercise by local authorities of statutory discretion (*X and Others (Minors)* v. *Bedfordshire CC* [1995]; *M (A Minor) and Another* v. *Newham LBC and Others* [1995]; *E (A Minor)* v. *Dorset CC* [1995]). In respect of other local authority services, it did allow the possibility of such redress if there was a failure by practitioners to take due care when offering services. This judgement has been criticised since, irrespective of how serious the negligence might be, children and parents cannot commence proceedings for the harm suffered (Hamilton and Watt, 1995).

Deprivation of civil liberties

This is a key area where ethical practice, accountability and the proper exercise of responsibility are crucial. Given the alacrity with which the media criticise social workers, the temptation is to use statutory powers in seeking to control 'risky' situations. All practitioners confront disturbing behaviour, unsettling in its effects on them. How, when using or considering control and compulsion, should practitioners act?

The Mental Health Act 1983 is again unusual in requiring Approved Social Workers to interview patients in a suitable manner and to satisfy themselves that detention is, in all the circumstances of the case, the most appropriate means of providing the necessary care and medical treatment (section 13(2)). The Code of Practice (DoH, 1993c) provides guidance on appropriate interviewing and on deciding between particular sections. It emphasises the obligation to consider and implement the most humane and least threatening method of conveying patients, consistent with ensuring their safety and that of others. The Code itemises good practice principles in respect of guardianship, including comprehensive care plans, regular monitoring and reviews, and providing clear information to patients on their rights. In relation to care and treatment in hospital it also emphasises patients' rights to information, promotes care plans, specifies principles governing treatment and restraint, and in welcome recognition that not all difficulties are the responsibility of service users, suggests that problem areas in the hospital environment should be pinpointed. However the disproportionate numbers of women and black people admitted compulsorily to hospital would seem to suggest that attention to principles of good practice is insufficient, and that monitoring of the attitudes and skills of the personnel involved is indicated. Even then, both the Act and the Code are silent on the social and economic factors associated with mental ill-health, and on how practitioners should weigh intervention here in the balance alongside admission. Accordingly, it remains easy for practice to individualise 'solutions' for 'individual ills'.

In relation to older people and vulnerable adults there is an absence of regulation and guidance. There is no statute by which social workers can protect older and vulnerable people from abuse or neglect by others. Indeed, proposals by the Law Commission (1993a, 1993b) concerning people without capacity will not form the basis of legislation. These proposals would have included a Continuing Power of Attorney, extending the remit of the Enduring Power of Attorney over property and affairs to personal welfare and health care. They would have introduced statutory protection for vulnerable people at risk, specifically through a duty on social services departments to investigate if a vulnerable person was suffering or likely to suffer significant harm, with powers of entry, assessment and protection. Moreover, whilst older people have the same basic rights as other citizens – liberty, freedom of expression, privacy, dignity and choice (DoH, 1989d) – no guidance exists which clarifies the use of section 47 of the National Assistance Act 1948. The legal position on restraining the freedom of movement of older people in residential care is unclear, except by consent, in self-defence and crime prevention. Legislation to protect and manage the finances of older and mentally disordered people exists (see Chapter 5), but how easily can people in residential care protest when, for administrative convenience, money is withheld from them? Norman (1980) argues that liberties should only be restricted in order to provide the level of care needed or to protect the quality of life of others. But who decides, following what consultation? What arrangements are made to overcome the imbalance of power between service provider and user? How clear are agencies in their policies about risks and what training do they provide staff in order to own and implement these policies?

Reliance solely on attitudes, skills and training is not the case in child care. As with the Mental Health Act Code of Practice, which states that patients should only be subject to the level of security appropriate to their individual needs and only for as long as required, so the principle in child care (DoH, 1989a) is the least coercive legal status consistent with meeting a child's needs, including no order at all. The Children Act 1989, while clarifying the duties and powers of local authorities in child care and child protection, strengthens the legal position of parents when emergency action is contemplated (Bainham, 1990). Before seeking orders local authorities must identify a child's needs and consider whether services to children in need would meet these needs. Options should be discussed with those with parental responsibility. A clear rationale for the use of compulsion will be required with legal advice sought and a multidisciplinary case conference held. Applications for child assessment orders should be preceded by a detailed investigation (DoH, 1991d, paragraph 4.11). Emergency protection orders should not be a routine first step in responding to child abuse allegations or initiating care proceedings (paragraph 4.30).

Similarly placements must be the least restrictive possible. Deprivation of liberty should only occur when no genuine alternative is appropriate, the last resort when all other options have been comprehensively considered and rejected. It should not be a response to the absence of other placements, staffing problems or a history of misbehaviour and absconding (DoH, 1991d). It should only be for as long as necessary. Similar regulations apply to independent schools (DoH, 1991c).

Contrast this with the introduction of secure training orders for young offenders aged between 12 and 14 (section 1, CJPOA 1994), and the extension to young people aged 10 of detention during Her Majesty's pleasure for grave crimes punishable in the case of an adult by imprisonment of fourteen years or more (section 16, CJPOA 1994 amending section 53, CAYP 1933), the compatibility of which with the best interests of the young person must be questionable. Here the emphasis is on punishment rather than rehabilitative care, despite the failures of similar regimes in the past. Moreover, the welfare of the child is a relevant but not the paramount consideration when a court is considering secure accommodation (section 25, CA 1989). The welfare checklist (section 1(3), CA 1989) does not apply here (*Re M (A Minor) (Secure Accommodation Order)* [1994]). The Children Act Advisory Committee (1993/94) is concerned about the complexity and divergence of civil and criminal rules in this area.

Is this adequate and sufficient regulation? There is evidence that young people are locked up needlessly, that is, not as a last resort (Travis, 1995), because suitable open accommodation is not available, and that units contain an inappropriate mix of children and young people. Levy and Kahan (1991) recommend that the law regarding the control and discipline of children in residential establishments be amended so that definitions of circumstances which amount to the restriction of children's liberty appear in law rather than being left to circulars and guidance. There can be no certainty that safeguards against ill-treatment, such as inspections of children's homes and prohibitions on types of punishment (DoH, 1991i), are now adequate (Hatchett, 1991) or that staff supervision, reviews and complaints procedures will enable children to complain about ill-treatment, or will enable practitioners to implement the spirit of the legislation. Attitudes to partnership will, therefore, be crucial since it is here that the imbalance of power between workers and users must be confronted.

Planning

Section 46 (NHSCCA 1990) requires local authorities to prepare, publish and review community care plans. This includes a duty to consult with district health authorities, family health service authorities, housing authorities and voluntary organisations. Guidance (DoH, 1990) has established that these plans should ensure that the needs of black and minority ethnic communities are included in the consultation process. Plans should cover a three-year period, annually reviewed and updated. They should detail how individual needs will be assessed, how needs will be incorporated into planning processes, and what the care needs of the local population are. Services and objectives should be detailed in relation to older people, disabled people, mental illness, domestic violence, HIV/Aids, with statements concerning how needs and services will be prioritised, and what practical help will be provided for carers. Plans should refer to:

1. quality: how this will be monitored and ensured, and the arrangements for inspection and complaints;
2. consumer choice: how this will be managed and what it will involve with various groups and agencies;
3. publicity: how information about services will be made known to potential users;
4. resources: the implications in terms of budgets, training and personnel;
5. future planning: how information from assessments and from community profiling will be gathered and analysed.

Voluntary agencies and the independent sector have complained about the degrees of involvement offered to them by local authorities. Accordingly, guidance (LAC(93)4) requires that the independent sector is fully involved in consultation processes during preparation and review of community care plans. The same is required for voluntary organisations representing users and carers. Basic principles of consultation are outlined (DoH, 1992a), including consultation on proposals rather than decisions, giving a reasonable time for responses, finding ways to meet different perspectives (purchasers – mapping; providers – local authority intentions on contracts), and taking all views into consideration.

Community care planning has been made more difficult by the absence of long-term information on budgets, unclear Department of Health priorities, a reorganisation of local government boundaries, and the failure to dovetail publication dates for the plans with budget cycles. Another problem remains tight financial budgets and the attendant legal implications of recording unmet need for individuals. The experience of multidisciplinary collaboration has been variable, and plans have been criticised for their failure to address performance evaluation and review (Wistow *et al.*, 1993). The Department of Health (DoH, 1993a) has found a widespread need to improve management and financial information and review systems, on which accurate monitoring of effectiveness in meeting needs has to be based. This has been reported again by Henwood and Wistow (1995). The Department of Health has also recognised that consultation does not necessarily equate with involvement (DoH, 1993b). It found that, despite progress in joint planning between agencies, not all groups were regularly covered, a finding mirrored by Bewley and Glendinning (1994) and Lovelock *et al.* (1995) in respect of deaf people, learning-disabled people, minority ethnic groups, and people with sensory impairment. Community care plans appeared to have little positive impact in helping these groups to access assessment and services. Links between consultation and decision-making on resource allocation were unclear, and community mapping or profiling of need was unsophisticated. Put another way, there is limited systematic alignment of needs and resources.

Research has found wide variations between local authorities on community care plans for learning-disabled people, with consequent doubts about the adequacy of plans as monitoring and planning documents (Turner, 1995). Concerns here include the absence of measures and statistics, and a failure to incorporate the needs of minority groups. This is despite guidance on social care for adults with learning disabilities (LAC(92)15) which lists the supports which learning-disabled people might need and advises that services should be planned on an individualised basis, not stereotypical notions and predetermined services. It requires the involvement of other sectors to meet people's housing, education and health needs, and of user and carer groups to ensure that learning-disabled people receive appropriate support and opportunities to promote their personal development. The evidence would suggest that planning is some way from equating services to needs, and from defining objectives in terms of outcomes for users which enable them to perform an effective planning and monitoring role.

A similar planning structure has now been established for children's services. Initially optional (LAC(92)18), children's services plans are now mandatory (the Children Act 1989 (Amendment) (Children's Services Planning) Order 1996). As in community care they should be strategic and collaborative, agreed between local, health and education authorities, inter-agency working documents with clearly agreed definitions of need, levels of local need, long-term aims to meet need, priorities and monitoring mechanisms. However, no format has been specified for the plans, resulting in variations surrounding, for example, the inclusion of targets, needs assessment, financial information, inter-agency plans, and identified service priorities linked to resources (SSI, 1994c). Consultation with minority ethnic groups has proved variable, and difficulties establishing joint registers between health authorities, education departments and social services departments have restricted their usefulness for planning in respect of disabled children (AMA, 1994). Most authorities are reported as being unclear concerning who these plans are for (SSI, 1995b). Mapping of needs is variable. Few plans adequately address implementation and are considered too vague to be useful.

Other worrying findings in respect of planning come from other reports, namely:

1. inadequate incorporation of residential child care services within a strategic approach to children's services overall (SSI, 1993a);
2. ineffective registers of disabled children, with consequent unreliable planning information (SSI, 1994a) and an inability to judge the range and levels of services required;
3. reviews of day care and childminding provision (section 19, CA 1989) have helped to develop inter-agency co-operation but further analysis is required of services for children in need and for minority ethnic group children (Trinder, 1993). Planning is descriptive rather than analytical.

This does not augur well for inter-agency collaboration on meeting the housing and social care needs of care-leavers and homeless families, where the potential for buck-passing has drawn judicial criticism (*R* v. *Northavon DC, ex parte Smith* [1994]), or for meeting the Audit Commission's recommendation (1994) that local authorities should broaden their remit whilst health authorities target their services more closely.

Evidence suggests that users and carers have a valuable role in pinpointing problems and potential solutions, and in contributing through collaboration to improvements in planning and service delivery (Buckley *et al.*, 1995; Goss and Miller, 1995). Partnership research (Everitt *et al.*, 1992; Whitaker and Archer, 1994) has potential here for organisations committed to making it possible to engage with and respond to the judgements of users and carers.

Partnership with service users

Increasingly user involvement has become a feature of social work practice: open records, attendance at case conferences and reviews, participation in decision-making, and access to complaints procedures. Besides serving as a check on the way practitioners use authority, this development is based on the centrality to effective and ethical practice of:

1. honesty and openness;
2. providing information and checking understanding;
3. developing and retaining clarity of purpose by clarifying expectations, defining and agreeing problem areas and tasks, and reviewing work regularly;
4. taking users' comments seriously, openly acknowledging differences;
5. identifying and promoting users' strengths and skills;
6. mobilising the active support of significant others; and
7. using contracts or working agreements.

In this development the law has been tardily responsive rather than pace-setting. It does not embrace fully the concept of partnership, discriminating between different user groups regarding the degree of partnership it will underscore. The power imbalance between providers and users remains largely weighted in favour of service providers. Whilst users and their carers are given certain rights, ideologies of economy and paternalism remain highly influential (Braye and Preston-Shoot, 1992, 1994).

The Mental Health Act Code of Practice (DoH, 1993c) promotes the involvement, as far as possible, of patients in the formulation and delivery of care and treatment. It requires Approved Social Workers to provide reasons for their decisions, and to discuss and take into account, in so far as urgency allows, the views of relatives and friends. Guardianship is seen as requiring both parties to be willing to work together. Patients should be given, orally and in writing, as much information as possible about their care and treatment, and about their rights (section 132, MHA 1983). Questions should be answered openly and honestly, with checks made to ensure understanding of the information given. The information given should be clearly recorded.

Guidance on the discharge of mentally disordered patients (LASSL(94)4) urges that assessing potentially violent patients requires information about a person's background, mental state and social functioning, from the person concerned and from their relatives/carers. This is responding to a criticism (Ritchie *et al.*, 1994) that family members or carers are overlooked as providers of information.

However, the experiences of survivors of the psychiatric system are such as to question whether these principles of partnership are enacted and sufficient to protect people's rights. To what extent do mental health practitioners promote advocacy and self-advocacy, and address in their practice the imbalance of power between providers and users, and different understandings of mental ill-health? How is the care and skill of practitioners monitored when they are seeking consent to treatment or conveying information? How are attitudes monitored towards those who exercise their right of non-consent to treatment or to a hearing before a Mental Health Review Tribunal?

Sections 1–3 and 4b, Disabled Persons Act 1986, would have given disabled people, including mentally disordered people, the right to appoint representatives to assist them in dealing with local authorities, and requesting and receiving an assessment of their need for services. Procedures would have allowed for the appointment of representatives to be made when individuals, because of mental or physical incapacity, were unable to do so themselves. These sections have not been implemented. The provisions would not have extended to health authorities. They are not included in the NHS and Community Care Act 1990. Potentially empowering legislation remains dormant.

Moreover, whilst local authorities have a duty to consider the needs of disabled people for services under section 2, Chronically Sick and Disabled Persons Act 1970, when requested by a disabled person or their carer (section 4, DPA 1986), and to meet an established need for welfare services, in respect of other people who may need community care services local authorities control the decision whether to assess (section 47, NHSCCA 1990).

Perhaps more positively, the Community Care (Direct Payments) Act 1996 will allow people to purchase their own care. However, this right will be limited. The local authority may exercise its discretion here – there is no duty to provide such payments. The Secretary of State may issue regulations limiting the groups to whom the Act applies, and concerns exist that these might exclude those who can live independently in the community with support and who can make constructive choices about care plans if offered appropriate information, such as learning-disabled people and older people. There are concerns that the levels of direct payments will be insufficient to meet the full costs of community care services.

A key to effective partnership is the provision of information. Another is user involvement in policy deliberations. The Disabled Persons Act 1986 includes a duty on local authorities to provide information about services and to consult organisations *of* disabled people before cooptions to committees. There is, however, no duty to coopt. Section 46 (NHSCCA 1990) requires consultation regarding, and publicity of, community care plans. Implementation has been patchy and the intentions underpinning the Acts have not been translated into action: assessments have often been made on the basis of what is available rather than what is needed; users and carers have been insufficiently involved; little has been done to provide information relevant to needs in suitable formats (SSI, 1990b; Warburton, 1990; SSI, 1993c). Whilst there is some evidence of user involvement in planning, there remains a dearth of appropriate, user-friendly and culturally sensitive information about community care policies and service options, and a need for new ways to involve groups who usually do not participate. There is widespread evidence of marginalisation: older people and disabled people are excluded from participation in shaping community care and housing services (Laurie and Macfarlane, 1995; Thornton and Tozer, 1995); information is not available in appropriate forms, despite section 9 (DPA 1986); people are not well-informed about what to expect, about charges, and about how services are organised; people express scepticism about the likely impact of expressed views (DoH, 1993d; Baldock and Ungerson, 1994; Day, 1994; Buckley *et al.*, 1995). The Chief Inspector of the Social Services Inspectorate (SSI, 1995a) has noted that comments from users are not positive about how they have been consulted.

Social workers are more likely to be satisfied with the information they provide than are users and carers with the information they receive, both verbal and written. Users and carers are concerned both with the quantity of information provided and with how it is given. Assessment and decision-making is a process over time. Information-giving may be required not just at the outset therefore. It may need to be repeated, with social workers developing skills in exploring how information has been heard and retained (Buckley *et al.*, 1995).

The quality and effectiveness of services improve when users and carers work in partnership with managers, where there is good two-way communication, and when users and carers help to design and lead the consultation process. Local authorities can facilitate this involvement by, for instance, the provision of training and transport (Goss and Miller, 1995).

The NHS and Community Care Act 1990, and government guidance about it (DoH, 1989c, 1990), demonstrate most clearly equivocal attitudes towards partnership. A written statement of the outcome of an assessment should be provided if a continuing service is to be offered (DoH, 1990). Where agreement between the parties is not possible, points of difference should be recorded. Written statements should always be provided on request. The ultimate responsibility for defining need, however, rests with the assessing professional and it is their assessment which should be recorded (DoH, 1991m). Care plans should be put in writing when assessment is followed by service provision. This plan should contain statements of objectives, criteria for evaluation of their achievement, services to be provided and by whom, the cost to the user, other options considered, differences of opinion, unmet needs with reasons, location of responsibility for monitoring and review, and the date of the first review. The care plan does not have legal standing but contributors may be asked to signify their agreement by signing, to reinforce commitment to the plan. Reviews should also be recorded.

Assessment is then participative. Users and carers must be involved, and should feel that assessment and care management processes are aimed at meeting their wishes, with services tailored to meet assessed needs. However assessment is not user-led. Rather the objective is to determine the *best available* way to meet needs. Assessment must take account of the local authority's criteria for determining when services should be provided and the types of service *they* have decided to make available. Consequently choice, a feature of the policy, is compromised by the local authority's responsibility to meet needs *within available resources*. Even where choice appears endorsed, for instance in respect of residential care (LAC(92)27), this is only where the local authority deems a person's choice to be suitable in relation to assessed needs, and where it would not cost the authority more than they would usually expect to pay. Given that the local authority remains the only major source of provision and the gatekeeper to other provision by dint of holding the purse strings and being responsible for assessment, the power of users is severely limited.

Research findings (Robbins, 1993; SSI, 1993c; Lamb and Layzell, 1995; Warner, 1995) indicate limited choice, ignored preferences and unmet needs arising from inadequate services 'forced' on people. Users and carers report that assessment is subordinated to agency policy needs and procedures, with evidence that block contracts are producing a set list of services where choice becomes secondary to concerns about resource constraints (Day, 1994; Hoyes *et al.*, 1994). They do not appear to be routinely involved in assessment and review meetings (DoH, 1993b; SSI, 1993f; DoH, 1993a), in receiving information and copies of care plans, or in sharing recording. Attempts vary in relation to obtaining views from service users with communication difficulties (Ellis, 1993; Day, 1994; Hoyes *et al.*, 1994), whilst some users and carers appear unaware that they have been assessed and/or why services have been offered (Baldock and Ungerson, 1994). The picture is not entirely negative, with some users and carers reporting satisfaction with services and with sensitive and thorough assessments (Buckley *et al.*, 1995; Lamb and Layzell, 1995; Warner, 1995). However, criticisms continue of a lack of understanding of cultural issues, contact only at times of crisis, neglect of stress and emotional issues, and a failure to consider carers' needs. Furthermore redress through judicial review is only possible where a local authority has acted irrationally or illegally in response to specific needs. However, some local authorities have had judicial review against them for failing to consult and/or to involve users and carers in assessments and reviews (*R* v. *North Yorkshire County Council, ex parte Hargreaves* [1994]; *R* v. *Gloucestershire County Council, ex parte Mahfood and Others* [1995]). Rather than partnership, what exists at best is participation in a pre-set agenda. Much is dependent, therefore, on attitudes and approaches adopted by service providers. These values and skills in practising social work law are discussed in Chapter 7.

The Children Act 1989 and accompanying regulatory guidance, in attempting to reconcile the conflicting imperatives of state intervention and the rights of children and of parents, have brought partnership and written agreements in social work to centre stage. In child protection (DoH, 1988) and day care (DoH, 1991b) social workers must involve parents as fully as possible because this working partnership 'is usually the most effective means of providing supplementary or substitute care for children' (DoH, 1989a). It improves the quality of information and the realism of assessments and treatment plans (Bell, 1993; DoH, 1995b). Sharing decisions with parents is likely to reduce their scapegoating of the agency, lessen feelings of powerlessness, and maximise the potential for cooperation. Cornerstones of partnership, endorsed in the Act, are the provision of information (Schedule 2,1(2)), consultation (sections 22, 61 and 64), reviews of services (sections 19 and 26), access to complaints procedures (section 26) and advocacy by representatives (section 41(2); Schedule 2(17)). No notice is required from parents prior to removing children from accommodation. Rather there is informed participation, encapsulated in written contracts, based on clear understanding of the powers, duties and roles of agencies, the legal rights of parents and children and, where possible, negotiation and agreement.

Due consideration must be given, after consultation, to the wishes and feelings of children, parents and relevant other people who may or may not have parental responsibility. Written agreements with parents are required regarding children accommodated by the local authority or children in care and placed with parents (DoH, 1991a). These agreements include the purpose of the placement, contact arrangements, any delegation of parental responsibility to the local authority regarding children being accommodated, and plans for the children. They must specify review dates and the services to be provided by the local authority. Contingency plans in the event of placement breakdown should be clarified. The agreements are concerned with identifying children's needs, how these will be met, and by whom. In situations where children are in care, arrangements should be made with parental agreement where possible. In situations where children are accommodated, that is, looked after but not in care, the arrangements detailed in the written agreement and plan must be agreed between the local authority and a person with parental responsibility, or the young person if aged 16 or 17 (Arrangements for the Placement of Children (General) Regulations 1991). Placement agreements are also required with foster parents covering care for the child, contact with parents and the local authority, and circumstances in which the child could be removed (Foster Placement (Children) Regulations 1991; DoH, 1991a). Foster carers must also be provided with any information necessary to enable them to care for the child. In providing a framework for and detailing the substance of the work, these written agreements mirror contracts in social work practice (Corden and Preston-Shoot, 1987; Aldgate, 1989). Rights, goals, responsibilities and expectations are clarified, challenging thereby any notion that failure is always the user's fault.

The partnership approach extends to making reasonable efforts, prior to applying for a child assessment order, to secure parental cooperation and to involve parents fully in decisions about the process the assessment will take once an order is made. It extends to children in care as a result of a court order, with social workers required to consult and notify parents about decisions affecting children, to promote contact where appropriate to a child's welfare, and to work with parents to secure a safe return home or a satisfactory alternative placement (DoH, 1991a). It extends to the child protection process (DoH, 1995b) where local authority practice should be characterised by openness and honesty regarding concerns, roles and planning, negotiation where possible and allowed by the legal mandate, and parental involvement throughout – preparation for conferences and meetings, preparing a child for placement.

Several critical points arise concerning partnership and how the balance between autonomy and state intervention has been codified. In weighing the duty to safeguard and promote a child's welfare against partnership, there exists no guidance on how to determine whether provision of accommodation by agreement with parents is sufficient to safeguard the child's welfare if that child is suffering or is likely to suffer significant harm (DoH, 1991b), nor any safeguards for local authorities and children under 16 if parents wish to remove children from accommodation. Voluntary contingency plans in placement agreements will not be binding, although agreements could be used as evidence in legal proceedings subsequently. Furthermore it remains unclear how authorities, or foster carers, may use section 3(5) to do what is reasonable to safeguard or promote the child's welfare. Thus practitioners may have to use emergency protection orders to 'buy time' to safeguard the child's welfare.

Research findings suggest that children are sceptical about, and not routinely offered, involvement in decision-making. Parents may also find themselves encouraged to accept responsibility for young people they cannot control (Cloke and Davies, 1995; Colton *et al.*, 1995). Not all authorities are using comprehensive child-care plans and parents may feel that they have little information or control over procedures or proposed arrangements. Not all situations facilitate participation and social workers can experience difficulties in being participatory in their practice (DoH, 1995a). This should not surprise since partnership is often offered against a background of legal proceedings which can appear adversarial (King and Trowell, 1992).

The Children Act 1989 also assumes that people will be reasonable in relation to children in care. Local authorities and parents may act independently, the former only able to limit the latter's exercise of parental responsibility when necessary to safeguard and promote a child's welfare. Such cooperation will not always be possible. Social workers must record these cases fully, indicating in particular why collaboration proved impossible and how an order might improve it (Adcock *et al.*, 1991). Nor does regulatory guidance assist greatly when the views of children under 16 and parents conflict. The child's views do not have primacy and are not determinative. If a child requests to be accommodated and a parent objects, only a court order will settle the dispute.

The duty to give 'due consideration' to the wishes of children and parents may be interpreted broadly or restrictively. Authorities need not implement their wishes. Nor are they guided on the relative importance to attach to their respective views, other than that a child's age and understanding will affect the weight given to what the child says and wishes (Bainham, 1990). Indeed, law and practice reflect an ambivalent attitude towards partnership with children. The Mental Health Act 1983 Code of Practice (DoH, 1993c) recommends that young people should be kept fully informed about their care and treatment, their views should be taken fully into account, and they should be regarded generally as having the right to make their own decisions when they have sufficient understanding. Any intervention should be the least restrictive possible. Children can make an application in family proceedings, although they sometimes require leave to do so. They may refuse medical assessments and examinations as part of child assessment orders, emergency protection orders and interim care orders (sections 38(6), 43(8), 44(7), CA 1989) and may refuse medical and psychiatric treatment when on supervision (Schedule 3, CA 1989). However, cases (*Re R (A Minor) (Wardship: Consent to Treatment)* [1991]; *Re W (A Minor) (Medical Treatment: Court's Jurisdiction)* [1992]) have eroded many of the gains derived from these sections and the Gillick judgement. The Children Act 1989 requires a court to listen to and consider a child's views, but the court's view of best interests decides (*Re P (Minors)* [1992]). However, a young person with special educational needs cannot appeal to a Special Educational Needs Tribunal against a decision of the local education authority (*S* v. *Special Educational Needs Tribunal and the City of Westminster* [1996]). Only a parent has standing here.

There remains no right of attendance for children and parents at case conferences, nor any guidance on what chairs of conferences should consider, beyond a clear conflict of interests (DoH, 1991a) or continued hostility, persistent denial of abuse, or severe illness (DoH, 1995b), in determining whether parental attendance will preclude proper consideration of the child's interests, and whether children are old enough to participate (DoH, 1991e).

Many young people do not feel listened to (Clark, 1993). The opportunity to influence decisions is very important, but even where law and policy promote involvement, for instance in relation to disabled children, local authorities are missing standards (SSI, 1994a).

Once again attitudes and skills are central to practising social work law: respecting and building on the competency of children;

empowering users to ensure that services to children in need are informed by their views; working to overcome power imbalances by addressing the effects of previous experiences of welfare services, implementing anti-oppressive strategies and constructing accessible representations and complaints procedures. In particular, where anxiety to control outcomes is high, and where defensive practice could subvert partnership, social workers must guard against agreements becoming institutionalised coercion: hurdles for users to jump to obtain services rather than tools of negotiation and empowerment. Sharing information and, especially, critical opinions with parents may not be easy but, arguably, practice is often a long way from a reciprocal and emancipatory approach which acknowledges users' views as legitimate (Bell, 1993).

Partnership with professionals

Multidisciplinary practice is a key feature in mental health work. The Mental Health Act 1983 implies that the doctor's role is to determine care and treatment; the Approved Social Worker's role is to decide the best way of providing it (Hoggett, 1990). The Code of Practice (DoH, 1993c) pinpoints the need for good working relationships based on knowledge and understanding of roles and responsibilities, and agreement on how these can best be discharged. It outlines specific responsibilities of doctors and Approved Social Workers, and offers advice for resolving disagreements – consulting colleagues, exploring alternatives and positively reframing disputes as opportunities to safeguard patients' interests.

The NHS Act 1977 requires health authorities and social services departments to cooperate in exercising their respective functions (section 22) and requires health authorities to provide, so far as is reasonable, practical and necessary, services to enable local authorities to fulfil their functions (section 26(3)). Section 46, NHS and Community Care Act 1990 requires local authorities to consult with a range of organisations when formulating and reviewing community care plans. The roles and responsibilities of social services departments and health authorities have been delineated (DoH, 1989c, 1990a).

Initial guidance did not address the factors which can impede interprofessional collaboration and the Department of Health

(DoH, 1993a) has found it necessary to prioritise improvements in this area, especially with housing departments. Continuing organisational change is militating against effective collaboration (DoH, 1993b) and the emphasis on a seamless service has yet to address the obstacles which have traditionally undermined collaboration and a focus on the multidisciplinary needs of the individual: fragmentation of responsibility, non-coterminosity of boundaries, differences in planning cycles and horizons, differences on confidentiality, differing status and levels of knowledge, financial arrangements, lack of role clarity, overlap of functions, stereotyping, suspicion and competitiveness, and attitudinal and value differences (Robbins, 1993; Braye and Preston-Shoot, 1995). These obstacles have surfaced in relation to continuing care, despite a clarificatory circular on the responsibilities of health and local authorities (LAC(95)5, see Chapter 5). They remain in the relationship between Care Management and the Care Programme Approach. LAC(95)4, in discussing the Mental Illness Specific Grant arrangements, requires health and local authorities to submit a statement of intent regarding a joint protocol covering the relationship between the Care Programme Approach and Care Management, with agreed arrangements for following up severely mentally ill people who drop out of services. LASSL(94)4, guidance on the discharge of mentally disordered people and their continuing care in the community, calls for proper coordination of the two approaches and for systematic recording and arrangements for communication between professionals. It emphasises continuity of care in an effort to overcome poor service coordination (inadequate diagnosis, assessment, discharge arrangements and services) which was a major factor in the breakdown of care for Christopher Clunis (Ritchie *et al.*, 1994). Contact points, knowledge of each other's roles, contingency arrangements and needs-led assessments should be clearly understood. However, implementation of the Care Programme Approach remains patchy and further guidance (LASSL(95)12) on arrangements for inter-agency work for the care and protection of severely mentally ill people fails to clarify the relationship between the two approaches. The boundary between health and social care remains problematic, with users and carers reporting poor interprofessional communication and collaboration (Lamb and Layzell, 1995). The underlying causes cannot be managed locally (Henwood and Wistow, 1995). They require structural change which only central government can initiate.

The Disabled Persons Act 1986 and the Education Act 1993 require an inter-agency approach to services for young people with disabilities. The track record of multi-agency collaboration is unimpressive. The SSI (1990b) reported that a substantial amount of further work was required if sections 5 and 6, Disabled Persons Act 1986 and the statementing process (Education Act 1993) were to be implemented satisfactorily. The evidence is of *ad hoc* joint planning, limited knowledge of the roles of the different agencies involved, and limited consultation between education authorities, health authorities and social services departments. The slow progress has continued, with a survey of services to disabled children reporting no evidence of effective coordination of assessment (SSI, 1994a).

The fragile nature of inter-agency collaboration has been most obvious in child protection. Teamwork is crucial for the protection and well-being of children (DoH, 1988) and fundamental to the implementation of duties in the Children Act 1989 in respect of young people leaving care (section 24), children in need (section 17) and day care (section 18). Sections 27, 28 and 30 provide duties and powers involving cooperation between social services departments, education, housing, health and independent authorities (DoH, 1991b). Whilst a coordinated approach to policy-making and service delivery is required, collaborative working arrangements have been undermined by divergent ideologies or priorities, separate training, blurred roles and responsibilities, financial constraints, competitiveness and different views on approaches to cases. Accordingly reports regularly highlight deficiencies (DHSS, 1982; Butler-Sloss, 1988; SSI, 1990a), for example in inter-agency work post-protection plans, and in cooperation between police and social workers in respect of video records of children's evidence (SSI, 1994b; DoH, 1995a). This suggests again that law and guidance are insufficient to achieve role clarity and relationships which foster professional understanding and use of expertise. This message is reinforced in a critical evaluation of inquiry reports (Reder *et al.*, 1993) which documents the need to understand and monitor relational processes in interprofessional contacts if polarisation, exaggeration of hierarchy, isolation, and closed systems are to be avoided.

Concern about inter-agency collaboration has resulted in revisions to *Working Together* (DoH, 1991e), guidance which will now be regulatory. It is designed to promote multidisciplinary teamwork with a shared understanding of aims and good practice, and with an ability to act decisively when necessary. It requires social workers, when undertaking child protection investigations (sections 37 and 47, CA 1989), to gather information from key professionals, to liaise and act in collaboration with other agencies to protect children. In decision-making in respect of children being looked after by the local authority, social workers must seek the views of relevant people (section 22(4)(d)). Staff of other agencies must recognise their responsibilities to keep the local authority fully and immediately informed of all matters relating to children's welfare. The document calls for a full commitment to inter-agency participation to support social services departments. Local education authorities are to promote the understanding and involvement of their staff. Police and social workers must establish methods of joint working concerning consultation, pursuing enquiries, obtaining court orders and removing children. Besides prescribing daily work practices, Area Child Protection Committees are to develop and subsequently review the operation of policies and procedures. Finally joint training is recommended to promote good working relationships and understanding of roles.

However the document does not consider reasons for past difficulties in inter-agency cooperation. Moreover the Children Act only provides a power, not a duty on social services departments to seek assistance, with other authorities under a duty to comply only if it does not unduly prejudice the discharge of their functions (section 27) or if it is not unreasonable in the circumstances of the case to assist (section 47). There is, therefore, no duty to cooperate. Arguably partnership between professionals requires more than a reinstatement of previous guidance. Some prerequisite knowledge, attitudes and skills are considered in Chapter 7 (see also Braye and Preston-Shoot, 1995, Chapter 7).

Confidentiality

Confidentiality is where the tension between partnership and protective duties is particularly prominent. Confidentiality is a traditional social work value (Horne, 1987). However the public interest, or the rights of one individual, do sometimes require that confidentiality between a practitioner and another individual is not preserved. These different interests must be weighed in each case, an exercise which presents moral and practical dilemmas. Too tight an adherence to confidentiality can place users at risk; too loose and there emerge risks of labelling and injustice.

Professional codes of confidentiality allow disclosure when there is a risk of danger to others (DoH, 1988). In cases of abuse social workers must share information. Good practice also suggests that facts must be distinguished from opinion or hearsay, that information should be checked for accuracy and openly shared with service users, and that practitioners should openly declare their duties and responsibilities.

The law recognises that a strong public interest in disclosure may override a professional's duty to maintain confidentiality (LAC(88)17; *W* v. *Egdell* [1989]). Thus, statements made in mediation sessions should not be given in evidence in family law proceedings except in highly unusual cases where a statement clearly indicates that the maker had caused or was likely to cause serious harm to a child, and only then when the public interest in protecting the child's interests outweighed the public interest in preserving confidentiality (*Re D (Minors)* [1993]). Where children have both the capacity to consent to treatment and to enter into a confidential relationship, then, as with adults, the obligation of confidentiality is not total if disclosure in the child's best interests is compelling on the grounds of serious risk or harm (*Re C (A Minor) (Evidence: Confidential Information)* [1991]; *Re W (A Minor) (Medical Treatment)* [1992]).

Professionals are entitled to breach confidences when, otherwise, a real risk of danger to the public exists. In respect of the discharge of mentally disordered people and their continuing care in the community (LASSL(94)4), the disclosure of NHS-held information to social workers and others should only occur where the patient has 'expressed or implied consent, or where disclosure can be justified as being in the public interest'. In assessing potentially violent patients, the level of risk can only be ascertained, and appropriate services provided, if all relevant information is available, including a person's background, social functioning, mental health, and past behaviour. Regulatory guidance on interdisciplinary cooperation in child protection (DoH, 1991e) states that confidentiality is not intended to prevent the exchange of information, and requires that information received by professionals from colleagues is treated confidentially. However the guidance does not address the quoted and contradictory advice given to doctors, social workers, and health visitors by their professional associations. All three recognise that the public interest may require disclosure. Advice given to doctors and social workers appears unequivocal – a duty to disclose when there is reason to believe that a person is being abused or neglected, or that there is serious danger. More equivocal advice is given by the United Kingdom Central Council for Nursing, Midwifery and Health Visiting. This reflects uncertainty more widely about the duty to cooperate, evidenced most critically in child protection inquiries where failure to disclose or ask for information has been crucial in distorting assessment and decision-making (Goodman Report, 1990; Bridge Child Care Consultancy, 1991). It must remain doubtful, therefore, whether regulatory guidance alone is sufficient to overcome professional reluctance to cooperate.

Workers may disclose information to the police if (a) it can help prevent, detect or prosecute serious crime; (b) the crime is sufficiently serious for the public interest to prevail; (c) without disclosure, the task of preventing or detecting the crime would be seriously prejudiced or delayed; or (d) a senior police officer requests the information, and undertakes not to use the information for other purposes and to destroy it if the person is not prosecuted or is discharged or acquitted (LAC (88)17). Serious crime includes death, serious injury and substantial financial gain or loss (section 116, PACE 1984). Similarly, on medical advice, it may be necessary to disclose health information to prevent serious risk to the public.

Not infrequently social workers must consider whether to respect the confidences of children. Children's rights under the Children Act, for example to seek leave to apply for a section 8 order or for the discharge of a parental responsibility order, are not restricted by specific age limits but rather by concepts of maturity, welfare and sufficient understanding. Mature children have a right to seek independent advice and expect confidentiality (except in the circumstances discussed earlier). Immaturity in some areas does not remove all rights to independent action when seeking advice and counselling. However it remains unclear how far the Gillick judgement may be applied to children seeking psychological counselling or advice (*Childright*, 1989b). Exceptional circumstances would justify giving advice or treatment to immature children without parental consent. Good practice requires practitioners to discuss with the child parental involvement, to provide information in a manner they can understand, and to assess how far the child understands the advice given, appreciates its implications and significance, and comprehends the implications of the help sought. Also relevant is whether the practitioner believes that it is in the child's best interests to receive the advice or treatment. It is matter of judgement on which courts may sometimes have to rule.

Social workers can be compelled to give evidence and cannot, therefore, guarantee confidentiality except as to the identity of informants (*D* v. *NSPCC* [1978]). Guardians *ad litem* should not promise complete confidentiality since it is for the courts to determine what is disclosed to any or all of the parties (*Re D (Minors)* [1994]). The confidentiality of what a person says to a guardian *ad litem* is that of the court. The court's permission is required, therefore, before information is disclosed to any person or agency not a party to the proceedings (*Oxfordshire CC* v. *P* [1995]).

On whether parties to a dispute should disclose documents, whether or not they intend to rely on them in legal proceedings, it has now been held that professional privilege has to yield to the paramount interests of the child (*Oxfordshire CC* v. *M* [1993]) since to determine a child's welfare requires that reports are disclosed, irrespective of whether these contain unfair statements relating to a party. Those seeking disclosure of documents must show why they should be produced. The court will balance the public interest in protecting (social work) records against the public interest that parties should obtain information in order to secure legal redress (*Re M (Social Work Records: Disclosure)* [1990]). It remains possible for courts to authorise that the evidence of one party, and reports, are not to be disclosed to another party if there are exceptional circumstances relating to the welfare of the child that outweigh the normal requirements of a fair trial (*Re B (A Minor) (Disclosure of Evidence)* [1993]). A local authority must disclose documents to other parties in care proceedings, whether or not the documents support its case. The presumption is one of disclosure. Where a local authority believes that public interest immunity should apply, it should inform the other parties and apply to the court for permission to withhold a document (*Re C (CA 1989: Expert Evidence)* [1995]). The same strong presumption in favour of disclosure to a party of material relating to them applies to adoption (*Re D and Another (Minors) (Adoption Reports: Confidentiality)* [1995]). Again, the welfare of the child may justify use by a court of discretion not to disclose but a court must consider the degree of likelihood that harm will occur and the gravity if it does. Both likelihood and seriousness are required for refusal to disclose.

Access to information

This is one expression of partnership and accountability. The law has been slower than social work practice to endorse the rights to know (access) and to involvement (shared recording). Once again the legislation can be implemented passively or actively. Local authorities have a duty to publicise information about the services they offer (DPA 1986; CA 1989; NHSCCA 1990). The information should be accessible (language, location) to all potential users. It should be straightforward, relevant, accurate, and sufficient to enable people to make informed choices (DoH, 1991g), providing information on services, eligibility criteria, costs and timescales. However, inspections and research studies have been critical of performance here. Disabled children and their families have received very little information and of what was available little was translated appropriately (SSI, 1994a). Children and young people rarely receive information on their rights (Cloke and Davies, 1995). Community care service users report inadequate information about complaints procedures, available options across service sectors, and financial assessments (Buckley *et al.*, 1995).

Access to records is governed by the Data Protection Act 1984; Access to Personal Files Act 1987; Access to Personal Files (Social Services) Regulations 1989; five local authority circulars which are regulatory guidance – LAC (83)14, Personal Social Services Records – Disclosure of Information to Clients; LAC (87)10, on an individual's right of access to personal information held on computerised records; LAC (88)17, Personal Social Services: Confidentiality of Personal Information; LAC (89)2 and LAC(91)11, Access to Personal Files (Social Services) Amendment Regulations.

Subject to certain safeguards and exceptions, individuals may see what is written about them, although this is not obligatory concerning records made prior to April 1989. This includes children where the authority is satisfied they understand the nature of their request, at interview, or someone with parental responsibility approves. It includes parents on behalf of children where the authority is satisfied they have authorised parents to apply or where a child is unable to make a valid application, unless there are grounds to believe they would not consent to access.

Social services departments must have an access procedure, although there is no duty to publicise it actively or widely. Having received a written request and, if required, a fee, departments must inform applicants within 40 days as to what information is held, and provide access and copies when requested. Applicants can request amendment of recorded information which they regard as inaccurate. If a department disagrees, a notice must be attached to the record which specifies that disputed part. A copy of this notice must be given to the applicant. Departments must establish an appeals procedure to consider grievances concerning access to or amendment of information. Applicants may request a review within 28 days of receiving notification of the authority's decision. The review committee comprises three members, only one of whom should be from the social services committee.

Exceptions to access are:

1. adoption information;
2. some reports to court;
3. information held for purposes of crime prevention or detection, or the prosecution of offenders, and where disclosure possibly would prejudice such matters;
4. information which would reveal the identity of another person to whom the information partly relates or a source of that information, with that individual refusing to consent to the disclosure on written request from the local authority; this does not apply to social services employees or to those providing services to enable the authority to exercise its functions; moreover the information can be supplied in ways in which the identity cannot be discerned;
5. information which would cause serious harm to the physical or mental health of the applicant; the criteria for deciding serious harm are not specified other than that it should be serious and exceptional;
6. where disclosure would possibly prejudice the functions of the department, including any case for legal proceedings.

Where access would involve personal physical or mental health information given by health professionals, the authority must not disclose this information if the relevant professional, having been contacted within 14 days of the application, states that the information must not be disclosed because of the likelihood of serious harm to the physical or mental health of the applicant or another person, or of revealing the identity of another person, whether the source or someone to whom the information partly relates.

Parallel legislation exists in respect of health records made after November 1991 (Access to Health Records Act 1991). Again there are exceptions: where the applicant is deemed unable to understand the information; where the information is likely to cause serious harm to health; and/or where the information is about a third party. In *R* v. *Mid Glamorgan FHS, ex parte Martin* [1994] a health authority was ruled as entitled to withhold access because disclosure would be detrimental to a patient's health. However, there has not yet been a judicial definition of what constitutes serious harm to the physical or mental health of the applicant or another (Dimond, 1995).

Courts, Mental Health Review Tribunals, the Commission for Local Administration, and Registered Homes Tribunals can all order disclosure of records to them. Consent of third parties is not required here but they should be informed. Guardians *ad litem* have statutory rights of access to information relating to the children in question (section 42(1), CA 1989; *Manchester City Council* v. *T and Another* [1993]). Parents may seek access to a child's records if the child is not competent to make an application and access is in the child's best interests, or if the child is competent and consents.

For access to be effective, information must be accessible in terms of structure, language and style. Users and practitioners should be clear what is to be recorded, how, and why. Each should participate in compiling records, including assessments, reviews and closing summaries. Records should contain the process of decision-making, observed or verified facts. Opinions, when stated, should be clearly identified, with evidence for them.

Gathering information/evidence

Obtaining evidence is a key task if social workers are to be competent in using the law, but there are several problems here, especially in the law's expectations of social work and concerns about unreliable evidence. First, social workers believe that their practice and evidence are held in low esteem by lawyers and courts (DoH, 1994a; Foster and Preston-Shoot, 1995). This is then reflected in an increasing use of medical and psychology experts by local authorities and guardians *ad litem*, even in situations where social workers might be expected to be competent. Whilst there are cases where social work evidence has carried conviction (for example, *F* v. *Suffolk County Council* [1981]; *R* v. *Derbyshire County Council, ex parte K* [1994]), others have stated that the evidence of psychiatrists and psychologists carries more weight and credibility, for example when evaluating a child's statements about abuse or the emotional impact of a child's death on a parent (*R* v. *Norfolk County Council, ex parte M* [1989]; *Re E (A Minor) (Child Abuse Evidence* [1990]; *Re R (A Minor) (Disclosure of Privileged Material)* [1993]; *B* v. *B (Procedure: Alleged Sexual Abuse)* [1994]). The uncertainty about the value attributed to social workers' training, experience and contact with service users, together with expectations and images held by others of the profession, arguably creates defensive practice.

Second, collecting evidence is difficult, especially that about emotional and sexual abuse, when secrecy and confusion abound (Glaser and Frosh, 1988), particularly about what is indicative of abuse. The uncertain meaning of legal phraseology, such as 'significant harm', compounds this difficulty, as does the Children Act's principle of no delay and the short duration of child assessment and emergency protection orders.

One particular practice dilemma captures the difficulty in collecting evidence: gathering acceptable and increasingly high standards of evidence for legal proceedings versus therapy and support for the children involved. Regulatory guidance states categorically that the purpose of interviewing abused children is to investigate, not to treat (DoH, 1991e). Whether this is right or possible is ethically and practically a moot point. A distinction has been drawn between interviews for the purposes of investigation and those for assessment or therapy (*Re N (Minors) (Sexual Abuse: Evidence)* [1993]), assuming that interviews for the latter purposes would rarely be used. They may be admissible, however, if conducted in a way to satisfy the court that any questioning was acceptable. However, is such a distinction possible and should it be drawn? The memorandum of good practice on video-recorded interviews (Home Office, 1992), in an attempt to ensure clarity and precision in evidence collection, requires that:

1. interviews are held as soon as possible, allowing for proper inter-agency planning and avoiding unnecessary delay;
2. interviews are conducted with appropriate regard for a child's attention span, linguistic and emotional development, cognitive ability, cultural background, and ideas about trust and time;
3. interviews are conducted at a pace dictated by the child;
4. the child's consent is obtained;
5. interviews have clear objectives related to the case, and that interviewers are open-minded;
6. interviews are based on listening rather than direct questioning, do not stop free recall, record rather than describe non-verbal responses, and avoid leading questions;
7. interviews avoid supplementary interviews unless necessary to elicit further information;
8. interviews are conducted around four phases of establishing rapport, obtaining a narrative account in the child's own words, questioning, and closing.

Once the video is complete, appropriate counselling or therapy may be introduced. There are concerns, however, that the memorandum has made it more difficult for children to give evidence because the procedure fails to understand that children give different information in different settings and not necessarily in one interview; decreases rapport and the likelihood that children will feel understood; ignores the possibility of non-directive therapeutic work, free from worker suggestion, giving a clear indication of a child's views; and fails to give clear criteria for videoing (SSI, 1994b; Larcombe-Williams, 1994; Cloke and Davies, 1995; Ryan and Wilson, 1995). Few videos have been shown in court and the delays and adversarial nature of the system, with the defence determined to discredit a child's evidence, arguably undermine the child's welfare.

Similarly a conflicting imperative dominates the legal system: balancing child protection against justice to the accused. Widespread concerns exist about the trauma abused children experience in court, especially under cross-examination, but the government's response to the Pigot Committee's proposals on children and evidence was ambivalent (Temkin, 1991). The proposals for an informal preliminary hearing to obviate the need for abused children to appear as witnesses at trial, and for cross-examination by the defence to be video-taped prior to the hearing, were rejected. Video-taped interviews are admissible in cases of sexual or violent offences (section 54, CJA 1991) but only if the child is available for cross-examination. However the Criminal Justice Act 1991 does allow committal proceedings to be bypassed where child victims and child witnesses of violence and abuse will have to testify (section 53). Alleged offenders are not permitted to cross-examine these witnesses personally (section 55). However, children may now be asked further questions by the prosecution if some matters are not dealt with adequately in video-taped evidence (section 50, CJPOA 1994) Rather than being a radical overhaul of the way the law treats children, the conflicting imperative has produced a compromise which does little to ease the pressures on children or the trauma experienced by them.

The law and social work diverge most markedly in their under-standing of children, especially concerning their competence to provide evidence. Social work's principle is that children have a right to be believed and that, in an atmosphere of safety and belief, they will provide valuable and reliable evidence. Indeed little evidence exists that indicates that children's reports are unreliable, and none at all that they make false accusations of sexual abuse or misunderstand innocent adult behaviour (Berliner and Barbieri, 1984). When children retract or fail to disclose, or when they appear to accept a different version of events, they may be accommodating to the power of adults (Summit, 1983), afraid of the consequences of revealing the truth, despairing of being believed or lacking the language to convey their knowledge (Lomas, 1987). Young children can distinguish between truth and falsehood but may be unable to withstand adult pressure in or out of court. The Children Act (section 96) recognises children's competence to give evidence if they can understand the duty to speak the truth and have sufficient understanding. If children are asked questions in ways they can understand, if they are prepared for, and supported in, the court experience (see *Childright*, 1990c) and if adults understand the literal and concrete phraseology children often employ and seek to enable them to demonstrate a duty to speak the truth, then the legal system may become more child-focused, may appreciate more fully the ability and desire of children to be involved, and may understand the effect of involvement, of being believed and taken seriously, on a child's sense of worth (DoH, 1992b).

The Criminal Justice and Public Order Act 1994 (section 168(1); Schedule 9(33)) confirms section 52(1) (CJA 1991) that a child's evidence shall be received unless a court believes the child is incapable of giving intelligible testimony. A child is presumed competent unless there is evidence otherwise. However, the child's welfare is not the sole or overriding consideration here: distress to the child is weighed against the interests of justice and a 'fair trial' (*Re M (Minors: Interview)* [1995]; *Re F* [1995]). Whilst a guardian *ad litem* may advise the court in civil proceedings on the child's feelings and on case management, no such support or preparation exists in criminal proceedings, compounding a child's isolation and anxiety (Morgan and Williams, 1993). The Children Act Advisory Committee (1992/93) has expressed concern about the considerable difficulties in safeguarding the welfare of the child in civil and criminal proceedings, and has argued (1993/94) for further consideration of the Pigot committee proposals concerning taking the whole of a child's evidence before trial, the use of closed-circuit television for cross-examination, the child's need for therapy in concurrent care and criminal proceedings, and coordinating and limiting the number of times children are questioned.

There is growing unease about how social work evidence is gathered. Whilst the local authority's proposals must command the greatest respect (*Re B (A Minor)* [1993]), courts have sometimes found video recordings limited and no substitute for an overall view based on the evidence as a whole (*Re W (Minors) (Child Abuse: Evidence)* [1987]). The reliability of social work interviewing techniques is criticised, especially a failure to avoid preconceptions, leading and hypothetical questions and the sequence in which questions are put. Thus, local authorities should not act in a totally adversarial way but should present a case in a balanced manner, referring to factors which point in the opposite direction to that desired by the authority (*Re B* [1994]), and providing information to assist the court (*Re A and Others (Minors) (Child Abuse: Guidelines)* [1992]). Assessments should be fair and balanced (*B v. B (Procedure: Alleged Sexual Abuse)* [1994]). By comparison, there is little scrutiny of the way lawyers question children or of the effect of the adversarial nature of proceedings on 'the truth'.

If difficulty surrounds the collecting of evidence, it also pervades the type of evidence gathered. The law values precision and certainties, characterised by an either/or dichotomy (Carson, 1990b). The court must be satisfied on proper material affirmatively proved; cases must be proved on facts, not suspicion; the evidence and opinions derived from it should prove in causal terms the case being made (*Re H and R (Child Sexual Abuse: Standard of Proof)* [1996]). The likelihood of significant harm should be a real possibility which should not be ignored. Social work, however, deals in shades of grey, in possibilities and probabilities.

Reliability of evidence surfaces most prominently over hearsay: information repeated by someone other than its author and offered to demonstrate a point. The strongest evidence is that given by the person holding the information or responsible for original remarks. However, to reduce the need for children to give evidence, and to minimise the loss of potentially important information, hearsay is admissible as evidence in proceedings concerned with the upbringing, maintenance or welfare of children (Children (Admissibility of Hearsay Evidence) Order 1990). Three categories of statement are admissible: children's statements related by others; statements made by those concerned with or having control of a child that they have assaulted, neglected or ill-treated the child; statements in court reports. Courts still have to determine what weight to attribute to such evidence which may apply to first (A reports what B said) or to subsequent hearsay (A reports what B related D said to C) (Hersham and McFarlane, 1990).

Exercise 6:3

Using a case to prepare and practise evidence

Take a case with which you are working. Identify your expertise which you bring to this case and discuss with a colleague how you can best present this expertise. Then, consider the issues which you wish to highlight in your statement and why. Then, consider what might arise in cross-examination and plan your response.

In so doing, reflect on your previous experiences and note what learning you have derived from these events. Then, consider what research and practice evidence you draw on in your work, and how these sources of evidence might be applicable in the case you are working on now.

Case law (*Re E (A Minor) (Child Abuse Evidence)* [1990]; *B* v. *B. (Procedure: Alleged Sexual Abuse)* [1994]) and regulatory guidance (DoH, 1991e) provide direction for social workers by specifically endorsing the general points to be observed in conducting interviews with children listed in the Cleveland Report (Butler-Sloss, 1988):

1. The undesirability of calling them 'disclosure' interviews, which precluded the notion that sexual abuse might not have occurred.
2. All interviews should be undertaken only by those with some training, experience and aptitude for talking with children.
3. The need to approach each interview with an open mind.
4. The style of the interview should be open-ended questions to support and encourage the child in free recall.
5. There should be where possible only one and not more than two interviews for the purpose of evaluation, and the interview should not be too long.
6. The interview should go at the pace of the child and not of the adult.
7. The setting for the interview must be suitable and sympathetic.
8. It must be accepted that at the end of the interview the child may have given no information to support the suspicion of sexual abuse and the position will remain unclear.
9. There must be careful recording of the interview and what the child says, whether or not there is a video recording.
10. It must be recognised that the use of facilitative techniques may create difficulties in subsequent court proceedings.
11. The great importance of adequate training for all those engaged in this work.
12. In certain circumstances it may be appropriate to use the special skills of a 'facilitated' interview. That type of interview

should be treated as a second stage. The interviewer must be conscious of the limitations and strengths of the techniques employed. In such cases the interview should only be conducted by those with the special skills and training.

Social workers should critically examine what children say, recognise that second and subsequent interviews are likely to be of diminishing value, and consider the climate in which children make disclosures, whether they might have been influenced by adults, whether the children reported fact, fiction or a mixture of both, whether there is independent corroborative evidence and whether behaviour before and after disclosures was consistent with the truth (*Re E (A Minor) (Child Abuse Evidence)* [1990]). Social workers should avoid preconceptions, and choose techniques according to whether abuse is suspected or proven (*Re M (A Minor) (Child Abuse: Evidence)* [1987]). In cases involving suspected abuse, interviews should be video-recorded, to allow the court to assess the dynamics within the interview, particularly with reference to the questions asked, the oral and non-verbal responses, and how these are interpreted. Less direct questions should be used (*Re E (A Minor) (Child Abuse Evidence)* [1987]; *Re W (A Minor)* [1993]). Interviews should be recorded properly. Courts will treat with great caution evidence obtained without following these guidelines (*Re E (A Minor) (Child Abuse Evidence)* [1990]). An agency's view must be based on the evidence as a whole rather than rely on one source (*Re W (Minors) (Child Abuse: Evidence)* [1987]).

The emphasis is not just on obtaining information but on assessing how firmly and consistently held views are, how much they may have been influenced by preceding events, including cues given by interviewers, and how appropriate it might be for a child of that age to hold particular views (LBTC, 1989). Considerable skill is required in using free-flowing interviews with minimal use of prompting questions. Questioning may improve completeness but is seen as reducing accuracy (Douglas and Willmore, 1987). Whether the free-flowing approach will enable children to feel safe enough to disclose, especially given the limited time social workers have, is debatable. Practitioners and lawyers are left to negotiate the potential contradictions in the Cleveland guidance points 5 and 6, and 4 and 10. As 'elsewhere it becomes imperative that practitioners state clearly what is and is not possible.

Exercise 6.4

Reviewing a case as a method of preparation

Take a case with which you are working. Identify with a colleague the strengths, weaknesses, areas of uncertainty and concerns in this case. Identify what you might do (a) to resolve the areas of weakness and uncertainty, and (b) to present the information clearly for the local authority solicitor.

Imagine the worst possible scenario on your case. How might you approach your work on the case to avoid this?

Take the most difficult case with which you have worked. Why was it difficult? What ways did you find helpful to negotiate through the difficulties, or could you imagine might be helpful?

Directions hearings

In private law and in care proceedings courts are required to draw up a timetable with a view to disposing of the application without delay (sections 11(1) and 32(1), CA 1989). At these directions hearings, which have given a much clearer structure to proceedings and promoted communication between the parties involved, leave may be given by the court for the disclosure of documents, and for examinations and assessments, for the purpose of preparing (expert) evidence. The court will define and decide what expert evidence is necessary in order for the case to be resolved. Put another way, the problems on which the court requires assistance should be specific and identifiable.

The style of the court is expected to be non-adversarial (DoH, 1991d). This (new) approach is underpinned by two developments: advanced disclosure by the parties of their evidence, and the use of directions hearings to identify disputes and agreement on evidential matters. One purpose of directions hearings is the narrowing of the issues to be considered. Another is to facilitate, where possible and necessary, the instruction of one expert, with the agreement of all the parties. The final directions hearing will take place approximately two weeks before the final hearing (Children Act Advisory Committee, 1993/94). The guardian *ad litem*'s report, the bundle of evidence, and a chronology of events agreed by the parties should be available.

Having identified the purpose of directions hearings, local authority social workers should:

1. be clear about the mandate given to them by their agency and through child protection procedures concerning the case in question;
2. be clear what they want by way of directions from the court;
3. consult within their agency when issues arise which have not been anticipated, or when resource questions arise, such as the amount of supervised contact to which the agency can commit resources;
4. ensure a manager is present in complex cases; anticipate what may arise and plan accordingly in terms of who needs to be present and what is to be requested;
5. use the local authority solicitor as a source of advice but not instruction. Their role is to be there for the social worker's case;
6. be clear that their role is the protection and welfare of the child;
7. know that joint instruction of experts is encouraged, and be clear what the position of the local authority is in relation to this case and further assessments.

Experts

The reason for requesting an expert assessment may include:

1. to benefit from expert advice in complex or 'borderline' cases, or in relation to matters which are beyond the expertise of social workers to assess, such as medical conditions, or the effects of culture;
2. to supplement other assessments, or to provide an assessment in an area which might be relevant and where the local authority has not provided evidence or has provided evidence which requires investigation and possible challenge;
3. to provide as much information as possible for the court to assist in the decision-making process;

4. to ensure that all avenues have been explored from as many perspectives as possible;

5. to engage the parties in partnership activity for the welfare of the child, expressed particularly in joint instructions;

6. to seek a further view when a party indicates that they will not accept the expert evidence offered by the local authority.

The use of experts raises a number of practice dilemmas. An established child-care principle, codified in regulatory section 7 guidance for children's services (Local Authority Social Services Act 1970) (DoH, 1989a), is that the number of assessments or examinations on children should be kept to a minimum. The child's right is to the minimum intervention or least restrictive response necessary. When it is felt necessary to obtain further assistance, the child's welfare, as expressed through the principle of the least coercive intervention possible, has to be balanced with the duty to investigate.

Second, if indeed social work evidence is held in lower regard by courts than the evidence given by other professionals, this raises the possibility that leave may be sought to instruct experts as a defensive measure – to counter the perceived strength of the case being advanced by other parties, and/or to enhance the perceived strength of one's own case.

Third, it is by no means always the case that assessments will reduce the adversarial nature of care proceedings and assist decision-making. Local authorities may feel coerced in relation to their own decision-making processes, even though the information is provided to assist the court, whilst for parents the findings may confirm their view that the proceedings are loaded against them. There remains the danger of symmetrical escalation – the more you use experts, the more I will use more experts.

Fourth, the limited number of experts in particular geographic areas or fields of specialism may create delay, or may lead some practitioners to continue without an expert assessment. Each instance could prejudice the child's long-term welfare.

There is a view (see King and Trowell, 1992) that the use of experts in care proceedings, and indeed the whole fabric of the law as a means of deciding a child's welfare, requires reconsideration. The argument runs that experts are required in evidence to provide a snapshot and to defend tentative conclusions drawn from an inexact science. King and Trowell argue that this practice gives the misleading impression that the law can deal with difficult problems and establish 'truth'. They further argue that the adversarial nature of proceedings means that the child becomes lost in legal issues of evidence and the search for definitive answers.

Nonetheless, a number of points of good practice do emerge. First, the need to avoid duplication of investigations where possible, for instance by joint instruction of experts which will also reduce the time required for the preparation of evidence and for the final hearing (*Re G (Minors)* [1994]). Second, the importance of sharing copies of reports before the final hearing, and using experts to identify areas of agreement rather than to strengthen adversarial positions, to minimise delays in hearing the evidence (*Re C (Children Act 1989: Expert Evidence)* [1995]).

Third, in relation to choice of expert, the expert should be suitable for the issues requiring attention, should have proven reliability as a witness, should be able to discern and present findings impartially in order to allow a court to reach a judgement, and should be able to understand rules of evidence and the requirements of the party issuing the instructions. The role is a highly specialist one, requiring an ability to collate and present evidence in a comprehensive and impartial manner, and to communicate that evidence in reports and under the close inspection of cross-examination. It requires an ability to interact with and feel comfortable within the legal arena. The expert should have sufficient experience to denote professional standing – this might embrace teaching and consultancy, but will include positions of responsibility in the specialism in question.

Fourth, when choosing an expert, the instructing party must consider what information they are looking for and whether any person currently involved is in a position to provide this. They should also reflect on the instructions or directions they might provide for the expert, indicating the precise questions which the expert is asked to address. Instruction should be by letter setting out the context in which an opinion is being sought and the specific questions they are being asked to consider. Relevant documents should be listed and sent and all this material filed into court with the expert's report. Experts should all give evidence on one day in order that they may comment on what each says (*Re M (Minors) (Care Proceedings: Conflict of Children's Wishes; Instruction of Expert Witnesses)* [1994]).

Fifth, the brief should be discussed with both the expert and the subjects of the assessment, planning how to involve those subjects in the process of assessment and mechanisms for ensuring that the final report is clear and balanced.

Applications for leave to instruct independent experts should be made as early as possible in proceedings (*Re D (Minors) (Time Estimates)* [1994]). The expert or area of expertise should be defined before leave to instruct is given: the category of evidence which the applying party seeks to adduce; the relevance of the expert evidence to issues for decision in the case; whether or not evidence could be properly attained by joint instruction or adduced by the party. The local authority has a positive duty to disclose information to the court. When leave is given, directions should be given regarding timescales, disclosure of material to parties, and discussion between experts to identify areas of (dis)agreement (*Re G (Minors)* [1994]).

Only experts are allowed to give opinions in evidence. Anyone with experience to give an informed opinion on a matter outside the court's experience may give expert evidence. They need not necessarily hold any formal qualifications. There is a general principle that courts will rely on expert evidence when they do not have the expertise themselves in order to resolve a particular issue. The evidence which they present will be a mixture of theoretical understanding, research studies, and observations derived from clinical practice, filtered through each case. It follows that the experts used must have experience of the matter(s) in question, must base their statements on clinical and research evidence, must know the literature, and must undertake a meticulous examination of the material available. They should only express opinions which they genuinely hold. They should not mislead by omission or bias but should cover all the material facts, supportive or otherwise of any opinion. (*Re R (A Minor) (Expert's Evidence)* [1991]); (*Re J (Child Abuse: Expert Evidence)* [1991]).

An expert's function is to make an assessment in their area of expertise. When advancing a hypothesis to explain facts, they must make this clear, consider evidence for and against it, and make material available to all other experts in the case. They must carefully consider all available material, and limit their areas of disagreement where possible since they are independent advisers of the court, not advocates of parties or causes (*Re AB (A Minor) (Medical Issues – Expert Evidence)* [1994]). A court, provided proper reasons are given, is free to depart from expert's views (*Re P (A Minor) (Contact)* [1994]).

Social workers should be able to undertake a comprehensive assessment, covering abuse and neglect, developmental history and direct observation, the care provided by parents including holding and security, emotional development and attachment, family interactions, and the personality and attitudes of significant adults. This includes their mental health status (DoH, 1988). From such an assessment, social workers should be competent in articulating causes for concern, factors facilitating or impeding change, and an action plan to achieve required change. When considering the question of significant harm and the exercise of statutory responsibilities, social workers should be able, on the basis of evidence gathered, to define the nature of the harm or impairment, its seriousness, and the degree of risk. From here, they should be able to define the child's needs, the capacity of the parents and others to meet these needs now or in the future, the changes required for the child's needs to be met, and how these changes might best be achieved (Adcock, 1991). Social workers and guardians *ad litem* should be competent in examining risk to children and the capacity of families to meet children's needs (DoH, 1992b).

In summary, key questions to ask include:

1. Is an expert needed? What is the assessment for? Who will benefit? Why is it necessary? What is the nature of the additional information which an expert will provide?
2. Is the decision to use an expert based on the case and/or other pressures?
3. Should the expert be invited to form an opinion on the evidence available, or should the instructions include direct contact with the child and/or the family?
4. What skills and expertise are required of an expert? Are there gender and cultural issues which should be considered in deciding that an expert is required, and in choosing one?
5. Will the other parties be encouraged to contribute to the expert's assessment, by way of joint instructions? This is less adversarial and may achieve the inquiry into the child's needs and welfare which is the focus of care proceedings.
6. Who will be responsible for the negotiations and, subsequently, discuss the findings with the person assessed?

7

Making Sense of Practice

This final chapter turns attention to the skills required in the practice of social work law within the context of an active commitment to social work values and principles. The law itself is a relatively blunt instrument. It is practice skills within a clear value base that enable it to be applied with any degree of precision. Skills and values are effective anchors against the temptations of defensive practice. They help to make sense of the complexity and dilemmas inherent in the task.

The chapter focuses on four interlinked areas in which knowledge, skills and values may be identified as foundations for effective practice: translating personal and professional values into practice; core skills for competency; effective interaction with other professionals; and developing resources for competency.

Translating personal and professional values into practice

Earlier chapters have demonstrated how the law embodies beliefs about how society should operate, beliefs based on principles which are collectively 'valued' and embedded within society's functioning. In addition to awareness of the law's value base, scrutiny is needed of the way *personal* values and organisational *culture* affect the practice of social work law. Personal and professional values, acquired from upbringing, training and experience, filter what is seen and the sense made of it. Organisational values determine the range of options open to practitioners and influence the way the law is applied. The professional values arena, however, is not a simple one. Two broad themes may be identified, with distinct and at times mutually exclusive characteristics (Braye and Preston-Shoot, 1995). Traditional social work values, such as respect for persons, and their contemporary incarnation in equality of opportunity and partnership, can be developed into a more radical agenda which tackles structural inequality and prioritises empowerment and citizenship. Faced with such complexity there is a danger that the term 'values' tends to be bandied about indiscriminately, rich in nuance and evocation but often thin in descriptive and informative content. There is, therefore, a responsibility for questioning and critical appraisal, for debates on both personal and organisational levels.

The following exercises help readers to clarify the personal value base in relation to key themes affecting social work law in practice: values about families and relationships, authority and power, and discrimination and oppression.

Families and relationships

Practitioners are inevitably affected by, and in turn affect, the family and relationship patterns they observe in their work. Underlying an individual's professional functioning is a complex personal history that will influence where they stand in relation to the conflicting imperatives and practice dilemmas of using the law.

Exercise 7.1

Think of something you learned in your family that is still important to you now. Think of something you did not like and have discarded. How do these two things affect your work with families?

Early experience and subsequent learning will profoundly affect what practitioners want to use the law to achieve – what are the merits of permanent placement for children as opposed to continuing contact and possible rehabilitation with birth families; how far should community presence and participation be promoted over protection from possible danger and exploitation; what work should be prioritised with young people living in the public care system? Such decisions are often value-led.

Exercise 7.2

What was the role of the people who looked after you as a child? What did they do for you? What do you believe parents and carers should do for children? Are there differences for men and women? How do these beliefs affect your work?

Children's experience of family life and of substitutes for family care have been the subject of extensive exploration, demonstrating key differences both of focus and quality in areas deemed fundamental for successful transition to adulthood, and resulting in the introduction of a system which attempts to promote a common value base about what children need and what should be prioritised (Parker *et al*, 1991; Ward, 1995).

Authority and power

Ironically, for a profession deemed by many to possess limitless and sometimes inappropriate power, social work faces its social control function with considerable unease, and individual practitioners often describe feeling *powerless*, both within their employing bureaucracies and in relation to helping people change their lives.

An analysis of the power that resides in the social work role, balanced with an understanding of the factors that influence personal authority in that role, is essential if the law is to be used appropriately. It must be accompanied by an awareness of power in the lives of service users if empowerment is to become a practical reality.

Exercise 7.3

When have you accepted or not accepted authority from others? What factors influenced your acceptance?

Exercise 7.4

When (in your work) do you feel powerful? Where does that power come from? Do you feel comfortable with that power?

When (in your work) do you feel powerless? What is it like to feel powerless?

What power do service users have? How are service users disempowered? How does your power affect people you work with?

The law is one obvious source of power since it confers the capacity to make decisions, to allocate resources, to coerce and ensure compliance. Individuals will again carry personal experiences which affect the way they value the power of the law.

Exercise 7.5

How does the law affect, or has it affected, your own life? When has the law helped or hindered you? How does the law help or hinder service users?

It is tempting to conflate the law with power to restrict, control and coerce in a negative sense. A more positive view is necessary which recognises the empowering aspects of legislation also – how it enables protection and resources to be offered.

Other sources of power include the helping role, the advantage of professional status, access to information and resources, agency status, knowledge and expertise, and membership of dominant groups. By contrast, service users can be disempowered by material and social disadvantage, by lack of knowledge of agency role and status, by jargon and the mystique of professionalism, by discrimination and oppression on both a corporate and an individual level. A 'power audit' of this kind is useful because it can be developed into action.

Exercise 7.6

Ask yourself the following questions:
   Is my power legitimate? Do I need it to do my job effectively?
   What power do I have that I can legally transfer? What power do I want to transfer? What power must I/do I want to keep for me?

Choosing to empower, however, presupposes the possession and transferability of power in the first place. Empowerment is not just a matter of transferring a finite amount of power, but also of working with people to discover their own sources of power, sometimes through the law, and valuing those in encounters with professionals.

Prejudice, discrimination and oppression

The theme of personal values and power leads to exploration of both personal and professional understandings of the use of power to oppress. Social work has struggled to recognise the impact of racism upon its professional task, of white power and privilege in relationships with black people and to overcome value judgements about the superiority of white culture and norms (Dominelli, 1988). The same may be said in relation to gender and class, as major structural oppressions in which social work is implicated. Personal values and awareness are an important part of this process. It is this awareness that influences when, how and why social workers reach for the law, and that underpins the skills necessary to combat the differential use of the law in relation to certain groups of people. It can be built from clarification of the patterns of understanding, messages, mottoes, anxieties and feelings arising from early learning and experience.

Exercise 7.7

How would I describe my racial identity?
   When was I first aware of my racial identity?

When was I first aware of people whose racial identity was different from my own?

What messages did I receive about my racial identity and about the racial identity of others? What effect have these had on my outlook and work?

Exercise 7.8

Ask yourself the same set of questions in relation to gender, sexual orientation, class and disability.

Exercise 7.9

Ask yourself the following questions:

When have I felt myself to be discriminated against? On what grounds did it happen? What did I feel? When have I discriminated against others? Why did it happen? What did I feel? How would I wish to be treated?

Exercise 7.10

When in my professional capacity I work with someone whose sex, racial origins or class are different from my own, what is the effect of this on our relationship? What is the impact of who I am and of my behaviour? What is the impact on me of who they are? What boundaries do I/they cross?

Hanmer and Statham (1988) emphasise for example the importance, in developing women-centred practice, of female workers working to establish commonality with women who are service users, commonality that arises from awareness of the problematic impact of female life experience, and which can be incorporated into their practice. Recognition of difference is also important; men have a different task of working to increase their understanding of women's lives and to examine the impact of their behaviour. The tendency is to notice only what one can see from one's own position and to prefer it as the 'true' version of reality. Developing awareness of what the world looks like from other people's perspectives brings new information that can be incorporated into an anti-oppressive position.

Organisational debates

The nature of the interaction between the law, agency policy and individual practice makes it essential that individual practitioners are not left to grapple alone with the intricacies of ethical decision-making in relation to the use of legal powers and duties. To be effective, social work policies and procedures need to be under-pinned by a clear philosophy and value base (DoH, 1988). Clearly articulated organisational values can provide considerable support to workers attempting to make sense of conflicting imperatives and practice dilemmas. Formal policy statements provide the security and anchors necessary to promote effective decision-making.

Exercise 7.11

Questions for managers

Does policy guidance on each sector of the work clearly articulate the legal content of that work? Is there written guidance on how the authority interprets its legal duties? Are there commonly agreed criteria and standards for triggering statutory interaction? Where there are powers rather than duties, is it clear how and when the authority uses that power?

In relation to antidiscriminatory practice, are there clear guidelines on prescribed and proscribed behaviours and on standards of service provision? How is the authority monitoring effectiveness? What do social workers do when they 'take race, culture, language and religion into account'?

In relation to partnership, what does the authority expect in terms of everyday practice? Do social workers know what is expected? How will service users know the authority regards them as partners?

In relation to protective functions, what risks is the agency prepared to back workers in taking? What risks are we never prepared to take? What can workers do to protect people from abuse in the absence of adequate legislation? Where do workers stand in taking action to promote welfare, for example in administering medication, in the absence of positive consent?

There are dangers in written guidelines. One is that they remain glowingly rhetorical about principles but, in offering no guidance about how to prioritise principles, they leave practitioners with the same insoluble dilemmas as the legislation itself. Indeed mention of practice dilemmas has been noticeably absent in policy documents (Robbins, 1990), as if refusing to name them will make them go away. But it is vital that consideration is given to prioritising: when must workers be gatekeepers of resources and when may users have free choice; when may the rights of carers take precedence over the rights of people being cared for; when does inspection become more important than support and guidance; at what point may the need to safeguard welfare overtake the right to autonomy?

Another danger is that, in attempting to give clear guidance, procedures tend to encourage linear thinking and solutions, as if by working through the procedures one will arrive at a good enough solution, almost without the use of professional judgement. A third danger is that written guidelines remain inaccessible, unlinked to practice realities, leaving practitioners to rely more frequently on informal understandings (Hardiker *et al.*, 1991). In the absence of an observable progression from principles through policy and objectives to strategy, organisational values remain distant, unachievable goals or resented constraints that seem irrelevant to practice. A balance will not be achieved without organisational debates taking place. This must involve active monitoring and wide discussion of when, how and why decisions to use the law are made; identification of where decision-making power and responsibility are located, what influences the way it is exercised, what objectives are to be achieved and how learning from outcomes is incorporated into future practice.

Core skills

The core skills for competency in the practice of social work law are of course no other than core skills for practice in general. There are, however, some emphases that must be given to skills that are particularly significant in the light of a critical understanding of the law. Individual competency will be emphasised alongside the organisation's responsibility to provide a competent context for practice.

Challenging discrimination

Social work law offers both opportunities and responsibilities for antidiscriminatory practice: using the law to challenge discrimination, and vigilance to ensure that the law is not applied in a discriminatory way. The wider context of oppressive law and legal structures makes it necessary to prioritise awareness of legislation such as the Race Relations Act 1976 and the Children Act 1989 which lay down specific responsibilities that can be used as standards against which other proposed actions involving the law can be measured. The skills that follow will take the challenge forward.

Skills in thinking systemically. The law encourages individually pathologising explanations for social problems and their solutions. Even where the law recognises discrimination it individualises the solution. In requiring a focus upon a presenting problem, such as 'significant harm' or 'mental disorder of a nature or degree that warrants detention in hospital', most welfare legislation obscures the presence of structural oppression in the lives of individuals. Emphasis on 'assessment of individual need' diverts attention from evidence of collective unmet need in black communities (Dutt, 1990a). Women's mental distress is seen as individual inadequacy rather than distress in relation to women's role in society, and treatments emphasise either biological or psychological adjustment on the personal level (Llewelyn, 1987).

Thinking systemically helps practitioners to balance the individual and the structural elements in explanations of and solutions to problems. It recognises the impact of social definitions of femininity upon women's experience (Hanmer and Statham, 1988), of gendered notions of caring which restrict women's opportunities (Grimwood and Popplestone, 1993), and of racism in the lives of black people (Dominelli, 1988). It recognises that confusing disability with disease and counting people with disabilities for registration (as required under the NAA 1948 and CA 1989) does little to establish a true picture of social need arising from disability (Phelan, 1986) and that changes of policy in resource allocation are as important as individual assessment (Dutt, 1990a).

Such recognitions enable the law to be directed much more accurately in intervention, allowing for both its potential and limitation as a short-term corrective solution, and avoiding an over-reliance on its provisions at the expense of more long-term changes.

Challenging normative or stereotypical assumptions. Practitioners must avoid the twin pitfalls of either failing to recognise difference or doing so in a way that uses stereotypical understandings. Current legislation and the way in which it is applied contain the potential for both. On the one hand, normative explanations and expectations which treat everyone the same are pervasive throughout welfare law and the practice it supports. The ideology of the NHS and Community Care Act 1990 reflects firmly entrenched social values and beliefs that have white cultural underpinnings. In following normalisation principles which tackle discrimination of one form, practitioners must avoid the danger of taking white values as the norm and thus perpetuating other forms of discrimination. Widely used systems, such as 'Individual Programme Planning' and 'Program Analysis of Service Systems', give rise to concerns about the extent to which they cross cultural boundaries (Baxter *et al.*, 1990). White eurocentric norms have also influenced expectations of child development, family patterns and parenting styles.

On the other hand, attempts to recognise difference and to move away from a colour-blind approach have resulted in cultural stereotyping rather than appropriate ethnic sensitivity (Ahmad, 1988). Powers to provide services have been under-used in relation to black elders, a policy justified by assumptions that 'families will care' or 'they go back home' (Marshall, 1990). Acts of abuse may be overlooked because they are assumed to be condoned by a culture only partially and stereotypically understood (Dutt, 1990b). It is vitally important that recognition of cultural diversity takes place in the context of a broader understanding of racism, that a balance is achieved between sensitivity to culture and sensitivity to structural inequality. This is particularly so in relation to the way protective legal measures are used, where assumptions can result in both over- and under-use.

Stereotypical assumptions about gender roles and family structure are also a danger to practitioners in that they define both the focus and outcome of intervention. Interventions such as family therapy, mediation and reparation, derived from a family welfare model rather than from criminal justice considerations, can serve to bind women even more strongly to violent relationships (Hanmer *et al.*, 1989). Gendered assumptions must not result in monitoring and judging women for their effectiveness in protecting children from abuse by men (Hanmer and Statham, 1988); or in reporting inappropriately on the domestic accomplishments of women offenders, or even the women partners of male offenders (Eaton, 1985); or imposing conservative family values which restrict the protection of women and children from male violence (Harne and Radford, 1994).

Challenging myths and stereotypes takes place on a variety of levels, from the personal to the political. Legislation such as the NHS and Community Care Act 1990, underpinning the provision of services matched to individual need, offers the opportunity to move away from stereotypical assumptions and to take full account of race, culture, language, religion, class, gender and ability. In relation to race in particular, the emphasis under the legislation on the provision of an 'available and affordable' service should not mean perpetuating one that is inappropriate for black people (Dutt, 1990a). Monitoring must include consideration of whether services are being used by all sectors of communities, not just the white sector. Purchaser/provider functions offer opportunities to purchase services from black voluntary organisations, not as a way of avoiding having to make relevant mainstream provision but for positive reasons, and agencies can facilitate tenders for business from such organisations (Dutt, 1990a). Additionally the Race Relations Act 1976 empowers local authorities to be much more proactive than hitherto in examining the relevance of services purchased from independent providers and whether they provide equality of opportunity and a non-discriminatory service.

Developing a language. Skill in communicating *about* discrimination is crucial to the development of a strong challenge. Practice is strengthened by appropriate language, underpinned by shared understandings about definitions and terminologies.

Exercise 7.12

What do I mean by the words 'equal opportunities'? How will I check whether a service is appropriate to a child's racial, cultural, linguistic and religious needs? What questions will I ask? How will I phrase them? How do I tell someone I think they are discriminating?

Misconceptions are common – such as that equal opportunities is a matter of treating everyone the same. There is an urgent need for organisations on a corporate level to agree the content of an organisational vocabulary (LGTB, 1990). A shared vocabulary then gives a strong base from which to challenge discriminatory language and to offer positive suggestions for substitute phraseology. The language used to frame communications is a powerful indicator and influencer of values; the words that are used to describe actions are challenges in themselves to discriminatory processes. In talking about domestic violence, for example, the use of criminal language such as 'assault' or 'murder' conveys a powerful message to counteract euphemisms such as 'a domestic incident' (McCann, 1985).

Skills in campaigning and empowering. Challenging discrimination at a wider level than in individual practice involves taking a personal and corporate stance against practices that are oppressive yet condoned by legislation. Immigration, housing and income support are three examples of areas in which practitioners will find themselves called upon to advise, assist and support. Where discrimination is covered by legislation, as with race and gender, it is important to encourage and support individuals to take action through tribunals and courts, and to involve the investigative powers of the Commission for Racial Equality and the Equal Opportunities Commission. This may mean initiating action through the channels of organisational hierarchy, and using legal knowledge and equal opportunity policy statements to empower such action, where discrimination against service users is apparent in the workings of one's own employing organisation. Working with groups of disabled people for the politicisation of disability issues and an impact on the profile and ethos of services will remain important, despite the

Disability Discrimination Act 1995, because of the limited powers of enforcement contained within the Act, the exclusion of some disabled people from its terms of reference, and the weakness of some of its scope and provisions (see Gooding, 1996).

In the absence of protective legislation, action on a policy level can be effective. The law does not protect people from discrimination on grounds of their sexual preference, but policy documents can include this in statements of equality (NAPO, 1990). Indeed, in the absence of protective legislation the position taken by an organisation becomes even more crucial (Hirst, 1995).

It is vital, while working to challenge discrimination at an individual level, to work in partnership with groups, both of service users and others, who, through validating the strengths and upholding the rights of oppressed groups, can begin to make a difference. Social workers have a key role in linking individuals into groups of common interest and experience, thereby enhancing their opportunity for collective action and access to political processes (Braye and Preston-Shoot, 1993a, 1993b). Taking this one step further, it can be argued that social work's concern with power leads inevitably to engagement with political action as an integral component of activity, and to training for skills in community organisation, lobbying and campaigning (Jackson and Preston-Shoot, 1996).

Working in partnership

The word 'partnership' is ill-defined, meaning a variety of different things to different people. It remains undefined in legislation and thereby open to infinite interpretation in practice. Essential to the development of skills in partnership is a clearer understanding of what is covered by the term and what the aims of working in partnership are.

Exercise 7.13

What do you understand by the term 'partnership'? With whom are you in a partnership? Why is partnership important?

The concept of partnership in social work has a complex aetiology, reflecting influences from such extremes as controlled consumerism and liberationist politics. The term is used to describe anything from token consultation to a total devolution of power and control (Braye and Preston-Shoot, 1995).

Understanding of partnership must be linked to understandings about power, and a recognition that partnership and empowerment are linked in a dynamic developmental process; that certain aspects of partnership – consultation, participation in social processes that affect people's lives – are in themselves empowering, and that transfer in the balance of power alters the nature of subsequent partnership.

The implications of a partnership ethos for practising social work law are that recognition must be given to the nature of the power at the centre of the relationship. Wilding (1982) proposes that professionals, service users and society are in a tripartite partnership which recognises the publicly mandated nature of professionals' power yet avoids their total subordination to the state by emphasising accountability to service users. A major factor must be the acknowledgement that partners in a relationship do not always have equal power. Social workers have power, and indeed duties, to act in certain circumstances. They cannot deny, delegate or ignore this. Service users and the communities to which they belong also have power and strengths. One of the skills of partnership is recognising the realities of the way power is distributed in the relationship, and for professionals to promote the exercise of users' power within it (A. Ahmad, 1990). An analysis of partnership that involves power must also take account of who is participating in the relationship and what function it is serving (Windle and Cibulka, 1981). It is tempting to assume that partnership is easier to achieve when exercising service provision (helping) functions than when exercising protective (controlling) functions. This is not necessarily the case, however, and skills are transferable from one to the other.

There is evidence that partnership remains stuck at the level of 'good intentions' within social work agencies, and that practitioners struggle to translate the rhetoric into reality (Marsh and Fisher, 1992). There are a number of components to this task, notably having a conceptual frame for practitioners' understanding, an organisational commitment to facilitate, a personal 'will', and a practice skills base (Braye and Preston-Shoot, 1993a).

Skills of partnership in service provision will certainly involve the following:

- conveying accurate information about the powers, duties and responsibilities of the local authority; information that is jargon-free in language accessible to local communities and conveyed through effective channels of communication;
- involving service users in problem definition and analysis of need, at both an individual and general planning level; this will involve the recognition of knowledge and skills that users possess as well as professionals' skills of assessment;
- the joint devising of strategies, taking account of what legislation empowers or requires and how appropriate intervention is; this must be in an atmosphere which encourages calculated risk-taking, with education about choices available and support to make difficult decisions (Brandon and Brandon, 1987);
- widening of consultation: service users' agendas must be in-cluded alongside those of professionals; there are many different opinions about what is the right service development to follow, and consultation with one group may lead in the opposite direction from consultation with another; care must be taken not to assume that one view is a representative view: black people's views may not be taken account of; women may not have a voice; competing ideologies lead to widely differing views; strategies must take account of the need to communicate in widely different ways with different groups of people, to set aside false assumptions about people's ability or willingness to become involved (Thornton and Tozer, 1995), and to take account of differing abilities to participate; material and financial help and support should be provided as well as insight and advice-giving under professional authority (Westcott, 1995);
- clarifying the aims of consultation: what is the purpose; what is the power structure; do the people being consulted have the means to influence the outcome; how will their views be taken forward?
- locating collaboration within a relationship based on respect which is maintained even when opinions differ (Beresford and Trevillion, 1995);
- developing practice tools such as written agreements that enable workers to reflect open and honest negotiation and reciprocity,

rather than coercive requirements (Braye and Preston-Shoot, 1992).

The extent of partnership will be influenced by what is authorised and legitimated by the political system and how far power may be transferred. Original policy guidance on community care (DoH, 1990) made it quite clear, for instance, that legislation forbade cash payments in lieu of services, thus limiting the extent of control a service user may ultimately have. The Community Care (Direct Payments) Act 1996 has changed this position for some service users, enabling a shift of power in determining how money to purchase individual services is used. Partnership of necessity however has to recognise both users' rights to self-determination and the local authority's wider responsibilities for and control of budgets (Walker, 1991).

But what of the more coercive and controlling aspects of practising social work law, the points at which self-determination and self definition of need may be overruled for purposes of control or protection?

Exercise 7.14

Is it possible to act in partnership when depriving someone of their liberty? Is it possible to act in partnership when intervening in the exercise of parental responsibility without that person's agreement?

Think of a time when you have been involved in using compulsory powers in relation to either children or adults. How could you achieve partnership in this context? How would the people concerned know you regarded them as partners?

Guidance (DoH, 1995b) stresses that partnership is not an end in itself but, in the child protection arena, has the objective of the child's protection and welfare. It is recognised that 'words such as equality, choice and power have a limited meaning at certain points in the child protection process', and that 'efforts to work in partnership should not put the child at risk'. Nonetheless, a bare minimum is advocated, namely that professionals must be open and honest, and keep parents informed about their rights and about what action is being taken. The same guidance identifies opportunities for good partnership practice at key stages through the child protection process, and additionally recognises the importance of a facilitative organisational framework involving senior managers, elected members, and Area Child Protection Committees.

It is entirely consistent with an ethos of partnership, and indeed imperative, to identify what cannot be changed – that the social worker has a duty to act – but within that context to use the authority positively, applying the same skills of informing, involving and consulting. Underpinning skill in the positive use of authority are:

- role clarity: the clear setting of boundaries and understandings of who has what powers, duties and resources; what principles are used in their application; what can or cannot be done; what is or is not negotiable;
- clear communication about what is happening and why, avoiding jargon and the mystique of legalistic language; using clear and unequivocal language – avoiding euphemisms that keep things nice and friendly on the surface;
- clarity of purpose: how the use of compulsory legal powers fits in with the overall purpose and goals of intervention;
- clarity about foregoing consent to a course of action if judgement indicates this is required, and then using the minimum coercive action necessary to secure safety or protection;
- openness to other possible means of achieving goals; the over-use of controlling legislation can sometimes be seen as a defensive strategy to reduce the anxiety inherent in the levels of responsibility carried by practitioners;
- the use of formal structures for participation in decision-making processes, such as case conferences, and skills in preparing, informing, educating and managing group process to ensure participation rather than tokenism (FRG, 1989).

Finally skills in partnership include the ability to join networks as well as individuals, tapping the strength that can arise from facilitating collective action (Mullender and Ward, 1991): putting individuals in touch with resources such as law centres, offering information about rights and complaints procedures, proactively encouraging independent representation and advocacy so that the power of social work law may be balanced by active strengthening of users' rights, opinions and perspectives.

Skills in assessment

The importance of assessment in contributing to the skilled and effective use of legislation has been emphasised in child protection (DoH, 1988), in family support (DoH, 1991b) and in adult services (DoH, 1989c, 1991h). The principles of open, accessible and needs-based assessment have, however, been difficult to translate into practice. Studies (DoH, 1991f) have found arrangements to be service-led, confined to statutory sector provision, segmented rather than holistic, and not promoting user or carer participation. Professionals and service users occupy very different power positions to influence the outcomes of assessment (Ellis, 1993). There is widespread dissatisfaction with the assessment process as experienced by people who use community care services (Lamb and Layzell, 1995), service users having low expectations about their involvement in the process, and given little information on which to make choices (Day, 1994). Whilst the belief that there exists a 'true' or 'correct' assessment of any situation remains a myth (Preston-Shoot and Agass, 1990), a number of key component skills can sharpen practice and contribute to a more accurate use of the law.

Clarity of purpose. The reasons for undertaking assessment will vary according to the legal framework. *Caring for People* (DoH, 1989c) specifies that the objective of assessment is to determine the best available way to help the individual, and guidance describes it as 'the understanding of an individual's needs with a view to establishing their eligibility for assistance, and to agreeing the priorities and objectives for any intervention' (DoH, 1991h). Under section 4 of the Disabled Persons Act 1986 assessment of the need for services is mandatory. Both the Mental Health Act 1983 and the Children Act 1989 permit coercive action in order to facilitate assessment and involve using judgement about degrees of risk. Since the legislation prioritises different objectives at different times, it is important in every assessment to understand the primary focus of the legal mandate. Some situations may contain a range of legal mandates.

Assessment under the NHS and Community Care Act 1990 may run parallel to one under the Disabled Persons Act 1986 and another under the Carers (Recognition and Services) Act 1995. As assessment becomes more formalised as a process, particularly under community care, further differentiation is required about the nature of a service user's involvement with the agency. Is advice and information sufficient, is it a priority to establish eligibility for an immediate service, or is full assessment required (DoH, 1991f)?

An associated issue is clarity over *who* is being assessed – in certain circumstances the needs of carers may be prioritised over and above the person being cared for (DoH, 1991g). The need for social services provision arises not from an individual's need alone but from the pattern of relationships available to that individual, thus requiring that the social situation is the appropriate unit of assessment (Stevenson and Parsloe, 1993). Clearly there will be changes over time, so that the purpose and focus of assessment will need to be kept under review.

A systematic process. The process of assessment can be broken down into stages or steps. Guidance for needs assessments under the NHS and Community Care Act 1990 (DoH, 1991h) offers a ten-step process, the key stages of which are:

- Negotiating the scope – what level of assessment is required, simple or comprehensive?
- Promoting participation – assessment takes place within a relationship.
- Defining need – by reference both to individual factors and social and care networks.
- Determining eligibility, prioritising and setting objectives – by relating needs to the policies and priorities of the authority.

Working through a systematic process will help practitioners to operationalise the principles of needs-based assessment – keeping the resource availability issue firmly out of play until allocation is necessary.

Of a different order of systematisation are the *components* of comprehensive assessment offered to structure child protection (DoH, 1988) and mental health (DoH, 1993c) assessments. These lead practitioners through a range of areas of enquiry deemed relevant to the task. Of importance here also will be internal departmental procedures and guidelines, which may specify structure of both process and content. Departmental children in need policies, for example, are likely to specify the areas contributing to assessment of a child's health and development, and the degree of prioritisation given to differing levels of need. The *Looking after Children – Assessing Outcomes* materials cover an exhaustive range of areas for ongoing assessment and attention in relation to looked-after children.

An important caveat, however, is not to allow the structure to dominate to the extent that it preempts the exploration of factors 'not on the list'. An essential stance is one of curiosity, an openness of mind that makes room for the 'not so obvious' and avoids prescribing the solution before defining the problem (Preston-Shoot and Agass, 1990).

Matching information to criteria and standards. It is crucial to define the criteria against which assessment is being made, and within those criteria to set standards, expressed in terms of specific behaviour, against which presenting information can be judged.

Exercise 7.15

What is the 'nature or degree' of mental disorder (section 2, MHA 1983) that warrants detention in hospital? What would you think definitely warranted hospitalisation? What definitely does not? Where is the cut-off point at which you would hospitalise?

What is 'seriously inadequate' care in a day care centre (section 74, CA 1989)? What would be good enough, what would be seriously inadequate? What is the difference between inadequate and seriously inadequate?

The skill, then, is in matching the information to the criteria, which must have organisational backing. It is important to be specific in terms of language used, and to recognise the power of legal definitions as opposed to, for example, medical definitions. 'Mentally impaired' is a phrase commonly used about a whole range of learning and behavioural difficulties, yet within the context of the Mental Health Act 1983 it has a precise legal meaning. The use of terminology, particularly that which confers legal status and thus requires legal action, such as the duty to admit to hospital, must be made with precision and understanding of the implications.

A danger when setting criteria and standards is that they can reflect white dominant norms and thus discriminate against black people in the context of assessment. Theoretical frameworks of child development presented in formal guidance on assessment (DoH, 1988) can be criticised as potentially leading to adverse judgements of black families; a family life-cycle approach is presented as if universally applicable, and there is insufficient attention to the disproportionate effect on black families of socioeconomic factors (Phillips, 1990). Practitioners matching information against standards must critically appraise the standards and ensure that in neither content nor application do they lead to discriminatory assessment.

Skills in opening up assessment to a process of participation. Despite emphasis upon openness and accessibility, government guidance locates assessment very firmly in the domain of professional activity. Participation/consultation is seen as a step on the way (DoH, 1991h) rather than integral to the whole process. Some service users are even unaware that they are being 'assessed' (DoH, 1991f). Clearly there are skills of communication and openness that need to be developed if involvement is to be more than token. Enabling people 'to describe their situation in their own words using their preferred language' (DoH, 1991g) demands time and sensitivity, and the routine involvement of people such as advocates and interpreters who can offer assistance in self-expression. Recognising that some service users may be the best assessors of their own needs and solutions (DoH, 1991g) suggests the need to widely publish criteria and procedures so that professional opinion does not control the process. Skills of negotiation in this context become crucial if assessment is to become truly participative (Ellis, 1993).

As social work attempts to move away from paternalistic assumptions of vulnerability and need towards a more open assessment, a major issue is how to involve service users who traditionally have not been judged to have decision-making capacity. An important factor is not to assume incapacity for judgement, but to check levels of comprehension at each decision point. Capacity can fluctuate and is functions-specific – different levels of capacity can be required for different decisions. Capacity can be affected by time, medication, treatment, location and company (Lush, 1996). The micro skills of communication – listening, building trust, non-verbal interaction, styles of questioning – can all help to facilitate self-expression (Marshall, 1990). Additionally, communication that takes place within a supportive and trusting relationship can maximise the understanding necessary for consent to be established (Pearce, 1994).

Law Commission proposals (1993a, 1993b) are based on the principle that people should be encouraged to take decisions they are able to take. This includes anticipatory decision-making by a competent person making arrangements for future incapacity. Knowledge of an individual's former views and wishes on an issue are therefore of great importance to ascertain and this may involve consultation with a wide range of people. Where capacity does not exist, both the current and proposed legal mandates promote the concept of 'best interests' as a key foundation for professional judgement. The Law Commission (1991) has also drawn attention to a possible alternative 'substitute judgement' test whereby the decision-maker thinks him/herself into the shoes of an individual and takes that individual's empathised personal perspective into account. There may remain a valid place for such a test in social work practice, particularly where decision-making rests on proactive choices between alternative but equally beneficial courses of action.

Children's views and children's choices are increasingly emphasised in recent legislation, so that the traditional views of capacity must of necessity be challenged in everyday practice. The use of interpreters in outlining, clarifying and taking forward assessment processes is a skill not yet widely developed, but crucial to effective communication: a skill not merely in working with a 'linguistic technician' but in valuing and drawing upon crucial knowledge and interpretation of fine nuance and detail in what is being communicated.

Decision-making about the ultimate application of the law inevitably remains the responsibility of the local authority. Resource allocation has to take place within strict constraints. Individual practitioners are accountable for their decisions and, in assessments which have a high political profile, such as child protection, the stakes are high. Within that broad framework, however, there is considerable scope for processes of greater equality between professionals and service users, and for assessment to be enhanced by fuller levels of partnership between the parties involved.

Skills in recording

Chapter 4 described in some detail the intricate processes of decision-making, particularly in situations where professionals have the dilemma of choosing between options none of which are risk-free. It is not uncommon for this thinking to take place in supervision, or in *ad hoc* consultation sessions where urgent action is required. As such, an accurate record of the decision-making *process* is unlikely to be made. At best, the outcome or final decision may be logged, but without detailed reflection of the thinking behind it. Yet it is precisely this thinking, or balancing act, that may be called to account in order for professionals to justify their actions. The implications of this for record-keeping are clear – where decisions to pursue one course of action in preference to another are being made, records must clearly demonstrate the attention paid to the advantages and disadvantages of each course of action.

King and Trowell (1992) point to concerns that professionals' worries about scrutiny of their files in the legal arena lead to less rather than more recording – that practitioners are less inclined to note impressions, opinions and hypotheses which could be challenged by lawyers. Clearly, the form of recording is important, and unsubstantiated judgements can and should be open to challenge. Hypotheses and impressions should be clearly identified as such, but do have a place in the formulation of professional judgement and are thus legitimately recorded.

Skills in court craft

The practice of social work law will inevitably bring practitioners into the legal arena of the courts. This is often experienced as something quite alien to common daily experience, and as a test both of character and of credibility (Carson, 1990b). However social work practice has a legitimate place in the courts and the skills involved, while different from those used in less formal arenas, are equally important (Wilson and James, 1989).

There are two areas of skill development. One concerns the preparation and presentation of evidence, where both cognitive and behavioural skills are important. Techniques of reasoning and logic, fact analysis and categorisation and interpretation, need to be matched by deliberately chosen techniques of presentation, both verbal and non-verbal, with attention to and preparation for the linguistic exercises likely to be encountered in cross-examination (Carson, 1990b). Social work of necessity deals in shades of opinion, probability and uncertainty. Legal process emphasises factual evidence, and social workers operating in the courts need to recognise and join the system in order to use it effectively. Familiarity with court rules, clarity of roles and relationships of court personnel can contribute to the ability to assert one's position with credibility and authority. Familiarity with relevant research can make an important contribution, and may indeed be needed in cross-examination as well as in the presentation of evidence.

Since implementation of the Children Act 1989, courts' traditional reliance on oral evidence has been replaced by increasing emphasis on written statements (Hedley, 1996). Practitioners need to maintain high standards of reporting in order to derive maximum benefit for children of court actions. A key skill lies in accurately linking the content of statements and reports to the legal context in which they will be read, and to the requirements of the relevant parts of the legislation being used. A systematic and thorough approach is advocated by Plotnikoff and Woolfson (1996) who offer the following overall checklist to ensure that social workers' statements are well-focused:

- take account of the principles of the Children Act 1989;
- reflect the requirements of the relevant sections;
- ensure balance and overall fairness;
- include all relevant facts, whether or not supportive of the local authority's conclusion;
- verify significant facts and justify opinions;
- avoid repetition;
- present information with sensitivity;
- make relevant references to race;
- avoid applying cultural/moral values;
- take account of changes during the court proceedings.

The second area of skill is in supporting service users through court processes, ensuring that people have information about their rights, about the nature and cause of proceedings, and being sensitive to the emotional impact of the occasion (Wilson and James, 1989). In the adversarial atmosphere of the court, such support may be difficult to give. However, in the wider context of the law as a necessary part of the relationship with service users, the court setting is no different from other situations where power and authority are key factors, to be incorporated positively.

Skills for interaction with other professions and agencies

The statutory foundations for inter-profession and inter-agency collaboration outlined in Chapter 6 cannot alone guarantee effective and efficient multidisciplinary working. Yet such collaboration is crucial to effective use of the law to protect, to promote welfare and to provide services. The emphasis in the NHS and Community Care Act 1990 on multidisciplinary assessment and collaboration in planning and providing services balances long-standing concerns about inter-agency processes in child protection. Yet research (DoH, 1991f) shows considerable mistrust between agencies regarding assessment, and demonstrates that there does not even exist a common language for articulating social care needs. Traditional barriers of professional role, ethos and ideology still exist (DoH, 1995a) and include differing legal roles, budgetary constraints, differing professional disciplines and cultural values (Mental Health Foundation, 1994). More recently, the 'inquiry culture' has prejudiced inter-agency work by creating paranoia and protectionism about what agencies become involved in (Sandford, 1995).

Much can be learned from analyses of what goes wrong in both inter-profession and inter-agency communication and processes: there are implications both for skills development and for procedures. A series of studies and reports (Hallett and Stevenson, 1980; DHSS, 1982; Whittington, 1983; French, 1984; Corby and Mills, 1986; Corby, 1987; Butler-Sloss, 1988; DoH, 1988; SSI, 1990a; Bridge Child Care Consultancy, 1991; Reder *et al.*, 1993; Ritchie *et al.*, 1994; DoH, 1995a) have identified a number of problems:

- lack of clarity about the contributions of various agencies and individuals, arising from unclear roles and responsibilities;
- differing levels of knowledge;
- individual workers asked to fulfil several roles at once, but those roles not clearly distinguished;
- failure to communicate, and to share information and decision-making;
- responsibilities allocated, to give a semblance of the task being done, but lack of attention to the resources required or the realities of resource constraint;
- overlap of functions common to more than one agency;
- lack of differentiation between degrees of risk;
- stereotyping, competitiveness, hostility and hidden agendas between different professional groups;
- attitudinal differences, for example about the involvement of service users, the culpability of victims, the treatment/punishment of offenders, the credibility of children – leading to goal differences and conflicts about how to proceed;
- a tendency to avoid contentious areas of difference and to consider only those which can be agreed upon;
- lack of recourse to specialist advice (legal/medical);
- differences in professional power and status affecting decision-making;
- dysfunctional patterns of relationships within professional networks;
- inappropriately closed or open professional systems in relation to their interaction with others outside the system.

These findings point to the skills that need to be developed.

Skill in differentiating

A key to more positive interaction is recognising how professional roles differ from one another, in terms of legal mandates and professional culture, ideology, attitudes and expertise. For instance, most professions in regular contact with service users would maintain that they have a role in assessment; yet within that generic concern there are a number of specialist areas that would become the focus of different professional groups. It is essential that knowledge is shared about the legal boundaries which determine the focus for work, that legal duties are made explicit and limitations on powers are understood. This can contribute to understanding how each profession thinks and approaches its task, its agendas and priorities.

Exercise 7.16

Take any case study from Chapter 5. List the different professional groups that might have a contribution to make in this case. What would be the legal responsibility of each? What would their professional expertise equip them to do? What are the areas of overlap? Are there any gaps?

Skill in negotiating

A next step from the recognition of difference is the negotiation of position – who is going to fulfil what role? Who is accountable for what to whom? The aim is to avoid overlap and gaps, to reach for a workable compromise. Of related importance is clarity of responsibility for decision-making and for implementing decisions. This will depend both on individual agency accountability structures and upon the power accorded to any joint forum. Written notes of agreements made can often be helpful, and form the basis of continuing review and evaluation.

Establishing a common value system

Guidance is increasingly emphasising the implications of values for practice, particularly in relation to partnership and anti-racist practice (DoH, 1991e, 1995b). Such statements provide a foundation for discussion and development of a shared value system: collective understandings about dynamics such as racism, the dangers of reliance on cultural explanations, the need for sensitivity to stereotyping. Dialogue between professions must take issues further into an understanding of the dynamics of professional/institutional power in people's lives. This is crucial if decisions to use the law are to reflect antidiscriminatory values, and the law is to be used positively to counteract oppression and abuse rather than maintain and institutionalise it.

Skill in networking

The task here is to bring the inter-agency system together, balancing views and opinions, working for clear definitions of need and articulation of risk, backed by understanding of the need for hard evidence in the legal arena. Where all parts of the system in reality congregate together, as in case conferences, the skill is extended into the arena of group process, ensuring it is a positive rather than a negative force. The existence of chairpersons who are independent of line management responsibility or agency allegiance makes an important contribution to establishing constructive processes in such forums.

Also important is a forum for inter-agency networking that is independent of the need to meet for decision-making on individual situations. Local liaison groups or local inter-agency planning mechanisms can promote the channels of communication and trust which can then facilitate effective collaboration in day-to-day decisions.

Skill in working within power structures

It is important to understand and respond to the ways in which power and status influence inter-professional communication. In addition to the differences of status between professions, there are hierarchies of gender, race and other individual characteristics which make interaction more complex. Attention must be given both to others' participation and to asserting one's own position and ensuring appropriate account is taken of this.

Although applicable across the range of inter-agency activity, the forum in which these skills are most immediately apparent is the case conference, described (DoH, 1991e) as an 'essential feature of inter-agency co-operation'. It is essential to establish clarity of purpose, with the emphasis on sharing of knowledge rather than decision-making (Bridge Child Care Consultancy, 1991) resulting in recommendations for action to each agency, though with a clear expectation that failure to implement recommendations should be reported back (DoH, 1991e). Careful thought must be given to ensure representative attendance, involving both those who 'need to know' and those who have a specific contribution to make. Independent chairing is stressed, with clear tasks outlined. The guidance also emphasises the availability of 'specialist' information and advice, on matters of race and culture, religion, disability and sexual abuse, and prioritises with that the need for professional legal advice to be available. The importance of written action plans is emphasised, again to specify roles and undertakings from the agencies involved. Increasing emphasis is being placed on inter-agency coordination in planning and reviewing the needs of and care outcomes for children looked after by local authorities (DoH, 1995c). This moves away from a model which assures all parties involved with a child meet together, partly because the dynamics of such meetings are often not facilitative of children's participation. Interagency consultation is nonetheless promoted, and seen as crucial to the development of positive outcomes for young people.

The emphasis upon the development of skills must be extended to include not only systematic individual collaboration between members of different professions in relation to specific pieces of work, but also collaboration at the structural level of agency organisation. The differing emphases of the NHS and Community Care Act 1990 and the Children Act 1989 may require differing relationships with other agencies and different styles of working, but the essential purpose remains one of facilitating the assessment of need and the delivery of services in accordance with available resources (DoH, 1991b). Agencies must consider what need for collaborative structures arises from the legal duty to coordinate services, what model of agency leadership is appropriate and how joint strategies can be developed while maintaining clear responsibility and accountability (Cambridge, 1990). Efficiency, cost-effectiveness and user-friendliness may indicate the sense of developing single transferable assessment procedures, with straightforward entry rather than a number of different points of assessment for different services (DoH, 1991g). This would require prior work on communication channels and the development of inter-agency trust. 'Bottom-up' initiatives in agency collaboration between professionals in the field need to be matched by 'top-down' approaches such as policy statements and guidelines (Butler and Ward, 1991).

Inter-agency protocols are vital in other fields also. Where housing and social services authorities can agree joint definitions of need in relation to the accommodation of young people aged 16 and 17, for example, this increases the likelihood of vulnerable young people being accepted as eligible for accommodation (McCluskey, 1994). Such protocols give practitioners a viable framework within which to communicate cooperatively and constructively.

The need for more effective inter-agency working in the use of the law to protect implies responsibility at managerial level for facilitating communication. *Working Together* (DoH, 1991e), for instance, requires key Health Authority personnel to be identified to coordinate and facilitate effective contributions from other health authority staff to the child protection process. The differing priorities of police and social services must be negotiated. Methods of joint working must take account of the first principle of child welfare, but also of the likelihood of gaining evidence which will secure child welfare through court processes.

Whilst child protection has received great emphasis, growing concern about abuse to other members of society, and review of legislation to protect vulnerable adults, has resulted in the development of inter-agency collaborative procedures which can promote good coordination of services even where a clear legislative mandate for protection does not exist.

A further dimension to inter-agency or inter-professional skills lies in the new arena of care management, in particular in the commissioning and coordinating of care packages following assessment (NHSCCA 1990). Care management itself is a complex concept and the term may be used to describe a range of quite different models (Huxley, 1993). Clinical models which bring the care manager close to the service user for direct work will draw on interactive and possibly therapeutic skills that would be less appropriate in an administrative model in which provision is deliberately separate from assessment and purchase of service. It will be important to clarify which model practitioners are expected to follow in any individual organisation.

Guidance (DoH, 1991h) identifies seven key stages of care management which may be carried out by one or several practitioners, depending on the complexity and level of provision:

- publishing information;
- determining the level of assessment;
- assessing need;
- care planning;
- implementing the care plan;

- monitoring;
- reviewing.

The skills required include many that are familiar in traditional social work practice, others that are transferred from elsewhere, and new approaches designed to accommodate the changed organisational environments. There has been a wide emphasis on the need for care managers to have skills in business planning, financial management, contract negotiation, tendering and marketing, particularly where the role is construed as brokerage and service allocation (Challis, 1994). Models of care management that are less driven by purchaser/provider organisational splits have retained an emphasis on human relations skills. Stevenson and Parsloe (1993), for example, emphasise the importance of core qualities such as authenticity, empathy and respect for joining with people and creating collaborative relationships. The skills of care management identified are those of engaging with, but remaining distinct from, networks of people and relationships, conceptualising and reframing information about circumstances, and arranging responses to those circumstances in partnership with others.

In entering such negotiations, however, care managers have to confront the challenge that there are complex organisational boundaries around the services that form the key components of care packages, yet the distinctions between the different roles involved are increasingly arbitrary (Warner, 1994). In such an environment it becomes important to identify and articulate the distinctive contribution of social work to the effective application of legal mandates for community care provision, and to maintain a profile for its values and commitments within the market-place of service provision (Braye, 1996).

The organisational context for effective and competent practice in social work law

In the discussion thus far there has been frequent reference to the organisational context – the role of policy, procedures, decision-making structures and forums – in which good practice is located. Competence in social work law requires a competent organisation which will show a number of features: a culture which models and supports empowerment, in relation to its employees as well as the people who use its services; a set of organisational goals which are disseminated at all levels and which give rise to clear procedural and policy guidance; a range of measures designed to support staff in achieving those goals and objectives (Braye and Preston-Shoot, 1995). Three specific mechanisms will resource practitioners to develop their practice of social work law.

Supervision and consultation

Supervision of the practice of social work law has two functions to fulfil: the accountability function, to ensure that legal duties and powers are being used appropriately and that policies and procedures are being complied with; and the reflective function, where the dynamics of the work being undertaken can be explored in detail (Bridge Child Care Consultancy, 1991). Supervision has been criticised (SSI, 1990a) as taking place with inadequate frequency and having an unclear influence on case management, despite its inclusion as one of the essential components of an effective organisational context for the high levels of responsibility carried by practitioners (DoH, 1988).

The practice of social work law is fraught with uncertainty, concern about rights and liberty, potential for discrimination, anxiety about risk management, ambiguity from conflicting imperatives and practice dilemmas, culminating in fear of getting it wrong and pressure to get it right. Decisions to use the law to protect or control may bring workers into situations where they are more likely than in any other activity to face violent protest (Brown *et al.*, 1986), to be fearful and apprehensive. Action is often required quickly, with inadequate information to strengthen judgements. Decisions not to act under the law, not to allocate resources or offer services can leave workers facing hostility, blame, disappointment and distress.

All of this must be the substance of supervision, along with exploration of the processes that affect decision-making, personal attitudes and values, feelings about the use of authority, the draining emotions in the situations in which the law requires or sanctions intervention, the effects of anxiety and defence in human interaction, and the interplay of personal values and agency priorities. The role of the supervisor is to provide a sufficiently supportive environment for challenges to be made constructively, to help practitioners consider alternatives of interpretation and action, to reflect on and weigh in the balance the likely effects of differing interventions, to acknowledge the fears and feelings, to face the task to be done, to gain courage and to see the law as a positive tool for practice rather than a constraint or imposition; in short, to attend both to task, the job to be done, and to process, how it is done and how it leaves the person doing it.

Exercise 7.17

Recall a time when you took action using powers of compulsion, control or protection under the law. What did you feel before and afterwards? What did others feel? How did this affect you? Who did you go to for support?

It is unlikely that all that practitioners need will be forthcoming from one supervisor. Consultation will be important with people with specialist knowledge, from other disciplines, and in particular with lawyers whose interpretations can clarify areas of uncertainty for practice and help build up the detailed working knowledge that contributes to confidence. There will be times too when groups or networks of practitioners, in operating within the tensions posed by the joint demands of legally and professionally accountable practice, need access to a 'reflective space' to examine the feelings and interpersonal processes that can arise and, if unchecked, will adversely influence future practice (Preston-Shoot, 1996c).

Access to information

Qualified social workers will have benefited from the emphasis placed on the law and legal knowledge within DipSW qualifying courses (Ball *et al.*, 1995). The complexity of social work law, however, can lead to a feeling of being swamped, and a rapidly changing and diversifying legal context can exacerbate this. Commentaries and interpretations abound; guides and manuals line up on the shelves. There is, however, key information to which every practitioner should have easy access. There is no substitute for returning to basics and referring to what the law as written down in Acts of Parliament actually says. Basic information must also routinely include associated legal instruments such as regulations, guidance and codes of practice. The third essential component is information on local policies and procedures – how the law is interpreted and implemented in criteria and standards by the employing authority; what strategies and priorities for policy implementation the organisation has devised. Of equal importance are the Appeal Court judgements which themselves alter, amend, clarify or innovate in relation to legal duties, powers and processes. Clearly there is agency responsibility here, but access to journals, newssheets and reports can help individual practitioners to keep in touch with developments which will be influencing lawyers and courts in their interpretations of the law.

At a wider level, practitioners have been publicly criticised for not having read key texts – notably the Cleveland Report (Butler-Sloss, 1988), and practitioners must expect to be familiar with key texts that both support and challenge the position they are taking in relation to a given situation. Since the mid-1980s there have been greater efforts to disseminate key findings of research to practitioners (DHSS, 1985; Sinclair, 1988; Kahan, 1989; Robbins, 1993; DoH, 1995a; Ward, 1995). Social work and research have not had an easy relationship. 'For many practitioners, research conjures up statistics, experiments and questionnaires . . . at best, [they] experience research as irrelevant, at worst as the process of being ripped off' (Everitt *et al.*, 1992). Yet the better integration of research into practice is a key process in the task of reclaiming professionalism from the control of managerialism and bureaucracy. Training sections have a key role in using this material as a resource for updating experienced practitioners on research outcomes.

Action planning

Finally, standing back to monitor one's work and to review its effectiveness is a vital process that can help in identifying impediments to the practice of social work law and in planning the necessary personal and organisational resources. The results of such scrutiny may usefully be incorporated into action planning for the future.

Exercise 7.18

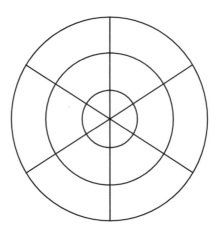

Action plans

In the centre of the diagram make a note of what concerns you about using the law in your practice. In the second circle, indicate what effect this has on your practice. In the outer circle specify the tasks, however small, that will enable you to start addressing the issue that is of concern, who else will need to be involved, when you will do these tasks and when you will review progress. Now commit yourself to your action plan by sharing it with a colleague and using discussion to develop your tasks.

Action plans can be both personal and organisational, carried out individually or in teams, involving both personal developmental tasks and corporate approaches to intervene on a structural level. By promoting open communication they help practitioners and managers to take a proactive stance in creating a work environment that facilitates the effective use of law within the wider context of practice. They work on the principle of breaking down apparently big or insoluble problems into smaller, more manageable parts, making commitments to strategy and tackling each step in turn. It is of crucial importance to identify those in an organisation who have the power and authority to take issues forward, to establish dialogue and engage key people in processes of development and change.

Action plans – examples

Possible concerns about using the law which might appear in the central circle of the diagram:

- appearing in court and being cross-examined;
- involving parents in case conferences;
- not enough factual knowledge about what I can and cannot do;
- no guidance on acceptable risk definitions;
- no legislation to protect older people from abuse;
- I'm not sure I should be crushing these tablets up into her food;
- our services discriminate;
- I have to admit people to psychiatric hospital because there are no suitable community alternatives;
- I don't know if the standards we apply are discriminatory against black families;
- I'm supposed to take into account the needs of both Ms Y and the person who looks after her, but they are diametrically opposed.

The beginnings of an action plan might look like the diagram overleaf, taking two concerns from this list.

I'm not sure I should be crushing these tablets up into her food

Relatives have questioned me and my replies have felt evasive

I do not know what I should do if she appears to refuse

I fear I may be infringing her rights

I cannot find any departmental guidance

Clarify why this is being done. Clarify why I do not like it

Talk to colleagues and ask what they think. Talk to managers – is this a problem for others? Ask for policy guidance

Ask her if she agrees to take the medication. Examine what her behaviour may be trying to tell me. Ask the doctor what effect crushing has on medication

Does she have the capacity to consent? What do I think? Find out who decides. Find out the legal position – talk to legal section

---

I have to admit people to hospital because of lack of suitable alternatives

Admissions may not be in line with the Code of Practice

Inappropriate admissions are oppressive and abusive of the individuals concerned

People don't get the services they need

What does legislation require me to do? Check Mental Health Act 1983. Discuss legal implications of being constrained to deprive someone of their liberty because of lack of resources

Determine what resources would help. Talk to colleagues, users and doctors. Find out from voluntary groups what resources they need to develop viable services

Make representation to health and social care purchasers about budget allocations

References

Adcock, M. (1991) 'Significant Harm: Implications for the Exercise of Statutory Responsibilities', in M. Adcock, R. White and A. Hollows (eds), *Significant Harm: Its Management and Outcome,* Croydon, Significant Publications.

Adcock, M., White, R. and Hollows, A. (eds) (1991), *Significant Harm: Its Management and Outcome,* Croydon, Significant Publications.

ADSS (1991) *Adults at Risk. Guidance for Directors of Social Services,* London, Association of Directors of Social Services.

Age Concern (1995) *Disability Rights and the Local Government Ombudsman. A Study of English Social Services Reports,* London, Age Concern England.

Ahmad, A. (1988) *Social Services for Black People. Service or Lip Service?* London, Race Equality Unit/National Institute for Social Work.

Ahmad, A. (1990) *Practice with Care,* London, Race Equality Unit, ACC Publications.

Ahmad, B. (1990) *Black Perspectives in Social Work,* Birmingham, Venture Press.

Ahmad-Aziz, A., Froggatt, A., Richardson, I., Whittaker, T. and Leung, T. (1992) *Improving Practice with Elders. A Training Manual,* London, Northern Curriculum Development Project, CCETSW.

Alcock, P. and Harris, P. (1982) *Welfare Law and Order. A Critical Introduction to Law for Social Workers,* London, Macmillan.

Aldgate, J. (ed.) (1989) *Using Written Agreements with Children and Families,* London, Family Rights Group.

Aldgate, J., Tunstill, J. and McBeath, G. (1994) 'Implementing Section 17', *Children Act News,* February, 3.

Algie, J. (1976) *Six Ways of Deciding,* Birmingham, British Association of Social Workers.

Allen, H. (1986) *Justice Unbalanced: Gender, Psychiatry and Judicial Decisions,* Milton Keynes, Open University Press.

AMA (1994) *Special Child: Special Needs. Services for Children with Disabilities,* London, Association of Metropolitan Authorities, Child Care Services No. 4.

Appio, H. and Rudgard, E. (1995) 'Women and Children First', *The Guardian,* 2, 4 July, 13.

Arden, A. (1986) *The Homeless Person's Handbook,* London, Allison & Busby.

Audit Commission (1992) *The Community Revolution: Personal Social Services and Community Care,* London, HMSO.

Audit Commission (1994) *Seen but not Heard,* London, HMSO.

Bainham, A. (1990) *Children – The New Law. The Children Act 1989,* Bristol, Family Law, Jordan & Sons.

Baldock, J. and Ungerson, C. (1994) *Becoming Consumers of Community Care: Households within the Mixed Economy of Welfare,* York, Joseph Rowntree Foundation.

Ball, C., Harris, R., Roberts, G. and Vernon, S. (1988) *The Law Report. Teaching and Assessment of Law in Social Work Education,* London, CCETSW, paper 4:1.

Ball, C., Preston-Shoot, M., Roberts, G. and Vernon, S. (1995) *Law for Social Workers in England and Wales,* London, CCETSW.

Bamford, T. (1989) 'Power to the People', *Social Services Insight,* 4(31), 24–5.

Banton, M. (1990) 'Racial Discrimination at Work: Bristol Cases, 1980–89', *New Community,* 17(1), 134–9.

Banton, M. (1994) *Discrimination,* Buckingham, Open University Press.

Barn, R. (1993) *Black Children in the Public Care System,* London, Batsford.

Barnes, M., Bowl, R. and Fisher, M. (1990) *Sectioned: Social Services and the 1983 Mental Health Act,* London, Routledge.

Barry, N. (1990) 'Unfit to Plead', *Social Work Today,* 21(22), 24.

BASW (1977) *Mental Health Crisis Services – A New Philosophy,* Birmingham, British Association of Social Workers.

BASW (1990) *Proposed Legislation – Adults at Risk: Parliamentary Briefing,* London, British Association of Social Workers.

Baxter, C., Poonia, K., Ward, L. and Nadirshaw, Z. (1990) *Double Discrimination. Issues and Services for People with Learning Difficulties from Black and Ethnic Minority Communities,* London, Kings Fund Centre/Commission for Racial Equality.

Bean, P. (1980) *Compulsory Admissions to Mental Hospitals,* Chichester, Wiley.

Bebbington, A. and Davies, B. (1993) 'Efficient Targeting of Community Care: The Use of the Home Help Service', *Journal of Social Policy,* 22(3), 373–91.

Beckford Report (1985) *A Child in Trust,* London Borough of Brent.

Bell, C. (1994) 'Images of Deviance – the Persistent Young Offender', *Justice of the Peace and Local Government Law,* 158 (June), 362–64.

Bell, M. (1993) 'See No Evil, Speak No Evil, Hear No Evil', *Community Care* (Inside Supplement), 28 October, 2–3.

Bentovim, A. and Gilmour, L. (1981) 'A Family Therapy Interactional Approach to Decision Making in Child Care, Access and Custody Cases', *Journal of Family Therapy,* 3(2), 65–77.

Bentovim, A., Elton, A. and Tranter, M. (1987) 'Prognosis for Rehabilitation after Abuse', *Adoption and Fostering,* 11(1), 26–31.

Beresford, P. and Trevillion, S. (1995) *Developing Skills for Community Care: A Collaborative Approach,* Aldershot, Arena.

Berliner, L. and Barbieri, M. (1984) 'The Testimony of the Child Victim of Sexual Assault', *Journal of Social Issues,* 40(2), 125–37.

Best, D. (1994) *Purchasing and Contracting Skills,* London, CCETSW.

Bewley, C. and Glendinning, C. (1994) *Involving Disabled People in Community Care Planning,* York, Joseph Rowntree Foundation.

Birchall, E. and Hallett, C. (1995) *Working Together in Child Protection,* London, HMSO.

Blackwell, G. (1990) 'In on the Act', *Community Care*, 813, 13–15.

Blaug, R. (1995) 'Distortion of the Face to Face: Communicative Reason and Social Work Practice', *British Journal of Social Work*, 25 (4), 423–39.

Blom-Cooper, L. (1988) 'A Patch for a Punctured Ideal', *Social Services Insight*, 3 (18), 12–14.

Booth, T., Bilson, A. and Fowell, I. (1990) 'Staff Attitudes and Caring Practices in Homes for Elderley', *British Journal of Social Work*, 20(2), 117–31.

Bourlet, A. (1990) *Police Intervention in Marital Violence*, Milton Keynes, Open University Press.

Brandon, A. and Brandon, D. (1987) *Consumers as Colleagues*, London, Mind Publications.

Braye, S. (1993) 'Building Competence in Social Work Law for the Diploma in Social Work', in M. Preston-Shoot (ed.), *Assessment of Competence in Social Work Law*, London, Whiting & Birch, Social Work Education.

Braye, S. (1996) 'Social Work with Adults: Is There a Future?' in S. Jackson and M. Preston-Shoot (eds), *Educating Social Workers in a Changing Policy Context,* London, Whiting & Birch.

Braye, S. and Preston-Shoot, M. (1990) 'On Teaching and Applying the Law in Social Work: It Is Not that Simple', *British Journal of Social Work*, 20(4), 333–53.

Braye, S. and Preston-Shoot, M. (1991) 'On Acquiring Law Competence for Social Work: Teaching, Practice and Assessment', *Social Work Education*, 10 (1), 12–29.

Braye, S. and Preston-Shoot, M. (1992) 'Honourable Intentions: Partnership and Written Agreements in Welfare Legislation', *Journal of Social Welfare and Family Law*, 6, 511–28.

Braye, S. and Preston-Shoot, M. (1993a) 'Empowerment and Partnership in Mental Health: Towards a Different Relationship', *Journal of Social Work Practice*, 7(2), 115–28.

Braye, S. and Preston-Shoot, M. (1993b) 'Partnership Practice: Responding to the Challenge, Realising the Potential', *Social Work Education*, 12(2), 35–53.

Braye, S. and Preston-Shoot, M. (1994) 'Partners in Community Care? Rethinking the Relationship between the Law and Social Work Practice', *Journal of Social Welfare and Family Law*, 16 (2), 163–83.

Braye, S. and Preston-Shoot, M. (1995) *Empowering Practice in Social Care,* Buckingham, Open University Press.

Braye, S., Corby, B. and Mills, C. (1988) 'Local Authority Plans on Client Access to Social Work Case Records', *Local Government Studies,* March/April, 49–67.

Brayne, H. and Martin, G. (1995) *Law for Social Workers*, 4th edn, London, Blackstone Press.

Brearley, P. (1979a) 'Gambling with Their Lives?', *Community Care*, 289, 22–3.

Brearley, P. (1979b) 'Gambling with Their Lives? Calculating the Odds?', *Community Care*, 290, 24–5.

Brearley, P. (1982) *Risk and Social Work*, London, Routledge & Kegan Paul.

Bridge Child Care Consultancy (1991) *Sukina – An Evaluation Report into the Circumstances Leading to Her Death*, London, Bridge Child Care Consultancy Services.

Brindle, D. (1994) 'Rights for Disabled Plan Disappoints Campaigners', *The Guardian*, 16 July, 5.

Brophy, J. and Smart, C. (eds) (1985) *Women-in-Law. Explorations in Law, Family and Sexuality*, London, Routledge & Kegan Paul.

Brown, R., Bute, S. and Ford, P. (1986) *Social Workers at Risk*, London, Macmillan.

Brownlee, I. (1990) 'Compellability and Contempt in Domestic Violence Cases', *Journal of Social Welfare Law*, 2, 107–15.

Buckley, J., Preston-Shoot, M. and Smith, C. (1995) *Community Care Reforms: The Views of Users and Carers – Research Findings*, University of Manchester School of Social Work.

Busfield, J. (1986) *Managing Madness*, London, Unwin Hyman.

Butler, T. and Ward, D. (1991) 'The Hampshire Approach', *Community Care*, 847, 22–3.

Butler-Sloss, E. (1988) *Report of the Inquiry into Child Abuse in Cleveland*, London, HMSO.

Byng-Hall, J. (1988) 'Scripts and Legends in Families and Family Therapy', *Family Process*, 27, 167–79.

Bynoe, I., Oliver, M. and Barnes, C. (1991) *Equal Rights for Disabled People. The Case for a New Law*, London, Institute for Public Policy Research.

Cambridge, P. (1990) 'A Decade of Opportunities', *Community Care*, 836, 17–19.

Campbell, D. (1990) 'Beating the Wife-Beater', *The Guardian*. 12 December, 23.

Carlen, P. (ed.) (1976) *The Sociology of Law*, Sociological Review Monograph 23, University of Keele.

Carlile Report (1987) *A Child in Mind. Report of the Commission of Inquiry into the Circumstances Surrounding the Death of Kimberley Carlile*, London Borough of Greenwich.

Carson, D. (1988) 'Risk-Taking Policies', *Journal of Social Welfare Law*, 5, 328–32.

Carson, D. (1989) 'The Sexuality of People with Learning Difficulties', *Journal of Social Welfare Law*, 6, 355–72.

Carson, D. (1990a) 'Reporting to Court: A Role in Preventing Decision Error', *Journal of Social Welfare Law*, 3, 151–63.

Carson, D. (1990b) *Professionals and the Courts. A Handbook for Expert Witnesses*, Birmingham, Venture Press.

Carson, D. (1990c) 'From Risk Policies to Risk Strategies', in D. Carson (ed.), *Risk-taking in Mental Disorder; Analyses, Policies and Practical Strategies*, Chichester, SLE Publications.

Carson, D. (1990d) 'Risk-Taking in Mental Disorder', in D. Carson (ed.).

Carson, D. (1995) 'Calculated Risk', *Community Care,* 26 October–1 November, 26–7.

CCETSW (1989) *Requirements and Regulations for the Diploma in Social Work* (Paper 30), London, Central Council for Education and Training in Social Work.

CCETSW (1995) *Assuring Quality in the Diploma in Social Work – 1. Rules and Requirements for the DipSW,* London, Central Council for Education and Training in Social Work.

Challis, D. (1994) 'Care Management', in N. Malin (ed.), *Implementing Community Care,* Buckingham, Open University Press.

Chamberlin, J. (1988) *On Our Own: Patient Controlled Alternatives to the Mental Health System,* London, Mind.

Child, J. (1984) *Organisations,* London, Harper & Row.

Children Act Advisory Committee (1992/93) *Annual Report,* London, HMSO.

Children Act Advisory Committee (1993/94) *Annual Report,* London, HMSO.

Childright (1989a) 'Smacking Ban for Foster Care', *Childright,* no. 62 (December), 3.

Childright (1989b) 'Children and Confidentiality – the Legal Position', *Childright,* no. 58 (July/August), 11–14.

Childright (1990a) 'Child Witnesses, a Step Forward', *Childright,* no. 64 (March), 2.

Childright (1990b) 'The UN Convention on the Rights of the Child', *Childright,* no. 63 (January/February), 13–20.

Childright (1990c) 'The Child Witness', *Childright,* no. 63 (January/February), 9–12.

Childright (1991) 'At the Police Station. The Role of the Appropriate Adult', *Childright,* no. 74, (March), 9–16.

Childright (1995a) 'UN Committee Criticise UK Rights of Child Report', *Childright,* no. 114 (March), 3–5.

Childright (1995b) 'Draft European Convention on the Exercise of Children's Rights', *Childright,* no. 121 (November), 9–12.

Childright (1995c) 'Young Black People and Homelessness', *Childright,* no. 120 (October), 10–12.

Clark, S. (1993) 'Children Call on Councils to Listen', *Community Care,* 8 July, 3.

Clark, S. (1995) 'SSI Exposes Scandal of Small Children's Homes', *Community Care,* 9–15 February, 1.

Clements, L. (1992) 'Duties of Social Services Departments', *Legal Action,* September, 15–16.

Clements, L. (1993) 'Community Care: Legal Structure', *Legal Action,* July, 10–12.

Clements, L. (1995) 'Judgement Daze', *Community Care,* 13–19 July, 24–5.

Clode, D. (1995) 'Balancing Your Budget', *Community Care,* 17–23 August, 14–15.

Cloke, C. and Davies, M. (eds) (1995) *Participation and Empowerment in Child Protection,* London, Pitman.

Coles, J. (1991) 'Taking on the System', *The Guardian,* 23 January, 25.

Colton, M., Drury, C. and Williams, M. (1995) 'Children in Need: Definition, Identification and Support', *British Journal of Social Work,* 25(6), 711–28.

Commission on Social Justice (1994) *Social Justice: Strategies for National Renewal,* London, Vintage.

Cooper, J. (1990) *The Legal Rights Manual. A Guide for Social Workers and Advice Centres,* Aldershot, Gower.

Cope, R. (1989) 'Compulsory Detention of Afro-Caribbeans under the Mental Health Act', *New Community,* 15(3), 343–56.

Corby, B. (1987) *Working with Child Abuse,* Milton Keynes, Open University Press.

Corby, B. and Mills, C. (1986) 'Child Abuse: Risks and Resources', *British Journal of Social Work,* 16(5), 531–42.

Corden, J. and Preston-Shoot, M. (1987) *Contracts in Social Work,* Aldershot, Gower.

Cornwell, N. (1992/93) 'Assessment and Accountability in Community Care', *Critical Social Policy,* 36, 40–52.

Counsel and Care (1993) *The Right to Take Risks,* London, Counsel and Care.

CRE (1989) *Racial Equality in Social Services Departments,* London, Commission for Racial Equality.

CRE (1995) *Local Authorities and Racial Equality,* London, Commission for Racial Equality.

Crisp, A. (1994) 'Children First', *Community Care* (Inside Supplement), 28 July–3 August, 2–3.

Croall, J. (1991) 'Special Needs, Muddled Deeds', *The Guardian,* 26 March, 25.

Curnock, K, and Hardiker, P. (1979) *Towards Practice Theory. Skills and Methods in Social Assessments,* London, Routledge & Kegan Paul.

Dale, P. (1984) 'The Danger Within Ourselves', *Community Care,* 501, 20–2.

Davies, M. and Brandon, M. (1988) 'The Summer of 88', *Community Care,* 733, 16–18.

Day, P. (1994) 'Ambiguity and User Involvement: Issues Arising in Assessments for Young People and Their Carers', *British Journal of Social Work,* 24 (5), 577–96.

Day, P., Klein, R. and Redmayne, S. (1995) *Why Regulate? Regulating Residential Care for Elderly People,* Bristol, Policy Press.

Dean, H. and Hartley, G. (1995) 'Listen to Learn', *Community Care,* 30 March–5 April, 22–3.

DFE (1994) *Code of Practice on the Identification and Assessment of Special Educational Needs,* London, Department for Education.

DHSS (1982) *Child Abuse: A Study of Inquiry Reports, 1973–1981,* London, HMSO.

DHSS (1985) *Social Work Decisions in Child Care,* London, HMSO.

Dimond, B. (1995) *Legal Aspects of Health Care*, London, Open Learning Foundation/Churchill Livingstone.

Dingwall, R., Eekelaar, J. and Murray, T. (1983) *The Protection of Children*, Oxford, Blackwell.

DoH (1988) *Protecting Children. A Guide for Social Workers Undertaking a Comprehensive Assessment*, London, HMSO.

DoH (1989a) *The Care of Children. Principles and Practice in Regulations and Guidance*, London, HMSO.

DoH (1989b) *An Introduction to the Children Act 1989*, London, HMSO.

DoH (1989c) *Caring for People; Community Care in the Next Decade and Beyond*, London, HMSO.

DoH (1989d) *Homes are for Living In*, London, HMSO.

DoH (1990) *Community Care in the Next Decade and Beyond; Policy Guidance*, London, HMSO.

DoH (1991a) *The Children Act 1989 Guidance and Regulations, Volume 3, Family Placements*, London, HMSO.

DoH (1991b) *The Children Act 1989 Guidance and Regulations, Volume 2, Family Support, Day Care and Educational Provision*, London, HMSO.

DoH (1991c) *The Children Act 1989 Guidance and Regulations, Volume 5, Independent Schools*, London, HMSO.

DoH (1991d) *The Children Act 1989 Guidance and Regulations, Volume 1, Court Orders*, London, HMSO.

DoH (1991e) *Working Together. A Guide to Arrangements for Inter-Agency Co-operation for the Protection of Children from Abuse*, London, HMSO.

DoH (1991f) *Assessment Systems and Community Care*, London, HMSO.

DoH (1991g) *Getting the Message Across. A Guide to Developing and Communicating Policies, Principles and Procedures on Assessment*, London, HMSO.

DoH (1991h) *Care Management and Assessment: A Guide to Practice*, London, HMSO.

DoH (1991i) *The Children Act 1989 Guidance and Regulations, Volume 4, Residential Care*, London, HMSO.

DoH (1991j) *Care Management and Assessment. Summary of Practice Guidance*, London, HMSO.

DoH (1991k) *Care Management and Assessment. Managers' Guide*, London, HMSO.

DoH (1991l) *The Right to Complain. Practice Guidance on Complaints Procedures in Social Services Departments*, London, HMSO.

DoH (1991m) *Care Management and Assessment. Practitioners' Guide*, London, HMSO.

DoH (1991n) *The Children Act 1989 Guidance and Regulations, Volume 6, Children with Disabilities*, London, HMSO.

DoH (1992a) *Implementing Community Care. Improving Independent Sector Involvement in Community Care Planning*, London, HMSO.

DoH (1992b) *Manual of Practice Guidance for Guardians Ad Litem and Reporting Officers*, London, HMSO.

DoH (1993a) *Letter to Local Authorities on Community Care (CI(93)35)*, London, Department of Health.

DoH (1993b) *Monitoring and Development. First Impressions, April–September*, London, HMSO.

DoH (1993c) *Code of Practice: Section 118 Mental Health Act 1983*, London, HMSO.

DoH (1993d) *Informing Users and Carers*, London, HMSO.

DoH (1993e) *Adoption: The Future*, London, HMSO.

DoH (1994a) *The Children Act 1989: Contact Orders Study*, London, HMSO.

DoH (1994b) *Mental Health Act Guardianship*, London, Department of Health.

DoH (1995a) *Child Protection – Messages from Research*, London, HMSO.

DoH (1995b) *The Challenge of Partnership in Child Protection: Practice Guide*, London, HMSO.

DoH (1995c) *Looking After Children. Management and Implementation Guide*, London, HMSO.

Dominelli, L. (1988) *Anti-Racist Social Work*, London, Macmillan.

Dooher, I. (1989) 'Research Note: Guardianship Under the Mental Health Act 1983 – Practice in Leicestershire', *British Journal of Social Work*, 19(2), 129–35.

Douglas, G. and Willmore, C. (1987) 'Diagnostic Interviews as Evidence in Cases of Child Sexual Abuse', *Family Law*, 17 (May), 151–4.

Dowie, J. (1989a) *Professional Judgement: Introductory Texts 5–7*, Milton Keynes, Open University Press.

Dowie, J. (1989b) *Professional Judgement: Introductory Texts 8–11*, Milton Keynes, Open University Press.

Doyal, L. and Gough, I. (1991) *A Theory of Human Need*, London, Macmillan.

Dutt, R. (1990b) 'Report of Study Day on Assessment and Case Conferences', in R. Dutt (ed.), *Towards a Black Perspective in Child Protection*, London, Race Equality Unit.

Dutt, R. (ed.) (1990a) *Black Community and Community Care*, London, Race Equality Unit/National Institute for Social Work.

Dyer, C. (1991a) 'Virgin Births and Human Rights', *The Guardian*, 13 March, 38.

Dyer, C. (1991b) 'Rochdale Children Returned to Parents', *The Guardian*, 8 March, 2.

Dyer, C. (1994) 'More Lesbian Parents Win', *The Guardian*, 6 July, 10.

Eaton, M. (1985) 'Documenting the Defendant: Placing Women in Social Inquiry Reports', in J. Brophy and C. Smart (eds), *Women-in-Law. Explorations in Law, Family and Sexuality*, London, Routledge & Kegan Paul.

Edwards, S. (ed.) (1985a) *Gender, Sex and the Law*, London, Croom Helm.

Edwards, S. (1985b) 'Gender "Justice"? Defending Defendants and Mitigating Sentence', in S. Edwards (ed.).

Edwards, S. and Halpern, A. (1988) 'Conflicting Interests: Protecting Children or Protecting Title to Property', *Journal of Social Welfare Law*, 2, 110–24.

Edwards, S. and Halpern, A. (1990) 'Regional "Injustice": Financial Provision on Divorce', *Journal of Social Welfare Law*, 2, 71–88.

Ellis, K. (1993) *Squaring the Circle. User and Carer Participation in Needs Assessment*, York, Joseph Rowntree Foundation.

Employment Gazette (1991) 'Registered Disabled People in the Public Sector', February, 81–6.

England, H. (1986) *Social Work as Art*, London, Allen & Unwin.

EOC (1988) *Equal Treatment for Men and Women*, Manchester, Equal Opportunities Commission.

EOC (1995) *Targeting Potential Discrimination*, Manchester, Equal Opportunities Commission.

Everitt, A., Hardiker, P., Littlewood, J. and Mullender, A. (1992) *Applied Research for Better Practice*, London, Macmillan.

Fahlberg, V. (1981a) *Attachment and Separation*, London, British Agencies for Adoption and Fostering.

Fahlberg, V. (1981b) *Helping Children When They Must Move*, London, British Agencies for Adoption and Fostering.

Farmer, E. and Owen, M. (1995) *Child Protection Practice. Private Risks and Public Remedies*, London, HMSO.

Faulkner, A. (1994) 'Mission Impossible', *Community Care*, 8–14 September, 22–3.

Fennell, P. (1989) 'The Beverley Lewis Case: Was the Law to Blame?', *New Law Journal*, 17 November, 1557–8.

Fennell, P. (1990) 'Inscribing Paternalism in the Law: Consent to Treatment and Mental Disorder', *Journal of Law and Society*, 17(1), 29–51.

Fernando, S. (1991) *Mental Health, Race and Culture*, London, Macmillan.

Ferreira, A. (1963) 'Family Myth and Homeostasis', *Archives of General Psychiatry*, 9, 457–63.

Fisher, M. (1994) 'Man-Made Care: Community Care and Older Male Carers', *British Journal of Social Work*, 24(6), 659–80.

Fisher, M. and Newton, C. (1985) 'Coming up to Expectation', *Community Care*, 556, 16.

Fisher, M., Newton, C. and Sainsbury, E. (1984) *Mental Health Social Work Observed*, London, George Allen & Unwin.

Flynn, N. (1993) *Public Sector Management*, 2nd edn, Hemel Hempstead, Harvester Wheatsheaf.

Forster, D. and Tiplady, P. (1980) 'Doctors and Compulsory Procedures: Section 47 of the National Assistance Act 1948', *British Medical Journal*, 8 March, 739–40.

Foster, B. and Preston-Shoot, M. (1995) *Guardians ad Litem and Independent Expert Assessments*, Manchester, Stockport, Tameside and Trafford GALRO Service and the University of Manchester.

Fothergill, J. (1994) 'The Colour Bar', *The Guardian*, 2, 19 July, 19.

Fox Harding, L. (1991) *Perspectives in Child Care Policy*, London, Longman.

Fox Report (1990) *Report into the Death of Stephanie Fox*, London Borough of Wandsworth.

Francis, E., David, J., Johnson, N. and Sashidharan, S. (1989) 'Black People and Psychiatry in the UK', *Psychiatric Bulletin*, 13, 482–5.

Francis, J. (1995) 'Cast Aside', *Community Care,* 28 September–4 October, 16–17.

Freeman, M. (1983a) *The Rights and Wrongs of Children*, London, Francis Pinter.

Freeman, M. (1983b) 'Freedom and the Welfare State: Child Rearing, Parental Autonomy and State Intervention', *Journal of Social Welfare Law*, March, 70–91.

Freeman, M. (1984a) 'Rethinking Family Law', in M. Freeman (ed.), *The State, the Law and the Family: Critical Perspectives*, London, Tavistock Publications, Sweet & Maxwell.

Freeman, M. (1984b) 'Legal Ideologies, Patriarchal Precedents and Domestic Violence', in M. Freeman (ed.).

Freeman, M. (ed.) (1990) *Critical Issues in Welfare Law*, London, Stevens & Sons.

French, C. (1984) 'Competing Orientations in Child Abuse Management', *British Journal of Social Work*, 14(6), 615–24.

FRG (1989) 'Working Together – Client Participation in Case Conferences', *Family Rights Group Bulletin*, Spring, 13–18.

Frost, N. and Stein, M. (1990) 'The Politics of the Children Act', *Childright*, no. 68, (July/August), 17–19.

Gardner, R. (1990) 'Children in Need', *Community Care*, 841, 28–9.

Garlick, H. (1990) 'Sex and the Single Parent', *The Guardian*, 5 December, 25.

George, M. (1991) 'Difficult Times, Little Help', *Community Care*, 846, 11.

George, M. (1995) 'Child Rights', *Community Care,* 12–18 October, 16–17.

Gibbons, J. (ed.) (1992) *The Children Act 1989 and Family Support: Principles into Practice,* London, HMSO.

Gibbons, J. and Bell, C. (1994) 'Variation in Operation of English Child Protection Registers', *British Journal of Social Work*, 24(6), 701–14.

Gilyeat, D. (1994) *A Companion Guide to Offence Seriousness*, 2nd edn, Ilkley, Owen Wells.

Glaser, D. and Frosh, S. (1988) *Child Sexual Abuse*, London, Macmillan.

Gooding, C. (1996) *Disability Discrimination Act 1995,* London, Blackstone Press.

Goodman Report (1990) *Report of the Inquiry into the Death of a Child in Care*, Derbyshire and Nottinghamshire County Councils and Area Child Protection Committees.

Gordon, R. (1993) *Community Care Assessments: A Practical Legal Framework,* London, Longman.

Goss, S. and Miller, C. (1995) *From Margin to Mainstream: Developing User- and Carer-Centred Community Care,* York, Joseph Rowntree Foundation.

Graham, H. (1993) 'Feminist Perspectives on Caring', in J. Bornat, C. Pereira, D. Pilgrim and F. Williams (eds), *Community Care. A Reader,* Basingstoke, Macmillan/The Open University.

Greengross, S. (1986) *The Law and Vulnerable Elderly People*, London, Age Concern England.

Greenland, C. (1987) *Preventing CAN Deaths. An International Study of Deaths Due to Child Abuse and Neglect*, London, Tavistock.

Grewcock, M., quoted in Thompson, A. (1995) 'A Share of Responsibility', *Community Care*, 3–9 August, 12–13.

Grimwood, C. and Popplestone, R. (1993) *Women, Management and Care*, London, Macmillan.

Guardian, The (1991) 'Disturbed Offenders in Limbo of Neglect', 21 March, 4.

Gunaratnam, Y. (1993) 'Breaking the Silence: Asian Carers in Britain', in J. Bornat, C. Pereira, D. Pilgrim and F. Williams (eds), *Community Care. A Reader*, Basingstoke, Macmillan/The Open University.

Gunn, M. (1986) 'Mental Health Act Guardianship: Where Now?', *Journal of Social Welfare Law*, May, 144–52.

Haley, M. and Swift, J. (1988) 'PACE and the Social Worker: A Step in the Right Direction?', *Journal of Social Welfare Law*, 6, 355–73.

Hallett, C. and Stevenson, O. (1980) *Child Abuse: Aspects of Inter-professional Co-operation*, London, George Allen & Unwin.

Hamilton, C. (1995) 'Report on Small Unregistered Children's Homes', *Childright*, no 122 (December), 14–15.

Hamilton, C. and Watt, B. (1995) 'Do Local Authorities Owe Children a Duty of Care?', *Childright*, no. 118 (August), 8–9.

Hamm, R. (1988) 'Clinical Intuition and Clinical Analysis: Expertise and the Cognitive Continuum', in J. Dowie and A. Elstein (eds), *Professional Judgement. A Reader in Clinical Decision Making*, Cambridge, Cambridge University Press.

Handy, C. (1985) *Understanding Organisations*, 3rd edn, Harmondsworth, Penguin.

Hanmer, J. and Statham, D. (1988) *Women and Social Work: Towards a Woman-Centred Practice*, London, Macmillan.

Hanmer, J., Radford, J. and Stanko, E. (eds) (1989) *Women, Policing and Male Violence: International Perspectives*, London, Routledge.

Hardiker, P., Exton, K. and Barker, M. (1991) 'Analysing Policy–Practice Links in Preventive Child Care', in P. Carter, T. Jeffs and M. Smith (eds), *Social Work and Social Welfare Yearbook*, 3, Milton Keynes, Open University Press.

Harne, L. and Radford, J. (1994) 'Reinstating Patriarchy: The Politics of the Family and the New Legislation', in A. Mullender and R. Morley (eds), *Children Living with Domestic Violence. Putting Men's Abuse of Women on the Child Care Agenda*, London, Whiting & Birch.

Harris, N. (1987) 'Defensive Social Work', *British Journal of Social Work*, 17(1), 61–9.

Harris, R. (1982) 'Institutionalised Ambivalence: Social Work and the Children and Young Persons Act 1969', *British Journal of Social Work*, 12(3), 247–63.

Harris, R. (1990a) 'A Matter of Balance: Power and Resistance in Child Protection Policy', *Journal of Social Welfare Law*, 5, 332–40.

Harris, R. (1990b) 'Out of Order', *Community Care*, 836, 24–5.

Hartman, A. (1969) 'Anomie and Social Casework', *Social Casework*, 50(3), 131–7.

Hatchett, W. (1991) 'An Act of Omission', *Community Care*, 866, 16–17.

Hedley, M. (1996) 'Preface', in J. Plotnikoff and R. Woolfson, *Reporting to Court under the Children Act. A Handbook for Social Services*, London, HMSO.

Henwood, M. and Wistow, G. (1995) 'The Waiting Game', *Community Care*, 2–8 February, 26–7.

Hersham, D. and McFarlane, A. (1990) 'Admissibility of Hearsay Evidence', *Family Law*, May, 164–6.

Hirst, J. (1995) 'Breaking Barriers', *Community Care*, 12–17 October, 25.

Hoath, D. (1990) 'Homelessness Law: First Aid in Need of Intensive Care', in M. Freeman (ed.).

Hodgkin, R. (1994) 'The Right to Consent to Treatment', *Children UK*, Winter, 4–5.

Hodson, D. (1990) 'The New Partner after Divorce. Part II – Children and Step-Parents', *Family Law*, (February), 68–71.

Hoggett, B. (1987) *Parents and Children: The Law of Parental Responsibility*, London, Sweet & Maxwell.

Hoggett, B. (1990) *Mental Health Law*, 3rd edn, London, Sweet & Maxwell.

Home Office (1992) *Memorandum of Good Practice on Video Recorded Interviews with Child Witnesses for Criminal Proceedings*, London, HMSO.

Home Office (1995) *National Standards for the Supervision of Offenders in the Community*, London, Home Office.

Horne, M. (1987) *Values in Social Work*, Aldershot, Wildwood House.

Howe, D. (1980) 'Inflated States and Empty Theories in Social Work', *British Journal of Social Work*, 10(3), 317–40.

Howe, D. (1990) 'The Client's View in Context', in P. Carter, T. Jeffs and M. Smith (eds), *Social Work and Social Welfare Yearbook 2*, Buckingham, Open University Press.

Howe, D. (1994) 'Modernity, Postmodernity and Social Work', *British Journal of Social Work*, 24(5), 513–32.

Howlett, M. (1995) quoted in Rickford, F. 'Risky business', *Community Care*, 24–30 August, 22–3.

Hoyes, L., Lart, R., Means, R. and Taylor, M. (1994) *Community Care in Transition*, York, Joseph Rowntree Foundation.

Hughes, R. D. and Bhaduri, R. (1987) *Race and Culture in Social Services Delivery*, Manchester, Social Services Inspectorate.

Huxley, P. (1993) 'Case Management and Care Management in Community Care', *British Journal of Social Work*, 23(4), 365–81.

Jackson, S. (1993) 'Family fortunes', *Community Care*, 9 December, 14–15.

Jackson, S. and Preston-Shoot, M. (1996) 'Social Work Education in a Changing Policy Context: An Introduction', in S. Jackson and M. Preston-Shoot (eds), *Educating Social Workers in a Changing Policy Context*, London, Whiting & Birch.

James, A. (1987) 'The Legacy', in *Decision Making in Child Care; Course Material*, East Sussex, Escata, 5–18.

Jones, C. and Novak, T. (1993) 'Social Work Today', *British Journal of Social Work*, 23(3), 195–212.

Jones, D. (1991) 'The Effectiveness of Intervention', in M. Adcock, R. White and A. Hollows (eds), *Significant Harm*, Croydon, Significant Publications.

Jones, E. (1993) *Family Systems Therapy. Developments in the Milan-Systemic Therapies*, Chichester, Wiley.

Jones, F., Fletcher, B. and Ibbetson, K. (1991) 'Stressors and Strains Amongst Social Workers; Demands, Supports, Constraints and Psychological Health', *British Journal of Social Work*, 21(5), 443–69.

Jones, K. (1991) 'An Educational Inconvenience', *Community Care*, 845, 7.

Kaganas, F., King, M. and Piper, C. (eds) (1995) *Legislating for Harmony. Partnership under the Children Act 1989*, London, Jessica Kingsley.

Kahan, B. (ed.) (1989) *Child Care Research, Policy and Practice*, London, Hodder & Stoughton.

Keep, J. and Clarkson, J. (1994) *Disabled People Have Rights*, London, RADAR.

Kelly, D. and Johnson, N. (1989) 'The Disabled Persons Act 1986: A Progress Report', *Social Work Today*, 20 (44), 30.

Kent, P. (1989) 'Detaching Law from the Real World', review of C. Ball (1989) *Law for Social Workers: An Introduction*, Aldershot, Gower, published in *Social Work Today*, 21(11), 30.

King, M. and Trowell, J. (1992) *Children's Welfare and the Law. The Limits of Legal Intervention*, London, Sage.

Kingston, P. (1982) 'Power and influence in the Environment of Family Therapy', *Journal of Family Therapy*, 4(3), 211–27.

Knapp, M., Cambridge, P., Thomason, C., Beecham, J., Allen, C. and Darton, R. (1992) *Care in the Community: Challenge and Demonstration*, Aldershot, Ashgate.

Knewstub, N. (1991) 'Guide for Police on Home Violence', *The Guardian*, 8 January, 8.

Lamb, B. and Layzell, S. (1995) *Disabled in Britain: Counting on Community Care*, London, SCOPE.

Lane, J. (1990) 'Sticks and Carrots – Using the Race Relations Act to Remove Bad Practice and the Children Act to Promote Good Practice', *Local Government Policy Making*, 17(3), 40–9.

Larcombe-Williams, N. (1994) 'Beyond Reasonable Doubt?', *Community Care*, 8–14 September, 30–1.

Laurie, L. and Macfarlane, A. (1995) *The Effect of Community Care on Housing for Disabled People*, York, Joseph Rowntree Foundation.

Law Commission (1989) 'Domestic Violence and Occupation of the Matrimonial Home', Working Paper No. 113, London, HMSO.

Law Commission (1991) 'Mentally Incapacitated Adults and Decision-Making: An Overview', Consultation Paper No. 119, London, HMSO.

Law Commission (1993a) 'Mentally Incapacitated Adults and Decision-Making. A New Jurisdiction', Consultation Paper No. 128, London, HMSO.

Law Commission (1993b) 'Mentally Incapacitated and Other Vulnerable Adults: Public Law Protection', Consultation Paper No. 130, London, HMSO.

Law Commission (1995) 'Mental Incapacity. Summary of Recommendations', Consultation Paper No. 231, London, HMSO.

Layton-Henry, Z. (1984) *The Politics of Race in Britain*, London, George Allen & Unwin.

LBTC (1989) *Training Together: A Training and Curriculum Model for the Children Act 1989*, London Boroughs' Training Committee.

Levy, A. (1995) 'Is Anyone Minding the Kids?', *The Guardian, 2,* 6 June, 13.

Levy, A. and Kahan, B. (1991) *The Pin Down Experience and the Protection of Children. The Report of the Staffordshire Child Care Inquiry, 1990*, Staffordshire County Council.

LGTB (1990) *Maximising Human Resources – Through Equal Opportunities*, Hounslow, Local Government Training Board.

Lindsay, M. (1992) *An Introduction to Children's Rights,* London, National Children's Bureau, Highlight No. 113.

Llewelyn, S. (1987) 'Ethical Issues in Psychotherapy for Women', in S. Fairbairn and G. Fairbairn (eds), *Psychology, Ethics and Change*, London, Routledge & Kegan Paul.

Lomas, P. (1987) *The Limits of Interpretation*, Harmondsworth, Penguin.

Lovelock, R. and Powell, J. with Craggs, S. (1995) *Shared Territory: Assessing the Social Support Needs of Visually Impaired People,* York: Joseph Rowntree Foundation.

Lush, D. (1996) 'Legal Tests of Mental Capacity', Conference paper to Joint Conference of the Law Society and the British Medical Association, Mental Incapacity, London, 19 January.

Lyon, C. (1988) 'From Diagnosis to Evidence – An Examination of Two Cases Illustrating the Problems of Such a Transition in Situations Involving Potential Emotional Abuse of Children', *Journal of Social Welfare Law*, 2, 88–93.

Lyon, C. (1989) 'Professional Decision-Making in Child Abuse Cases: The Social Worker's Dilemma – part 1', *Family Law*, 19 January, 6–10.

Macdonald, S. (1991) *All Equal Under the Act*? London, Race Equality Unit/National Institute for Social Work.

Mama, A. (1989) *The Hidden Struggle. Statutory and Voluntary Sector Responses to Violence against Black Women in the Home*, London, London Race and Housing Research Unit.

Manthorpe, J., Walsh, M., Alaszewski, A. and Harrison, L. (1995) 'Taking a Chance', *Community Care,* 19–25 October, 20–1.

Marchant, C. (1995) 'Care Managers Speak Out', *Community Care,* 30 March–5 April, 16–17.

Marsh, P. and Fisher, M. (1992) *Good Intentions: Developing Partnership in Social Services,* York, Joseph Rowntree Foundation.

Marshall, M. (ed.) (1990) *Working with Dementia. Guidelines for Professionals*, Birmingham, Venture Press.

Martin, T. (1990) 'Whose Duty?', *Social Services Insight*, 5(19), 20–1.

Mason, M. (1995) 'The Faulty Balance of Power', *The Guardian* 2, 7 June, 6–7.

Masson, J. (1994) 'Social Engineering in the House of Lords: Re M', *Journal of Child Law*, 6 (4), 170–73.

McCann, K. (1985) 'Battered Women and the Law: The Limits of the Legislation', in J. Brophy and C. Smart (eds), *Women-In-Law. Explorations in Law, Family and Sexuality*, London, Routledge & Kegan Paul.

McCluskey, J. (1994) *Acting in Isolation. An Evaluation of the Effectiveness of the Children Act for Young Homeless People*, London, CHAR.

McWilliams, B. (1992) 'The Rise and Development of Management Thought in the English Probation System', in R. Statham and P. Whitehead (eds), *Managing the Probation Service. Issues for the 1990s*, Harlow, Longman.

Mental Health Foundation (1994) *Creating Community Care*, London, Mental Health Foundation.

Miller, S. (1991) 'Driven to Destruction', *The Guardian*, 20 February, 19.

Mirza, K. (1991) 'Community Care for the Black Community – Waiting for Guidance', in CCETSW, *One Small Step Towards Racial Justice*, London, CCETSW.

Morgan, D. (1988) 'Re F (In Utero)', *Journal of Social Welfare Law*, 3, 197–203.

Morgan, D. (1990) 'Recent Cases: *F* v. *West Berkshire Health Authority*', *Journal of Social Welfare Law*, 3, 204–11.

Morgan, J. and Williams, J. (1993) 'A Role for a Support Person for Child Witnesses in Criminal Proceedings', *British Journal of Social Work*, 23(2), 113–21.

Moss, M. (1990) 'NAYPIC Report on Abuse in Care', *Childright*, no. 66, (May), 19.

Mullender, A. (1991) 'Nottingham Advocacy Group: Giving a Voice to the Users of Mental Health Services', *Practice*, 5(1), 5–12.

Mullender, A. and Ward, D. (1991) *Self-Directed Groupwork – Users Take Action for Empowerment*, London, Whiting & Birch.

NACRO (1992a) *Pre-sentence Reports. A Handbook for Probation Officers and Social Workers*, London, National Association for the Care and Resettlement of Offenders.

NACRO (1992b) *Statutory Criteria for Custodial Sentences*, London, National Association for the Care and Resettlement of Offenders.

NAPO (1990) *Working with Lesbians and Gay Men as Clients of the Service: Good Practice Guidelines*, London, National Association of Probation Officers.

NAREA (undated) *Black Community Care Charter*, Birmingham, National Association of Race Equality Advisers.

NCH (1994) *The Hidden Victims. Children and Domestic Violence*, London, National Children's Homes.

Norman, A. (1980) *Rights and Risk. A Discussion Document on Civil Liberty in Old Age*, London, Centre for Policy on Ageing.

O'Hara, M. (1994) 'Child Deaths in Contexts of Domestic Violence: Implications for Professional Practice', in A. Mullender and R. Morley (eds), *Children Living with Domestic Violence. Putting Men's Abuse of Women on the Child Care Agenda*, London, Whiting & Birch.

Official Solicitor (1989) 'Practice Note: Sterilisation', *New Law Journal*, 13 October, 1380.

Oliver, M. (1983) *Social Work with Disabled People*, London, Macmillan.

Ormiston, H. (1990) 'What's it all about?', *Community Care*, 825, 19.

Parker, H., Sumner, M. and Jarvis, G. (1989) *Unmasking the Magistrates: The Custody or Not Decision in Sentencing Young Offenders*, Milton Keynes, Open University Press.

Parker, R., Ward, H., Jackson, S., Aldgate, J. and Wedge, P. (1991) *Assessing Outcomes in Child Care*, London, HMSO.

Parton, N. (1981) 'Child Abuse, Social Anxiety and Welfare', *British Journal of Social Work*, 11(4), 391–414.

Parton, N. (1985) *The Politics of Child Abuse*, London, Macmillan.

Parton, N. (1986) 'The Beckford Report: A Critical Appraisal', *British Journal of Social Work*, 16(5), 511–30.

Parton, N. (1991) *Governing the Family: Child Care, Child Protection and the State*, London, Macmillan.

Parton, N. (1994) ' "Problematics of Government", (Post) Modernity and Social Work', *British Journal of Social Work*, 24(1), 9–32.

Parton, N. (1995) 'Child Welfare and Child Protection: The Need for a Radical Re-think', Conference Paper, Child and Family Support and Protection – A Practical Approach, London, 28 June.

Pearce, J. (1994) 'Consent to Treatment During Childhood', *British Journal of Psychiatry*, 165, 713–16.

Pearson, G. (1975) 'Making Social Workers: Bad Promises and Good Omens', in R. Bailey and M. Brake (eds), *Radical Social Work*, London, Edward Arnold.

Phelan, P. (1986) 'The Social Model of Disability: Ways and Means for Practice', paper given at 'Disabled People and Social Workers: Changing Philosophy, Changing Practice', 31 October, Birmingham, British Association of Social Workers/British Council of Organisations of Disabled People.

Phillips, M. (1990) 'Black and White Perspectives in Child Abuse – Conference Report', in R. Dutt (ed.), *Towards a Black Perspective in Child Protection*, London, Race Equality Unit.

Pierson, J. (1990) 'Decision-Making Notes', unpublished.

Pitts, J. (1995) 'Scare in the Community: Britain in a Moral Panic. Part 1. Youth Crime', *Community Care*, 4–10 May, i–viii.

Plotnikoff, J. and Woolfson, R. (1996) *Reporting to Court under the Children Act. A Handbook for Social Services*, London, HMSO.

Preston-Shoot, M. (1996a) 'A Question of Emphasis? On Legalism and Social Work Education', in S. Jackson and M. Preston-Shoot (eds),

Educating Social Workers in a Changing Policy Context, London, Whiting & Birch.

Preston-Shoot, M. (1996b) 'Contesting the Contradictions: Needs, Resources and Community Care Decisions', *Journal of Social Welfare and Family Law,* 18(3), 307–25.

Preston-Shoot, M. (1996c) 'On Retaining a Reflective Space: Making Sense of Interactions in Work and Work Groups', *Journal of Social Work Practice,* 10(1), 9–23.

Preston-Shoot, M. (ed.) (1993) *Assessment of Competence in Social Work Law,* London, Whiting & Birch/Social Work Education.

Preston-Shoot, M. and Agass, D. (1990) *Making Sense of Social Work: Psychodynamics, Systems and Practice,* London, Macmillan.

Pritchard, J. (1992) *The New Penguin Guide to the Law,* London, Viking.

RADAR (1995) *Annual Report 1994–95,* London, The Royal Association for Disability and Rehabilitation.

Redding, D. (1991a) 'The Not So Tender Trap', *The Guardian,* 9 January, 17.

Redding, D. (1991b) 'A Fundamental Review', *Community Care,* 849, 17–19.

Reder, P., Duncan, S. and Gray, M. (1993) *Beyond Blame. Child Abuse Tragedies Revisited,* London, Routledge.

Rickford, F. (1992) 'Courting Danger', *Social Work Today,* 24(7), 14–15.

Rickford, F. (1993) 'Why the Kids Aren't All Right', *The Guardian,* 1 September, 12–13.

Rickford, F. (1995) 'Country Living', *Community Care,* 19–25 October, 14–15.

Ritchie, J., Dick, D. and Lingham, R. (1994) *Report of the Inquiry into the Care and Treatment of Christopher Clunis,* London, HMSO.

Robbins, D. (1990) *Child Care Policy: Putting it in Writing,* London, HMSO.

Robbins, D. (ed.) (1993) *Community Care. Findings from DoH Funded Research, 1988–1992,* London, HMSO.

Robinson, A. (1994) quoted in Brindle, D. and Wintour, P. 'New Rights for Disabled Welcomed', *The Guardian,* 25 November, 8.

Robinson, B. (1987) 'Planning and Decision Making', in *Decision Making in Child Care; Course Material,* East Sussex, Escata, 68–86.

Rogers, A. and Faulkener, A. (1987) *A Place of Safety,* London, Mind.

Romans, P. (1991) 'Women with Much to Offer', *Community Care,* 855, 14–15.

Rowe, A. and Kent, N. (1992) 'Airtime', *Social Work Today,* 5 November, 21.

Ruddock, M. (1988) 'A Child in Mind, A Lost Opportunity', *Social Work Today,* 19(20), 14–15.

Ryan, J. and Thomas, F. (1993) 'Concepts of Normalisation', in J. Bornat, C. Pereira, D. Pilgrim and F. Williams (eds), *Community Care. A Reader,* Basingstoke, Macmillan/The Open University.

Ryan, V. and Wilson, K. (1995) 'Child Therapy and Evidence in Court Proceedings: Tensions and Some Solutions', *British Journal of Social Work*, 25(2), 157–72.

Sachs, A. (1976) 'The Myth of Judicial Neutrality', in P. Carlen (ed.).

Sandford, T. (1995) quoted in Rickford, F. 'Contrasting Opinions', *Community Care* (Inside Supplement), 30 November–6 December, 2–3.

Sashidharan, S. (1989) 'Schizophrenic – or Just Black?', *Community Care*, 783, 14–15.

Shaw, J. (1990) 'Sterilisation of Mentally Handicapped People: Judges Rule OK?', *Modern Law Review*, 53 (January), 91–106.

Sheppard, M. (1990) *Mental Health: the Role of the Approved Social Worker*, Sheffield, Joint Unit for Social Services Research.

Simmonds, J. (1991) 'Making Professional Judgements of Significant Harm', in M. Adcock, R. White and A. Hollows (eds), *Significant Harm*, Croydon, Significant Publications.

Simons, K. (1995) *I'm Not Complaining But . . . Complaints Procedures in Social Services*, York, Joseph Rowntree Foundation.

Sinclair, I. (ed.) (1988) *Residential Care. The Research Reviewed*, London, HMSO.

Smart, C. (1990) 'Law's Power, the Sexed Body, and Feminist Discourse', *Journal of Law and Society*, 17(2), 194–210.

Smith, G. and Harris, R. (1972) 'Ideologies of Need and the Organisation of Social Work Departments', *British Journal of Social Work*, 2(1), 27–45.

Smith, L. (1989) *Domestic Violence: Home Office Research Study 107*, London, HMSO.

Smith, T. (1990) 'Services for the Under Fives – What Children Need and Parents Want?', *Local Government Policy Making*, 17(3), 56–60.

Sone, K. (1995) 'Lack of Conviction', *Community Care*, 8–14 June, 22–3.

Specht, H. and Vickery, A. (eds) (1977) *Integrating Social Work Methods*, London, George Allen & Unwin.

Spencer, J. and Flin, R. (1993) *The Evidence of Children. The Law and the Psychology*, London, Blackstone Press.

SSI (1990a) *Inspection of Child Protection Services In Rochdale*, London, Department of Health.

SSI (1990b) *Developing Services for Young People with Disabilities*, London, Department of Health.

SSI (1992a) *The Children Act 1989 – Court Orders Study. A Study of Local Authority Decision Making about Public Law Court Applications*, London, Department of Health.

SSI (1992b) *Implementing Caring for People: Assessment*, London, Department of Health.

SSI (1993a) *Corporate Parents*, London, Department of Health.

SSI (1993b) *No Longer Afraid*, London, Department of Health.

SSI (1993c) *Whose Life is it Anyway? A Report of an Inspection of Services for People with Multiple Impairments*, London, Department of Health.

SSI (1993d) *The Inspection of the Complaints Procedures in Local Authority Social Services Departments*, London, HMSO.

SSI (1993e) *Local Authority Inspection Units: A Review of Progress During the First Year,* London, Department of Health.

SSI (1993f) *Social Services for Hospital Patients III: Users' and Carers' Perspective,* London, Department of Health.

SSI (1993g) *Planning for Permanence? An Inspection of Adoption Services in Three Northern Local Authorities,* London, Department of Health.

SSI (1994a) *Services to Disabled Children and their Families,* London, Department of Health.

SSI (1994b) *The Child, The Court and The Video. A Study of the Implementation of the Memorandum of Good Practice on Video Interviewing of Child Witnesses,* London, Department of Health.

SSI (1994c) *Report on the National Survey of Children's Services Plans,* London, Department of Health.

SSI (1995a) *Partners in Caring. 4th Annual Report of the Chief Inspector, Social Services Inspectorate 1994/95,* London, HMSO.

SSI (1995b) *Children's Services Plans. An Analysis of Children's Services Plans,* London, Department of Health.

Stevenson, O. (1974) *Minority Report in DHSS, Report of the Committee of Inquiry into the Care and Supervision Provided in Relation to Maria Colwell,* London, HMSO.

Stevenson, O. (1986) 'Guest Editorial on the Jasmine Beckford Inquiry', *British Journal of Social Work,* 16(5), 501–10.

Stevenson, O. (1988) 'Law and Social Work Education: A Commentary on the "Law Report"', *Issues In Social Work Education,* 8(1), 37–45.

Stevenson, O. and Parsloe, P. (1993) *Community Care and Empowerment,* York, Joseph Rowntree Foundation.

Stratton, P., Preston-Shoot, M. and Hanks, H. (1990) *Family Therapy: Training and Practice,* Birmingham, Venture Press.

Summit, R. (1983) 'The Child Sexual Abuse Accommodation Syndrome', *Child Abuse and Neglect,* 7, 177–93.

Swain, P. (1989) 'From Carney to Cleveland . . . to Chinkapook and Cottles Bridge or Lawyer and Social Worker . . . Can the Marriage Work?', *Journal of Social Welfare Law,* 4, 229–34.

Temkin, J. (1991) 'Doing Justice to Children', *New Law Journal,* 8 March, 315–17.

Thornton, P. and Lunt, N. (1995) 'Working to Rule', *Community Care,* 3–9 August, 21.

Thornton, P. and Tozer, R. (1995) *Having a Say in Change: Older People and Community Care,* York, Joseph Rowntree Foundation.

Travis, A. (1995) 'Children "Are Locked Up Needlessly"', *The Guardian,* 19 May, 5.

Trinder, L. (1993) 'Reviewing Day Care', *Children Act News,* December, 6.

Triseliotis, J. (1991) 'Maintaining Links in Adoption', *British Journal of Social Work,* 21(4), 401–14.

Trotter, J. (1991) 'Wanting Protection', *Social Work Today,* 22(31), 14–15.

Turner, S. (1995) 'Grand Plans', *Community Care,* 9–15 February, 26.

Utting, W. (1991) *Children in the Public Care. A Review of Residential Care,* London, HMSO.

Valentine, M. (1994) 'The Social Worker as "Bad Object"', *British Journal of Social Work*, 24 (1), 71–86.

Vernon, S. (1993) *Social Work and the Law*, 2nd edn, London, Butterworths.

Vernon, S., Harris, R. and Ball, C. (1990) *Towards Social Work Law. Legally Competent Professional Practice*, London, CCETSW, paper 4:2.

Walker, A. (1991) 'No Gain Without Pain', *Community Care*, 872, 14–16.

Walrond-Skinner, S. and Watson, D. (eds) (1987) *Ethical Issues in Family Therapy*, London, Routledge & Kegan Paul.

Warburton, R. (1990) *Developing Services for Disabled People. Results of an Inspection to Monitor the Operation of the Disabled Persons (Services, Consultation and Representation) Act 1986*, London, Social Services Inspectorate, Department of Health.

Ward, D. (1996) 'Probation Training: Celebration or Wake', in S. Jackson and M. Preston-Shoot (eds), *Educating Social Workers in a Changing Policy Context*, London, Whiting & Birch.

Ward, H. (ed.) (1995) *Looking After Children: Research into Practice*, London, HMSO.

Warner, N. (1994) 'Care Shared', *The Guardian (Society)*, 2 November, 8.

Warner, N. (1995) *Better Tomorrows? Report of a National Study of Carers and the Community Care Changes*, London, Carers National Association.

Wasik, M. and Taylor, R. (1991) *Blackstone's Guide to the Criminal Justice Act 1991*, London, Blackstone Press.

Waters, J. (1995) 'Direct Payment Plans in Queen's Speech', *Community Care*, 23–9 November, 8.

Westcott, H. (1995) 'Perceptions of Child Protection Casework: Views from Children, Parents and Practitioners', in C. Cloke and M. Davies (eds), *Participation and Empowerment in Child Protection*, London, Pitman.

Whitaker, D. and Archer, L. (1994) 'Partnership Research and its Contributions to Learning and to Team-Building', *Social Work Education*, 13(3), 39–60.

White, I. (1992) 'A Director's Perspective', in J. Gibbons (ed.), *The Children Act 1989 and Family Support: Principles into Practice*, London, HMSO.

Whitefield, R. (1991) 'Don't Give In to Pressure', *Community Care*, 848, 16.

Whiteley, P. (1995) 'Residents Booted Out as Care Gap Grows', *Community Care*, 30 March–5 April, 8–9.

Whittington, C. (1977) 'Social Workers' Orientations: An Action Perspective', *British Journal of Social Work*, 7(1), 73–95.

Whittington, C. (1983) 'Social Work in the Welfare Network: Negotiating Daily Practice', *British Journal of Social Work*, 13(3), 265–86.

Wilding, P. (1982) *Professional Power and Social Welfare*, London, Routledge & Kegan Paul.

Wilson, K. and James, A. (1989) 'Looking into the Law Report: A Two-Dimensional Affair', *Social Work Today*, 20(27), 12–13.

Windle, C. and Cibulka, J. (1981) 'A Framework for Understanding Participation in Community Mental Health Services', *Community Mental Health Journal*, 17(1), 4–18.

WING (1985) *Worlds Apart: Women under Immigration and Nationality Law*, London, Pluto Press.

Wistow, G., Hardy, B. and Leedham, I. (1993) 'Where Do We Go from Here?', *Community Care,* 21 January, 20–1.

Wolkind, S. (1988) 'Emotional Signs', *Journal of Social Welfare Law*, 2, 82–7.

Woodcock, M. (1989) *Team Development Manual*, Aldershot, Gower.

Wootton, B. (1959) *Social Science and Social Pathology*, London, George Allen & Unwin.

Yelloly, M. (1980) *Social Work Theory and Psychoanalysis*, Wokingham, Van Nostrand Reinhold.

Zander, M. (1974) *Social Workers, their Clients and the Law*, London, Sweet & Maxwell.

Index